Marybeth Harlan

Western Maryland College

Summer of '75

Language
for the Preschool
Deaf Child

Grace M. Harris

Supervisor,
Preschool Services for the Deaf,
The Society for Crippled Children
and Adults of Manitoba,
Winnipeg, Manitoba

Foreword by Dr. S. R. Silverman

Language
for the Preschool
Deaf Child

THIRD EDITION

Grune & Stratton

New York • London

First Edition   1950
Second Edition   1963

Third Edition

© *1971 by Grune & Stratton, Inc.*

All rights reserved. No part of this publication may be reproduced or transmitted in any form or by any means, electronic or mechanical, including photocopy, recording, or any information storage and retrieval system, without permission in writing from the publisher.

Grune & Stratton, Inc.
111 Fifth Avenue
New York, New York 10003

Library of Congress Catalog Card Number 77-167976
International Standard Book Number 0-8089-0733-6
Printed in the United States of America

Contents

Foreword

by *S. R. Silverman, Ph.D.*

Director, Central Institute for the Deaf;
Professor of Audiology, Washington University,
St. Louis, Missouri.

For the relatively small number of individuals who comprise
our profession of educating the deaf we are by tradition amaz-
ingly vehement about our differences of opinion concerning
the proper manner in which we must discharge our professional
obligations. Such classical issues as manual vs. combined vs. oral
methods, the day vs. the residential school, and "analytic"
methods vs. "natural" methods of teaching speech are still hotly
debated. But one point on which we have reached almost uni-
versal agreement is that *language is the keystone upon which
successful education of the deaf ultimately rests.* It is with this
language problem that Miss Harris comes to unusually effective grips at a critical stage in the child's development.

We are all aware of the relatively rapid mental, physical, psychological and social growth which takes place in the so-called
preschool period in a child's life. Miss Harris recognizes the
potentialities for effective learning in these early years. She
makes available a rich storehouse of sound advice and practical
procedures which enable not only the teacher but also the parent to take full advantage of the young deaf child's tractability.
Furthermore, the material assists the parent in gaining an in-
structive appreciation of the child's problems of communication which is frequently difficult for the layman to grasp.

Miss Harris' book is particularly timely. In our latter day concern for psychological and auditory assessment and diagnosis through various testing techniques, we seem to have attenuated our interest in practical educational techniques to the point where the testing fringe is getting larger than the teaching cloth. This trend, fortunately, has not been without its significant value. It has led to early detection and assessment of the deaf child and consequently to wider acceptance of the value of instruction at the preschool level.

Now we need to have increasingly effective teaching procedures to meet these instructional needs. Miss Harris' creative mind, nurtured by her own rich experience and that of her predecessors and contemporaries, has met the challenge superbly.

Above all, Miss Harris conveys to her readers a spirit of rational hope and optimism about the worthwhileness of our efforts on behalf of the deaf child. To the parent in particular, who could be a more constructive contribution?

In this new edition, Miss Harris has wisely recognized the need for guidance to those who would organize nursery schools and conduct programs of parent education. The demand for a new edition underlines the validity and usefulness of the previous ones.

Preface to the Third Edition

The title of this book remains, *Language For The Preschool Deaf Child.* One reason for retaining the word *deaf,* is that many of those children found in infancy and early childhood, who are specifically in need of the guidance put forth here, are in the beginning *deaf to spoken language,* by measurement, by response and performance, or both. There may be those who respond to sound of amplified voice under certain conditions, but who cannot and may never without appropriate training respond to and develop *language concepts.* There are others who may measure within the "moderately hearing impaired" limits, but who are, and may continue to be, without specific training, *educationally deaf.*

At least since the early part of the twentieth century, terminology to describe, briefly, the child with a hearing loss serious enough to warrant special training for educational advancement, has included: acoustically handicapped or impaired, deaf (mildly, moderately, severely, profoundly, extremely), hard of hearing (mildly, moderately, severely, extremely), borderline deaf, hearing handicapped, hearing impaired, auditorially impaired, and a host of other descriptive phrases.

We find children who, described as "moderately hearing impaired," depending on interpretation by which discipline, may, with full-time amplification and little specific training, find a suitable placement with hearing children. Others by the same description are, as far as educational requirements in the minimum are concerned, nothing less than educationally deaf by performance, at least in the beginning and perhaps for some time. Some children, after three or four or more years of good pre-school training, continue to have, by measurement without hearing aids, severe to profound hearing losses, still measuring between 90 and 110 decibels losses within the range most important for hearing speech. Yet, these same children at the end of that time may, when wearing hearing aids, measure much closer to the norm for ease in hearing spoken language, and may have begun to perform like children with no more than minimal hearing losses. Without the specialized training, particularly auditory training, these children would have remained "deaf," and indeed, without appropriate follow-up training to at least early adulthood, when the onus for retaining language competence becomes their own responsibility, could quickly and easily regress to "deafness."

Since *education* in its general and specific interpretation is the goal toward which the contents of this book are directed, and since education, learning, language, and experiences are interwoven, the word *deaf* is being retained. The child at the most extreme end of the continuum, therefore, can be provided for and trained toward peak performance with language. And, possibly some principles and practices outlined here may be used selectively and profitably, as they have been in the past, for those children considered to be less needful of intensive language training.

Any changes in presentation, any additions to, or reorganization of content material in this edition, in contrast to former editions, have been done to *further* emphasize: (1) active consideration of the whole child; (2) the need to be fully aware of what an increasingly complex society requires as a foundation toward a life of maximum achieving, which includes language interaction with others beyond the home, the school, and the disability; (3) the emphatic need for more, and more suitably trained educators with knowledgeable supervision; (4) the mandatory need for realistic parental guidance and continuous, responsible involvement of parents; (5) the responsibility of professionals to educate the child, however deaf, toward his highest potential; (6) and to be cognizant of the dangers for the deaf child when professionals in responsible positions could fall prey to unification in education of all hearing impaired children.

The many individuals—professionals, students, laymen, and parents—to whom I wish to express my indebtedness, are too numerous to list here. For many years, throughout North America and in other countries of the world, there are those with whom it has been my pleasure to be associated in some way, continuously or periodically, and from whom I have learned, and continue to learn more and better ways of helping individuals with hearing losses wherever I can. The sharing of information, even when some was not, at a particular time, applicable to children in the respective centers, has been an enriching experience for thought, for action, and sometimes for storehousing of ideas helpful at later dates. The foregoing refers also to persons associated with Early Childhood Education and Child Study, who have contributed so much to hearing impaired children who were able to attend nursery schools, kindergarten, and later levels, with hearing children. In some instances, the workers and teachers in day care centers, nursery schools, and kindergartens, have identified children with minimal to moderate hearing losses, who might otherwise have been missed until failure in elementary school occurred.

In particular I wish to thank the parents for their permission to use pictures of the children appearing in this book, and those teachers, students, and volunteers who have permitted use of pictures of them in action with the children.

I extend my continuing and sincere thanks to Dr. S. Richard Silverman, Director of Central Institute for the Deaf in St. Louis, Missouri, for his steadfast recognition of human endeavour on behalf of hearing impaired individuals, wherever they may be.

Once again, my thanks and sincere appreciation to the publishers for their patience and cooperation.

Grace M. Harris

Deafness in Childhood—
A Problem and a Responsibility

THE WHOLE AND THE PART

The importance of early and responsible guidance as a sound basis for the continuing education and achievement of hearing impaired persons, particularly those educationally deaf in their early years, has been universally recognized. The understanding of problems encountered in the *rehabilitation* of many young adults handicapped by deafness is motivating concerned educators in this field to place more emphasis on sound *habilitation* and *prevention* at the operational level. Early guidance of children with extreme hearing impairments does not eliminate the need for appropriate education and care in the future. It can, however, make it possible for more children to profit from educational opportunities.

The increased number of related professional disciplines, working at team level, has brought about earlier detection of hearing loss on a broader scale.[178] Subsequent referral for parent guidance and infant-child training has become more available and prompt. Follow-up professional attention from otologists, audiologists, psychologists, and pediatricians, in addition to continuing guidance in the home from social workers, is fast becoming more routine. The findings of these highly ·qualified indi-

1

viduals have clarified many situations for the teacher, allowing for better understanding of the individual child in less time. The well-disseminated information and reinforcement provided by the entire multidisciplinary team have helped many parents to cope more realistically with hearing loss in a family member.

The qualitative and quantitative growth in special provisions for the very young educationally deaf child has served to emphasize, rather than replace, his need to be recognized as a whole human being.[2] Part of the wholeness is the handicap. The little deaf child needs more specific training under the best of environmental conditions if he is to develop toward the worthwhile human achievement which approaches his full potential. No form of guidance works to the benefit of the child where it bypasses human development and, therefore, essential needs. Failure of hearing handicapped children to profit from the most expert and selective professional guidance, whatever the methodology employed, is being linked on a broader basis with environmental deprivation. Such deprivation can occur in any home, not just in those described as culturally deprived. However severe the hearing loss may be, the child is a human being with human needs.[40] The success of individual and combined efforts of professional workers and parents in coping with problems incurred by a hearing loss in a little child, depends strongly on this fact.

A CONSIDERATION OF PRIORITIES

Responsible, informed teachers and parents recognize language as the human method of communicating ideas and emotions, which the young hearing impaired child should be given every opportunity to establish. Since communication with a syntactic language of the resident society is becoming more and more essential for achievement in this changing world,[61] the desire of parents for their hearing impaired child to develop this human characteristic is quite understandable. Thus, the task of educating the child toward this end as early as possible tends to take priority over all other factors. We must remember, however, that language development in these children, as with hearing children, does not, and cannot occur on some continuum or plane separated from other developmental tasks of childhood. From time of diagnosis of hearing loss (hopefully in infancy), the child's environment *must be* language oriented. In reality, this necessary atmosphere is never established unless the priorities of human development are allowed to go into action early and continuously. The process of true language development is inextricably woven within the whole developmental pattern.

The developmental tasks of childhood, in the order of their priority, provide an essential frame of reference for all those persons directly responsible for constructive guidance of very young hearing handicapped children toward more normal human development. Each important step or task has its roots in some way at birth for every member of the human race. Each, however, becomes a functioning reality only as it is fulfilled in order, blended and carried forth to the next, until, toward the close of the preschool years, the child is prepared for ongoing intellectual endeavor.[71]

The order of tasks as presented by Child Study specialists are, in brief: (1) human relationship and learning in human interaction; (2) self-identity and discovery of self as a person; (3) emotional learning; (4) learning the skills of learning; (5) cognitive learning and intellectual endeavor.[104]

Consideration of these priorities within which lives the potential for *language,* inseparable from *learning* through needed and desirable experiences,[157] allows for much easier identification of deprivations preventing progress in the child as a whole, and therefore, in language development. It is a simple matter for educators and interested parents to learn about the progression of human development (and the principles involved in child learning), because it is orderly and a common denominator. It is not, however, easy for many parents (even with help), nor for some teachers, to provide the stimulating and motivating reinforcement that each child needs for satisfying, human achievement, which is bound to language.[13]

The deaf child who has not been embarked on a suitable training program until two or three years of age, and who has had inadequate home guidance to that time, demonstrates real deprivation in the first three developmental steps. Therefore, he *cannot* go on to learn the simplest skills of learning, unless, through cooperative effort, the responsible, concerned adults— teachers, social workers, and particularly parents—can make unlearning and relearning possible. It is not uncommon to encounter very young hearing impaired children, upon referral to hearing clinics and preschool centers, having already learned well how to defend themselves against learning. Their behavior may be dominated by fear, by anger,[82] or even by habitual retreat to hugging and cuddling, having learned to view this as desirable by adults and "a way out" which meets with approval.[78] The antilearning behavior of these children is too often attributed solely to frustration or intellectual incapacity arising out of hearing loss.[15]

The deprivation experienced by many young deaf children handicaps them to an extent that hearing loss alone could not possibly do. The hearing child in a similar situation would be seriously handicapped.[80]

Educators of young children with hearing losses must be knowledgeable about human development, and of how to blend into the total developmental pattern of the individual child the opportunity for experience which is language-learning based. They must also have the courage to inform parents in this regard. Teachers, social workers, and others working closely with parents have the responsibility of guiding parents in ways that will prevent misinterpretations, such as concluding that the early tasks to be achieved by young children are "taught" as curriculum subject-matter. The anxiety [42] and sense of urgency associated with desire for "speech" from the child, can result in rigid parental guidance for the sake of any vocalization that might be interpreted as "speech." At other times child-centered self-indulgence comes into play to the extent of becoming habituated. Some parents may become lax and decide that this is entirely the responsibility of the trained teacher. All such practices operate *against* the child.[14]

It is much too easy for unaware adults to confuse structure, direction, and planning with formality and inflexibility in establishing an enriched environment for learning by the young, hearing impaired child. The child must have the opportunity to play out his feelings and his thoughts, and to struggle like all children to put his findings into words. It is not logical to conclude that the unpreparedness of many young deaf children for percept-concept and language learning, after a few years of preschool training, is due to the child's being "too deaf." Highly perceptive involved adults, working together, can foster cognitive learning [39] in the deafest of little children within the framework of constructive play. The whole child must be given the opportunity to experience and to generate experiences that have worthwhile meaning.[29]

LANGUAGE AS A PRIORITY

Language is learned, and in the beginning, is learned auditorially. A child, if not physically restricted, will one day learn to walk on his own. Language, however, is not learned in any such predestined way.[143] It is understandable, therefore, that the infant or young child with a hearing loss will not develop language skills without special attention. The "average" hearing child is said to produce his first word at approximately one year of age, although he probably understands much more than he expresses. Up to approximately two years of age, symbolic language expression, referred to as speech, is so minimal that language acquisition cannot be considered established. From this time onward, however, the child begins to respond with spoken language to express his thoughts about himself, and his experiences within his environment. The delight of the parents with their hearing child's verbal responses, and the "gesture drop out," in addition to the social rewards the child receives each time he expresses himself with language, points out the priority position language assumes in human development.[109]

The importance of auditory stimulation and aural training in the guidance of hearing-impaired children has been emphasized for many years. Combined factors such as earlier diagnosis of hearing loss, immediate and continuing audiological assessments, full-time and appropriate use of two suitable hearing aids for any one child,[10] ongoing guidance of parents, and the knowledgable attention of educators have demonstrated on a broader scale, the extent to which the smallest remnant of hearing can be stimulated and developed as a real force in even profoundly deaf children, by measurement of hearing, developing truly practical language skills. Where professional personnel are well-educated, fully trained, experienced, and work well together, the possibility of maximizing opportunity for the severely hearing impaired child's developing language is favorable. However, the parents and the environment they provide for the child are also important.

Parents must be included in everything possible regarding the child as a whole being, and not approached only as instruments to produce language in a young human being. All little children need the first years for sensorimotor development and for the interwoven experiences of adult contact that express parental concern and care. It is only within the framework of such guidance, which includes hearing aids and wise use of situations created by the child himself that an internalized and expressive language can eventually evolve.[126] The little deaf child can easily be lost as a human being in the artificiality of misinterpreted language guidance. Until parents can maintain their morale, despite the sorrows imposed by the handicap of deafness, and can make communication a part of the common denominator of family life, the little deaf child may never learn how to be free, or how to make life's required choices.[127]

Every guidance program for hearing impaired children must be strongly oriented toward language. It is the task of responsible professionals to guide parents according to the child as a human being.[156] Subtle, fast changes continue to occur in our society, and some facets are eliminated without replacement. Although

Plate I.   Young child with severe to profound hearing loss, bilaterally, wearing two hearing aids, contained within "harness" made by the parent. The teacher has asked the child, "What color goes on first?" The child, listening only, replies, "Yellow," and places the section on the tower.

many of the innovations and deletions have proved to be bene-
ficial, it seems likely that the young child still needs the pro-
tection and guidance of an anchor-environment, commonly
known as "home." Today's greater demand for facility in human
symbolic communication as human development progresses on
its orderly way, depending for fulfillment upon motivation and
reinforcement, might be advising us of the greater need for
stability within the family. For the deaf child, it is still
mandatory.[161]

A REALISTIC APPROACH

Loss of hearing in the extreme tends to be associated automatically, at it was hundreds of years ago,[11] with lack of spoken
language, and parents confronted with this handicap in their
young child, may make generalized misinterpretations. The
potential absence of "speech" may cause them to act in most
unnatural ways toward the child. Human interaction involves
human communication. It is not always easy to continue speaking to any person when spoken response remains absent. Yet, a
hearing baby who does not use words meaningfully, or who has
not arrived at minimal level of understanding, eventually understands and uses spoken language only because others in his environment have provided for him, from birth, experiences with
spoken language. To use spoken language for communication
with others is only natural and human.[98] To decrease or warp
its use in any home, where there is a hearing impaired child
and where communication with spoken language has been a
common factor, may often affect the whole family in negative
ways. Father, mother, brothers and sisters begin and continue
to talk over the hearing handicapped child's head, to exclude
him more and more from the family group, and, in day-to-day
planning, "different" arrangements for this child grow in number and character. The lack of self-identity often leads to behavior problems which could have been prevented. In time,
these problems can "deaf-center" the home in an unhappy and
extreme degree. However, with appropriate training within a

communicating family the inclusion of the child could have been possible.

No matter how we may sidetrack the importance of spoken language, understood and used, and although we may use the excuse that language is just one form of communication, any attempts to use, and to deliberately restrict people who have severe hearing impairments to other symbolisms will only result in hiding ignorance in obscurity. Studies of the history of peoples and of the origin of languages reveal that spoken language has been a part of cultures for almost a million years, whereas written languages are only a few thousand years old. Where manual and body sign systems were used effectively and necessarily from hilltop-to-hilltop, men, when face to face, communicated with spoken language. There is evidence that the earliest inventions which eventually played a useful role in the establishment and advancement of civilization probably came into being only after spoken language was developed.[23]

In the total population of hearing impaired children, there will be those unable for just reason to develop real and true language. Among all peoples there are those who achieve at different levels of production and contribution, and in different ways. It is well to remember, however, that in spite of the emphasis placed on "individuality," there has been a growing tendency to encourage uniformity in education, as well as in many other areas, by governing bodies who only view children from a distance.[142] Doubtlessly, it makes the system of "educating" easier for those who rule and for those who think of education as an expense rather than an investment. But, attempts to educate hearing handicapped children at any age, in the same way, sometimes all "mixed" under the same roof in the name of integration, eliminates the possibility of any child reaching his potential and enjoying quality of life as an individual.

Teachers of the deaf who love their work, who know their area well, and who have real affection for the hearing impaired child, can, with the cooperation of responsible parents and administrators, educate more of these handicapped children in the development of real language skills and wholesome living.

Young deaf children who may have fewer chances of developing desirable and useful language may be those who are more severely multihandicapped. Some may have parents who are away from the home all day and are placed in Day Care centers or with a series of baby sitters, without full-time parent substitutes.[176] There are parents who are unable, even with the best available professional assistance, to cope with the home training requirements for oral-aural training of their hearing-impaired child. Indeed, records in some centers reveal that many such parents have also failed to take the responsibility for training their child by other systematic symbolic means of communication available to them. Attentional repertoire in any young human being is accumulated through training, and such training is necessary to the development of language for communication,[18] for socialization,[4] and much later, for job proficiency.[22] Preschool attendance alone will not fill this need for the young deaf child.

On the other hand, there are many examples of very deaf children, not at all "hard of hearing" by continuing audiological measurements, who, before entering elementary school, have been able to develop language skills that are so well "built-in" that needed, optional responses in conversational situations are habituated and selective. Such children have had the benefit of loving parents whose awareness of life's demands, and whose values and standards allow them to give direct support and assistance through correspondence.[162] Such parents come to the realization that there is never a time during their years of responsibility when, for such reasons as absence of required attention in the home, and/or inadequate education in the school, the child is immune from regression that will have lasting, derogatory effects. Of course they have problems and the children have problems. The parents, however, have the inner strength that permits them to seek assistance if necessary, and to see this action as mature procedure and not as a weakness.[24] As parents work cooperatively with knowledgable professionals in resolving environmental and educational problems, we observe each child gradually entering into the problem-solving process.[14] Such parents who tend to live out their lives happily in any given community, and whose deaf children grow up to do likewise, should be recognized by educators, and be given an opportunity to speak to other parents of hearing-impaired children.

No teacher can, with assurance, tell parents that their deaf child *will* "talk." In most cases, however, the parent should be told what is involved in this possibility. What the child *can* or *could do* should not be confused with "will do," as has often happened, particularly in published information, not only by parents but also by professional persons in related fields. Where possible, parents of deaf babies who may never have encountered other hearing impaired children, should have the opportunity of seeing such children in action. Some centers have a great variety of young hearing handicapped children who function at many different levels, even within one age group. There are those who, by measurement, are severely to profoundly deaf without hearing aids, and after three or more years of preschool training, are communicating with one another and with hearing children and adults with meaningful, spoken language that includes correctly used verb tenses, singulars and plurals, etc. There may be others who have had just as much individualized training and opportunity in the preschool center, but have had little or no follow-up home training, who have no real language skills, and whose deprivation could not be overcome by any amount of skilled professional attention or even by adding a second hearing aid.

Whatever the problems encountered by parents in the home or in the community, they should be helped particularly in relation to the child himself. Parents who can and do interact with affection and concern with their child provide the reinforcement he needs for full development, and allow training by trained teachers to work.[62] Where such guidance is continuously in process, the child achieves closer to potential, and when the time comes for school placement, it can be dealt with realistically on the basis of the child's actual functioning as a whole. Hopefully, of course, the stream of education into which the child should be placed at that time will exist in the community or will be established. Parents should be advised early in convincing ways, if possible, that school placement beyond preschool, if appropriately carried out, will rest heavily upon the child's performance as a whole, including how well he functions with language. Many parents are disappointed later when their child for justifiable reasons was not admitted to the school of their choice, or was, at some time following admittance there, referred out on the basis of not being prepared. Parents should be helped if necessary to guide the whole child, without which practice the process of "teaching language" is wasted effort.

SOME PROFESSIONAL RESPONSIBILITIES

Consideration of the whole child and priorities within the educational guidance of children handicapped in the extreme by hearing loss identifies for us a professional responsibility to carry out our tasks according to the absolute potential of each child, from time of his being discovered, and not on the basis of ease in administrative governing, or of ease in what may be mistaken for teaching, or on the basis of preconceived misconceptions of what the "deaf child cannot do."

Where professional workers in the field are well-prepared, and where supervision in skilled hands is close,[55] the training and guidance of hearing-impaired children, from birth, should be characteristically positive, mature, and cultivated. Under such conditions, highly selective and individualized guidance all along the educational continuum will not be viewed as "bad" versus "good," as "structured" versus "free," but as the means by which each young human being can best achieve the most for quality living. Quality living requires a background of, and current involvement with spoken language interaction with other human beings, and any dilution of or substitution for this experience cannot do other than weaken the individual's role in any environment.[3] It is our duty and responsibility to help every young human being, whatever the degree of his hearing loss, to develop this important living skill.

If, then, it is discovered, usually before school entrance, that such a goal is quite impossible for this particular child, there need be no feelings of bitterness, of guilt, or of failure in educator or parent. It is when, with a wealth of available information before us, the child is knowingly deprived of this potential achievement by inadequate training or by sparsely informed "leaders," who are controlled by expedient "methodology," rather than by knowledge of children, of the particular child, of the environment, and of the field, that we can call ourselves failures.

Any one individual is better prepared to speak and write influentially and convincingly about that which he has done and which he has experienced. Those educators who have lived with deaf children, and who have worked closely with the young children, parents, and other teachers and who have maintained contact with many of the grown children, continue to take a positive approach to the total educational potential of severely to profoundly hearing-impaired individuals, and thus recognize the need for oral-aural training throughout the pre- and postacademic years. This positive attitude is based on actual experience and on the successful performance of numerous graduates, who, although like most human beings have their own problems with which they must live and deal, are living independently. The means toward any goal must be put into action in its entirety, directly and continuously, expertly and positively, for that goal to be achieved. A means under the most desirable name but with little relation to the name will not, of course, lead to the associated desirable goal.

Back of every hearing-impaired child who eventually achieves full citizenship, there have undoubtedly been good, well-informed parents. Many young parents are almost completely uninformed about deafness in childhood, and many others have only the fragmented kind of information to which the public is often exposed and which is scarcely educational. Parents, who are so important in the early training of deaf children, need help,[152] which the multidisciplinary team, and, in particular, the real educator can and should be allowed to provide.

Part I

Fundamentals
of the Training

Chapter 1

Language

The language element must be given priority over any other in the training of the deaf child, especially the *young* deaf child. Each parent and each specialist has his own ideas concerning the deaf child's needs. The ideas may center upon speech, auditory training, hearing aids, lipreading, intelligence tests, reading, writing, psychological guidance for the parents, play therapy for the child, or upon nursery school activities, and each of these is important as a part of the total picture. However, it must be forcefully emphasized that no method can be effective nor any objective attained, unless it is viewed, understood, and employed in relation to *language*.

Language is not only the *objective* in mind for the deaf child; it is also the *means*. Creative activities and free play as means of expression are language experiences. Lipreading is merely a tool for the understanding of spoken language in relation to situations, people, and things. Sense training as a means of expression, and of developing the ability to concentrate, observe, and think, is a language experience. Auditory training is a tool for the development of better voice quality, a broader concept of spoken language, and a consciousness of language in the environment. Proficiency in reading is based on language experiences, and reading itself is a language experience. Speech or articulated language is dependent upon an understanding of spoken language in relation to other language experiences.

The child's thoughts as they are expressed in many ways are a form of language.[126] His feelings, as they are expressed in various ways—as a cry, in laughter, in negative reactions or cooperative attitudes, and, later on, through speech—are a form of language. His relationship with his parents, with children, with his teacher, and with other individuals, are each expressed in some way, and whether or not the avenues of expression are obvious or not, they constitute a language which may "speak" more forcefully than any words could. The language of feelings is very important and must not be overlooked while striving to cope with any other form of language necessary to the deaf child's development.[125]

It would be a great error to restrict our concept of the term "language" to the spoken form or to the printed form. Understanding of the spoken word and, much later, of the printed word, is essential to the deaf child, and steps must be taken from the earliest possible moment to reach such understanding. The attainment of the objective, however, is dependent upon á recognition of all other phases of the child's development as furnishing powerful tributaries in the total language system.[143]

The speech teacher must be a language teacher; the lipreading teacher is a language teacher; the teacher of reading is a teacher of language; the nursery school teacher is a language teacher; the parent who guides and cares for her child constantly is a teacher of language.

The educator who leads the way in setting up experiences conducive to language development and learning in the young deaf child knows that the child cannot progress if language is presented as one would teach "grammar," nor as adults learn a foreign language.[35] Grammar involves analytical study of language structure, where basic language concepts are already learned, and a means of learning more about and with language. And, no young child learns language as a foreign language is learned by adults.[85] It is the developmentally nourishing environment we must use to make every move, every glance, every sound a living, worthwhile learning experience for the child.

"Permissiveness" and "freedom," concepts often misinterpreted and abused in the name of "love," exist only within specific limits protecting the child from harm and from undesirable learning. Within that atmosphere, the little child, even the baby, is bound to establish in some way throughout his waking hours situations which are language-learning oriented in that the adult picks up a new idea, puts it into spoken language and builds on it.[43] Exposure of language concepts in relation to a child-initiated situation often holds attention longer, and helps the child begin to take unto himself what he feels is a part of him.[64]

Language and every aspect of the child's development are inter-related; and any particular area of that development, which may not be itself a language, will be related to language in some respect and will contribute to language.

In the pages that follow, it has been necessary to divide the total language training into parts, and to divide those parts into smaller sections, in order to clarify facts and ideas for a broader understanding and for more effective use. The worker, however, whether parent or teacher, is cautioned against losing sight of the *whole* while studying or using the *part*.

PRINCIPLES TO WORK BY

In guiding the young deaf child, in the home, in the nursery school, or in the play yard, two principles must be adhered to by parent and teacher: (1) His needs *as a child* must be provided for, by exposure to a normal, happy environment in which he may enjoy the activities and experiences of the hearing child.[17, 89] (2) His needs *as a deaf child* must be met, by special, consciously designed methods employed by the adults who guide him.

In practice, the parent and the teacher make every effort to combine both principles in such a way that the "special" skills which the child must acquire will blend into his everyday experiences. The person who is familiar with the problems of deafness and with the principles of child development realizes that failure to attend to both areas results in a limited and limiting training. It is quite possible to combine developmental growth and the special training, and the latter is more effective if it is made an outgrowth of the former.

These principles will be kept in mind as the *whole* language factor is divided, discussed, and read about under such headings as those that follow in this section. When the worker is concerned with speech, she considers not only the speech exercise, but also how the idea may be combined with lipreading, auditory training, sense training, developmental activities, and with the child's experiences and interests, to facilitate and accelerate language development.

Consider the Child

The implications of preschool education for the child who has a serious hearing loss, are frequently misunderstood or misinterpreted. *Misinterpretations can be disastrous.* This, of course, applies to many people; but, among those most personally concerned, it applies in most cases, probably, to the parents of these children, and occasionally, to teachers, who still are unfamiliar with the normal growth and development of young children, and with the fundamental needs of the very young deaf or hard of hearing child.

It should be made very clear that early education of any child, including the one who has a hearing handicap, is *NOT* an oversimplified version of elementary school education. For the young child with a hearing loss, preschool education implies training him to make the most of his abilities, all of them, from day to day, in order that he may enjoy to the utmost his one and only childhood, and in so doing, be better prepared in all respects to cope with elementary school education and all the years ahead. One has only to observe little hearing children at play to realize what a tremendous role oral communication plays in their lives. It is obvious that the little deaf or hard of hearing child must begin establishing communication skills if he is to have a chance of developing normally. We must also realize that these skills have to be established as a part of his total development.

Perhaps educators, in their attempts to ease parents into understanding, accepting and learning to live with the problem of deafness in the home, are prone to emphasize the possibilities of children with hearing losses, without, at the same time, revealing some of the difficulties and the hard work involved. It happens, of course, even when the whole problem is placed before them, that some parents expect results far beyond reason. Some are deeply disappointed when intelligible speech is not forthcoming within a matter of weeks. Others look for a miraculous restoration of hearing. Some parents, as soon as understanding and speech vocabularies have been established, expect the preschool age child, even a very deaf one, to begin reading and writing. They forget about children as human beings.

To overindulge is wrong; to expect too little is neglect; but to demand the impossible is disastrous. Keep in mind the "normal" child. If we do not expect the preschool age hearing child with good learning ability to excel in elementary school "subjects," how can we expect it of a child with a hearing loss?

The young child, during the first five years of life, goes through many cycles of growth and development. He is affected favorably or unfavorably by the people about him, and by the environment they create for him. He lays hold of his environment through eyes and ears and experiences. Eventually, he expresses himself through spoken language. The thinking processes are put to work early in life, and the capacity to think often accompanies the ability to understand and use spoken language. Without language, there is little that anyone can cope with adequately, including the first year in school.

We realize that there are certain difficult tasks to deal with. Hearing must be developed to the utmost. Understanding of spoken language must be developed. Speech must be developed. There are many aids, many teaching experts, and wonderful parents, but, *there are no short cuts.* Give the child a happy childhood, unmarred by rejection and overindulgence. Give him language that lives, and see that he uses it. Put his mind to work. Present language to him so that it grows with him.

Preschool goals should be concerned with language "know-how," with meanings, vocabulary, and practical speech. If the hearing-impaired child can start to school at five or six years of age after having such a start, necessary cognitive learning should be quite possible for him. Make oral communication a reality. Time must be used economically. Make the first few years count for something that with good follow-up education, can have a lasting influence for good. Don't bypass the potentialities of the young mind.

Deaf Children Achieve with Language

Young deaf children who have had a good and early start are, by their last year in preschool, usually accepting of reminding for better language usage. They, too, however, will take short cuts in speaking if allowed to. The deaf child needs to practice correct use of acceptable language. Use of poor language can easily become habitual.[73] People he knows may understand what he means, but language skills can break down quickly where expectations become consistently too low. The following is an example of a language "short cut." A five-year-old profoundly deaf child whose training began when she was 18 months old, came into a preschool one day and said to a teacher, "Rain." The teacher replied, "I don't know what you mean." The child immediately responded, as her eyes twinkled knowingly, "It's raining." The achieving deaf child should be encouraged to continue achieving.

Toward the close of the preschool years, teachers find that continuously well-guided deaf children take pleasure in working with language. The task has become an enjoyable adventure.[13] They enter into situations where they know that the teacher is going to make correct response more demanding of their thought and attention. They take up the challenge. They become more aware of what is more difficult to hear, and they learn to use and sift heard or visual language cues to clue themselves into meanings for happy, triumphant responses with language. They recognize in the situation what they don't know or understand, and say so, not with a sense of failure, but rather with discovery.

These are the children who, although still measuring below 80 to 90 decibels across the continuum of hearing, integrate into day classes for children with minimal hearing losses, or, where therapy for language, hearing, and speech is routinely provided, may attend regular classes with hearing peers,[36] and progress satisfactorily according to standards of the whole class so that referral out is not necessary. Some deaf children who qualified for such placement have been placed in foster homes in cities where appropriate educational services have been available. More cities are making required provisions for such children so that they need not leave home for best placement according to readiness. It should be pointed out that, since teachers in either of the foregoing placements may be trained only in the education of hearing children, the deaf child's receptive language and intelligibility of speech in use of expressive language must meet at least minimal requirements for reasonably facile teacher-child interaction with language.

It is quite unwise, and could be an unforgivable waste of time and lives, to act on the assumption that the best prepared *deaf* child will continue to progress satisfactorily in such placements following preschool without ongoing language reinforcement and regular conferences by concerned and responsible professionals. Although all known and pertinent factors about the child must be considered seriously and knowledgeably before school placement can be decided upon, the predominance of the child's actual functioning with language as the key factor in such decisions further emphasizes the importance of language for learning.[68]

Highly achieving deaf children may be best placed at school age in a day school or class for deaf children, in some instances within the same center as the preschool. If no day class exists in the home community, placement, if possible, in one of the relatively few truly "oral" residential schools for the deaf may be most appropriate. Under those conditions, where good teachers of the deaf understand and know how to educate the children, each child will have excellent opportunity to get a complete education in preparation for high school. No matter where the child goes to school, his performance for learning and living with language is a measurement of his maturity and of his readiness for the next step which once again requires more language.[37]

Although speech itself is not language, and many, many concepts of things, events, people, etc., must be realized through a vast number of experiences before spoken language becomes a reality, its role in human communication requires that educators make it possible for a greater number of deaf children to take on speech as an element of language.[103] Well-planned, continuous training in the development of sensorimotor skills with enriching experiences, not restricted to just single word-thing association, has for many years made this possible for an encouraging number.[51]

It is a fact that speech production as in articulation may be the poorest performance area of the very deaf child even after four or five years of appropriate preschool guidance. The receptive and expressive language may well approach the "norm" for hearing children—voluntary, habitual, and concept-based. If such prerequisites exist, the speech, through good therapy and training as to voice quality, tone, pitch, accent, and particularly breathing,[74] should become increasingly better. Having the speaking facility within his grasp helps the deaf child retain and enlarge upon language for learning. He then need not drop the paint brush, the toy, the crayon, or remove his hands from finger painting to gesture or use other signs to convey his ideas.[28] He has a better chance of being fully involved continuously and creatively with experiences that have an energizing impact on learning.[163]

Establishment of language in the young deaf child requires that environments and procedures allow for child-involvement rather than child-centeredness. Specific training with attention to the smallest detail is necessary. If, however, training in language understanding is restricted to learning to point to isolated objects or pictures, if training includes no more than speaking to the child incidentally at home or in the nursery school, or if training toward use of spoken language stops at imitation of an adult's utterance, which is not speech, the child will have little if any chance of developing language for thinking and learning.

Although teachers, parents, homes, and other services for deaf children are not equally good and appropriate everywhere, and although learning potential varies from child to child, it remains a fact that each deaf child must develop language if worthwhile education is to be possible for him.[65] Since experiences are fundamental to language, the child must be *involved* early in life in *unifying* ways with learning-based activity.[47]

Chapter 2

Auditory Training—Language

Studies and other data, published and unpublished, continue to advise us that language is learned, and is initiated auditorially.[107] Confronted with this information, parents and possibly some teachers who have not had a background of intensive training in this area may be prone to exclude or minimize the importance of auditory (aural) training in the guidance of young children who, by performance when first discovered, are deaf to spoken language.[115] Whereas a teacher may complete required training [131] or take another position, parental responsibility remains.[92] Parents must be factually and well-informed about training of existent hearing in their young child, about limitations as well as possibilities, especially where hearing at that time is known to be extremely limited. The use and care of hearing aids should be clearly explained. In spite of the advances made in auditory trainers and wearable aids, and in the expert use of them on a broader scale, it is most inadvisable to make glorified predications to any parent.

Following otologic diagnosis, audiological [38] and, if possible, developmental assessments, infants and young children are usually fitted with suitable body hearing aids.[69] Depending on the judgment of those experts in charge, any one of a number of fittings may be recommended. A child may be fitted with one hearing with a single cord, but with a mold for each ear for alternate use under continuing supervision. In some cases, one hearing aid with Y cord arrangement and a receiver for each ear may be deemed more suitable. More and more frequently, two hearing aids (one for each ear) are being recommended, even for infants.[9] Some children start out with one hearing aid, and later, upon recommendation, wear two, whether in two separate cases, or both aids in one case. For some years, the fully binaural arrangement has been in practice, particularly in centers where expert audiological supervision is routine and teachers are highly trained.

On occasion, parents have become targets for misleading opinions about hearing aids and hearing losses. They have been told, even in recent times, that language training for a deaf child was wrong and that for the child to wear a hearing aid was only to wire and mechanize him. At the other extreme, hearing aids were described as miracle cures for deafness. Parents may become very uneasy about the child's wearing of the appliance, in particular if two aids are recommended. Since the hearing aid was, or should have been, purchased following ethical and professional guidance, since no known child who has been adequately cared for has developed physical and psychological abnormalities specifically from the wearing of one or two hearing aids from his earliest weeks, parents should be reassured to overcome such fears. Unreasonable expectations should also be prevented, if possible.[101]

It should be made very clear to all parents that once the child has adjusted to the wearing of the hearing aid, he should wear it all day every day. It must be well cared for and used properly. The child who wears a hearing aid only during preschool hours, whose aid is usually in a state of disrepair or unclean, and who, therefore, may never understand its use and value, has little chance of benefiting from the appliance. The possibilities of his profiting from training only in the preschool with an auditory trainer and earphones are also few.

The child who wears one or two suitable aids full-time, which are kept clean and in working order, learns at an early age that without the aid he is cut off from many enjoyable events.

While still a preschooler he learns not to play with it, to keep it in the comfortable harness provided, to keep the microphone uncovered, to manage some of the switches carefully including how and when to switch from "mike" to "loop," and to be aware of lowered performance of the aid, at which time he will advise teacher or parent.

Many deaf children who have had concerned parents, continuing otologic attention, at least twice yearly hearing assessments by a qualified clinical audiologist, and expert educational guidance, use language at levels that cause even parents to wonder if the children really are as deaf as measurement indicates. Yet, in some cases such as prolonged illness, where the child has been without his hearing aid and the accompanying learning experiences, parents have noticed lowered performance (both in hearing responses and in language) for some time after the hearing aid could be worn again. A hearing loss, regardless of the best provisions made for the child, remains.

"HEARING" WON'T DO EVERYTHING

The child with a severe to profound hearing loss who, for some reason, is suddenly deprived of excellent aural training, even after three or four years, and who, during that time, has not had accompanying training in visual perception and enriched opportunity for sensorimotor development, can and has regressed at a startling rate. Studies have revealed that preschool age deaf children after a few years of good guidance and training are still below the norm in visual perception. There is a wealth of information available on the early development of children in general, when and how senses of taste, touch, smell, sight, and hearing function, predominantly or recessively. Under favorable conditions, the child remains a whole being with all senses, gradually developing more fully—sometimes of necessity operating two or more in unison, sometimes for prolonged periods or just fleetingly alone. (Plate II)

It is the responsibility of every educator of young hearing impaired children to be capable and highly informed about the

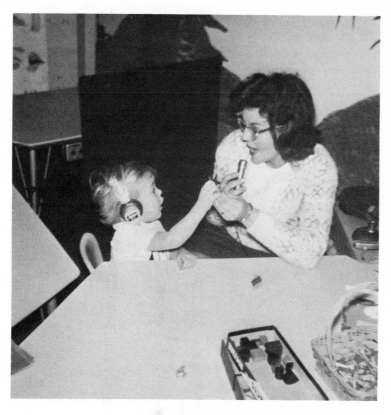

Plate II. Teacher and young, profoundly deaf child interacting with spoken language. The child, having learned to differentiate, through "hearing," between words "star" and "house," "car" and "mouse," is moving toward experiences with rhyming words, *house* and *mouse, car* and *star.*

auditory aspects of training.[150] For the child's sake and for the parents, who rely heavily on professional guidance, it is also our responsibility to prepare the child as completely as possible for ongoing education, for coping with the changes that education is subject to, and the changes education subjects him to.

Preschool guidance of hearing impaired children must be

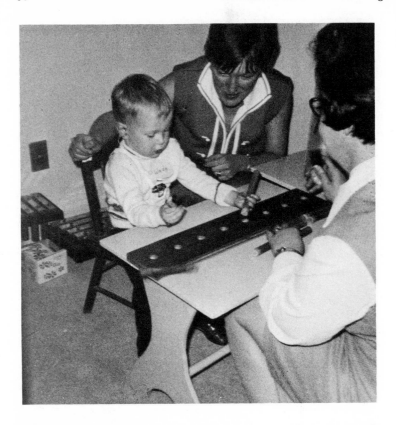

Plate III. Profoundly deaf child, almost two years of age, who, with his parents, comes to a preschool center for the first time. He is shown responding to the sound of a snapper by placing a peg in the pegboard.

identified with procedures that will help prevent problems for those children. One way is to bring each child to his highest hearing potential for language learning. This one sense can operate at maximum level only if the child is not deprived of other developmental opportunities. The indescribable importance of aural guidance cannot be disputed.[88] In preparing each child for cognitive learning within the framework of constructive experience, it is necessary for educators to plan scientifically and knowledgeably for each child, which necessitates isolating and blending techniques according to how the child learns best by doing.[17] Under such conditions, the child has a better chance of learning with language and being involved responsively with meaningful language spontaneously, whether the situation is oriented toward auditory or visual acuity or both. (Plate III)

Auditory experiences with well-planned training should play a prominent role in making the environmental provisions more effective for each child in carrying out the general and specific developmental tasks of early childhood, and in establishing the fundamentals for cognitive learning.[81]

Chapter 3

Sense Training—Language

Sense training might be described as the springboard to communication for the young deaf child.[109] It is one of his most useful tools in learning—in developing lipreading for language understanding, in speech preparation, in reading readiness—and it is a form of learning which is play for him. He can touch, manipulate, put together, take apart, match, experiment, and attain a feeling of success through constructing forms. (Plate IV)

The development of the senses of touch, sight, taste, smell, and hearing, which begins at the early levels through sense training, is closely related to the development of lipreading, speech, and reading, and also improves the quality of developed skills. The child's ability to observe, to match, to imitate, to experiment, leads to a proficiency in matching lip movements and speech patterns, in learning to recognize similarities and differences in printed forms, and in feeling free to express himself orally, physically, and creatively.

No parent or teacher who has an understanding of the child would underestimate the value of sense training activities in the guidance of the deaf child. In essence, speech training is sense training, auditory training is sense training, and every other special activity with which the worker is concerned for the promotion of the deaf child is related to sense training.

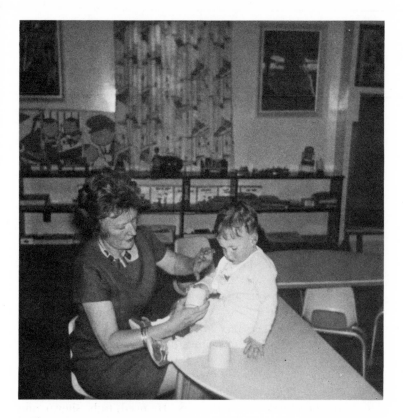

Plate IV. Profoundly deaf child, 11 months old, wearing binaural hearing aid (two hearing aids in one case), grasping section of stacking cups as teacher had done, and responding with hearing to the word, "Pull," as he attempts to remove the next cup.

The parent may feel that the time spent on matching colors, objects, pictures, etc., is a waste of time, and that someone should put a stop to this "play" and "get down to business." That parent should be reminded that in schools for hearing children, the children who have difficulty in reading and other language problems are taken through special programs that include the kind of sense training they should have had during the preschool years.[171]

Sense training assists in personality development. The activities often serve as means of expression and of emotional outlet, and so become tension reducers and security builders. Completion of a puzzle or form board results in a feeling of pride and achievement.

In the use of sense training exercises, all the constructive principles of parent-child relationships, teacher-child relationships, and of the child-guidance situation must be faithfully followed by the adult. Sometimes, there is a tendency to do the child's exercise for him, to try to make him understand that "this goes here" and "that goes there," instead of allowing him to satisfy his curiosity and his sense of achievement through touch, taste, smell, and sight, if he wishes to do so.

The young child will not tolerate for long an adult's interference with his exploratory measures without reacting and possibly refusing to cooperate with the adult in any learning situation. Guidance and direction are acceptable to the child, but interference is not, and the adult must recognize the fine line between the two.[41]

A teacher may say, very kindly. "This goes here, Johnny," and Johnny will proceed to remove the object and do something else with it. Early in the nursery years, reactions like that are to be expected.

However, the adult must not get the idea that the child should not be shown the "right" way. He needs to be shown, and he likes to "know how." The danger lies in how he is shown, and whether or not the adult is willing to accept his experimenting with the materials, and to continue showing him until he is ready to follow directions and to get satisfaction out of doing it correctly.

Sense training for the young child does not start suddenly and it never stops. While the child is still in infancy, the mother plays with his toes and tells him, "That's a toe, and that's a toe." She points to his nose and to her own, to his mouth and to her own, and talks about her actions. The child, in these instances, is getting a start in matching and in lipreading and speech.

One of the first "lessons" that the parent may *do* with the child is a form of sense training. The nature of sense training activities is such that it lends itself easily to use by the untrained person. Throughout the world, there are parents who have never had the opportunity of obtaining direct guidance from a teacher, who have had to rely on correspondence, and who are using sense training exercises effectively in guiding their respective children to oral communication.

Chapter 4

Speech Reading—Language

It has been mentioned that the eyes of the deaf child have to take over many of the jobs that the eyes and ears of the hearing child assume. In time, the hearing child is able to interpret what is being said through hearing alone, without having to watch the speaker, and he also develops an ability to interpret, through hearing, many things being *done* although the actions, within earshot, may be out of his line of vision. The deaf child is rarely in this fortunate position. He must use his eyes and other senses he possess in a normal capacity to make up for the lack of hearing.

He has to use his eyes in learning to understanding spoken language. This operation is referred to as *lipreading* or *speech reading*. In the discussion of methods it is described as the *visual* method.

Lipreading, although its obvious meaning would appear to be the reading of the lips, implies considerably more than that. Since the little deaf child must be given an early and "right" start in lipreading for the development of language understanding, the demands of lipreading and the difficulties involved should be made clear to those who are guiding the child.[66]

SOME DIFFICULTIES AND DEMANDS

Two hearing adults have only to try lipreading each other's natural speech as each stands on either side of a glass door, or by watching a silent movie with no captions, to get some conception of the difficulties involved in interpreting spoken language through lipreading. It becomes all too evident that spoken language has been developed as a means of communication between persons who hear.[82]

Every hearing person, especially one who works with deaf children or who plans to do so, should try to place himself in the position of *having* to lipread, for a better understanding of the child's problem. The person will find himself, no doubt, straining either to catch a thread of sound or squinting to see more, in the urge to tear down the barrier between himself and the speaker, or looking around frantically at the same time he is trying to watch the continuous speech of the speaker, in an attempt to get some clue as to what is being said.

Many a person who has subjected himself to such a situation, and who has tried with all his might to understand, sinks with relief into the nearest chair and groans, "It's AWFUL!" This is a normal reaction by people with a wealth of language experiences behind them.

The most "awful" part of the situation is that people tend to go through life taking language and its by-product, speech, too much for granted, whether one has hearing or no hearing. Factors which make understanding of speech a difficult task on occasion for the hearing person combine into an enormous problem for the person who does not hear.

Grammatical forms, rapid speech, very slow speech, slurred pronunciation, and facial expression or lack of it, on the part of the speaker, all affect the lipreader. It is the duty of every person to know *how* to talk. However, since many hearing people continue to think in terms of *what* they say rather than *how*, the deaf child must develop many qualities which will make lipreading of the majority more possible. He must develop quickness and alertness of mind, concentration, visual memory,

Plate V. Very young child, with severe to profound hearing loss, bilaterally, unzipping bag so that her bottle of milk may be put away, and watching and listening to her mother speaking of what is happening step-by-step.

subconscious grasp of meaning, and intuition, to supplement the speech which he is able to see and interpret.

Such abilities cannot be developed if training the young deaf child to lipread is restricted to the reading of the lips alone. Exercise in speech reading must be made a part of his everyday life.

LIPREADING TAKES TIME

This lipreading skill, which is necessary to the child's understanding of language in all respects and which must come before speech, must be developed as early in life as possible. In spite of its many real demands on the child, it can be developed while he is still at the preschool level in the course of daily living, depending on how it is done, and on the attitude of the person who is leading the way.

There must be neither hurry nor impatience, and there must be no discouragement if the child does not learn to lipread quickly. He will establish either positive or negative attitudes toward lipreading according to whether it is presented to him enjoyably or as a painful chore.

The first requirement in training the child to lipread is that everyone *talk* to him whenever it is possible and plausible to do so. The act of talking however is not sufficient. The parent and the teacher must talk about something related to the child in the situation where he is found, to something which the child can see, either as an object or an action.[144] (Plate V)

If he is exposed to speech in a happy environment, if everyone talks to him in real situations, and if he is encouraged, not forced, to watch the faces of speakers, he will begin to connect the movements of the speaker's lips and face with the object, the person, or the action of the moment. This recognition does not come swiftly. There are seldom immediate results in lipreading. The child must see the words spoken in the same relationship many times, just as the hearing child has to hear them many times, before understanding comes. It does come, however, to a gratifying and often surprising degree, if both parent and teacher are content to give the child the experiences and the time he requires.[147]

THE PARENTS' CONCERNS

Many parents, especially those who have been working with their children for a short time only, regard it as a problem that their respective children are often unwilling to watch their (the parents') faces. Far too much concern is aroused by this un-willingness.

Suppose the adult starts to train the child to lipread the word *ball*. She holds the colored object in her hand and talks to the child about it. "This is a ball, Billy. It's a pretty ball." What does the child see? He sees a mouth moving, or something happening to the whole face, but he also sees the ball, and that is more interesting to him.

He probably wants to hold it, to make it a part of himself, and to know more about this wonderful, bright thing before him. This is not only a normal reaction but a highly constructive one. After the child has had more experience with the ball and has derived some personal satisfaction from that experience, he will be more willing to look at the speaker's face. To some extent he realizes that the movements of the mouth and face relate to the plaything, and realizes more and more that everything which concerns him is related to those peculiar movements.

At first, the lip movements are merely a part of the whole expression in the whole situation. If the whole is attractive enough, and *if there is no compulsion to respond,* the child will begin to notice details. He will observe differences as well as similarities, and will notice that certain lip and facial movements go with one object or situation, while other movements go with another object or situation.

Many a parent has felt that the child pays too little attention to the lips, and too much attention to the whole face. This is only normal, as the whole means more to any young child than the part. Furthermore, the child's attention to the whole expression is essential to proficient lipreading.

In consideration of the child's tendency to notice the whole, with himself as the center, the teacher and the parent must know that a tense, harsh, anxious approach will cause him to withdraw before he realizes what the lip movements can mean to him.

It cannot be repeated too often that the parent or the teacher who is starting lipreading with the young deaf child must be content to "pour out" speech without asking the child to indicate at once that he understands. Some children take twice or three times as long as other children take to indicate understanding through lipreading. This apparent "slowness" in lip-reading is not necessarily a sign of retardation, of inability to learn to lipread, nor of any other negative factor. The indication will come in time, but it must come spontaneously if the child is to enjoy the process of learning to read the lips, and eventually to become a good lipreader.[108]

Once it is clearly understood that language understanding through lipreading is essential to speech development, the parents' anxiety for speech, which still prevails, sometimes leads to forceful methods in lipreading situations. A parent may have been told, and rightly so, that she should not attempt any formal "teaching" of speech, but that she may prepare for speech through starting lipreading with the child. Unless she is given further guidance in the lipreading process, all her drives and resources may be so concentrated in the lipreading training that she forgets the child, and does more breaking down than preparing.

One parent began to train her eighteen-month-old deaf child through the John Tracy Clinic Correspondence Course. She became disturbed almost immediately because he would not sit still and watch her as she talked. She was advised against attempting to "make" him sit still and watch her. A hearing child would not do this under the happiest of conditions, so why should the deaf child? She was further advised to attempt no formal lip-reading work at this time, but to use every opportunity to talk to him casually, to sing, to play with him, and to enjoy him.

When he was twenty-three months old, his mother brought him to a center to get an opinion from the teacher concerning his progress. He lipread simple words and directions for his mother and for the teacher, and no gestures were used by either adult. It was apparent too that the relationship between mother and child was a comfortable one.

The mother was asked how she had accomplished such results in lipreading. Her reply was that she didn't know exactly when the lipreading began, but that the child seemed to begin understanding what his mother and father said a short time after they stopped trying to "make" him read their lips.

Another parent, who had not started training until the child was four years of age, reported a somewhat similar experience with her child and made the following very cogent remark, "I suppose he figured that if *I* wanted to work so hard doing *his* job there wasn't much point in his doing it!"

GENERAL AND SPECIFIC ASPECTS

Lipreading may be divided into two categories, (1) *general* lipreading, and (2) *specific* lipreading.

General lipreading is the term applied to the comprehension of spontaneous and natural language encountered by the child during the day, in those situations which tend to be common to all children, and in which no effort is made to "teach" specific words, phrases, or other language forms. It is concerned mainly with general meanings, concepts, and understandings.

Specific lipreading is the term applied to the comprehension of specific words, to the conscious building of a lipreading vocabulary, and tends to take place in the "lesson" or deliberately contrived situation.

Specific lipreading tends to be an outgrowth of general lipreading. Both terms should be understood by the worker to enable her to give attention to all areas of lipreading and to keep closer check on the child's progress. Specific and general lipreading overlap in practice almost constantly.

In both cases, the parent and the teacher talk to the child in simple language suitable to his age and related to a familiar experience. Lighting should be good to avoid eyestrain and tension. The speaker uses normal conversational speech without mouthing, facial contortions, or exaggerations. Children have a tendency to exaggerate anyway, and if they are exposed constantly to exaggerated speech, they will learn to use speech of that nature, and may even exaggerate the exaggerated.

A discussion of each of these categories should give the parent and the teacher further assistance in organizing the child's program and in answering the question, "How do I know if he is getting all that he should be getting?"

Chapter 5

General Speech Reading

There are almost as many opportunities for general lipreading as there are incidents in the daily life of the child. Even before the child goes to nursery school, if that becomes a possibility for him, the parents talk to him and play with him just as the parents of any hearing child would do.[45] It doesn't matter if the child shows little or no understanding of what is being "said." The parents talk to him anyway. The hearing infant and young child do not "understand" all the things a mother says to either of them as each is being bathed, dressed, cuddled, etc., but this does not cause the mother to cease talking, laughing, and singing when she is with her child. Just as the hearing baby in time begins to recognize a connection between such performances, between things being *done* and things being *said,* so does the deaf child, although the ability of the deaf child to interpret specific *words* may take much longer.

Lipreading is not only an experience in itself, it is a part of every experience of the child.

"LIPREADING IDEAS" IS IMPORTANT

Real conversation is essential to the child's language growth. Expressions such as "Come to lunch," "It's time to go to bed," "Let's go to the store," "Where are your shoes?" "Get your coat,"

"Here's Daddy," and others, are a natural part of the daily life of any child, and both the parent and the teacher should grasp every opportunity to expose the little deaf child to the same expressions.

The deaf child learns to connect the lip and facial movements with events *that concern him* and which are therefore more meaningful to him. When he sees his mother working around the kitchen, setting the table, and finally saying to him. "Come to dinner," he is not only learning to understand the expression from reading the lips but also from making use of clues, such as his mother's activity, the food on the table, etc. His concept of the "words" is broadened through his understanding of the situation related to the words.

In such instances, the mother may say that Jimmy really isn't lipreading, that he is merely getting the idea from the situation. *It is extremely important that he does learn to get the idea from the situation.* That is actually the child's first indication of lipreading, and is as essential to language understanding and proficient lipreading as the comprehension of the isolated word.

Complete sentences uttered in connection with a given situation are as easily understood by the young deaf child as are single words, and if he sees them often enough in the same relationship, he eventually learns to lipread them "objectively." That is, he understands the phrases and sentences more and more independently of visible clues, such as the table, the food, etc., as in the above example.

The ability to get the general concept of a sentence, to "lipread ideas," is one of the fundamental requirements of language development. For this reason, the parent must be cautioned against restricting her training of the child to "lessons" or "drills" on isolated words. If a choice between general lipreading and specific lipreading had to be made by a parent, the wise choice would be general lipreading.

TALK: DON'T GESTURE

There is often a temptation to gesture to a deaf child, even while talking to him, especially if he does not understand immediately. For instance, while saying, "Go and get your coat;

we're going out," it may seem easy to make the gesture of putting on a coat. Unfortunately, the child will pay more attention to the gesture than to the speaker's face. This is natural for him since he tends to be impressed by the "bigness" of things, and the movements of the arms and the body are "bigger" and more noticeable than the movements of the mouth.[179]

If the child doesn't understand, the adult should go and find the coat, show it to the child, and talk about it—"This is your coat. Put it on. We're going out." In time, the child is able to understand the sentence without such assistance from the adult and without depending on the unnatural gesture. Constant exposure to such "gesturing experiences" could breed a dependence on gestures and could limit his growth in many respects.

No one with a knowledge of lipreading or of his own language would say merely "bed" if the occasion calls for using the word in a sentence. Furthermore, there are all kinds of beds in many different situations and all must be learned at some time by the deaf child; for example, "It's time to go to bed," or "Let's go to bed," or "The baby has gone to bed," or "Put the dolly to bed," or "Mother is going to make the bed," etc.

After the child has been exposed to the word *bed* in many different associations, he not only learns to lipread the word more easily in the specific lipreading situation, but also he understands that *bed* may be associated with a number of situations and people. The young child loves repetition (not drills) and through pleasurable repetition every object or action that is a part of his daily experience becomes associated, in his thinking and his understanding, with other words. And so he is learning about *language*.[96] (Plate VI)

USE "LANGUAGE" THAT LIVES

In the case of the child who is in nursery school, casual and enthusiastic talks between teacher and child, or parent and child (even though the adult does most of the talking), provide the earliest opportunities for tying up home and school activities.[104] Home and school should harmonize as much as possible, to make the child's life an integrated whole.[108]

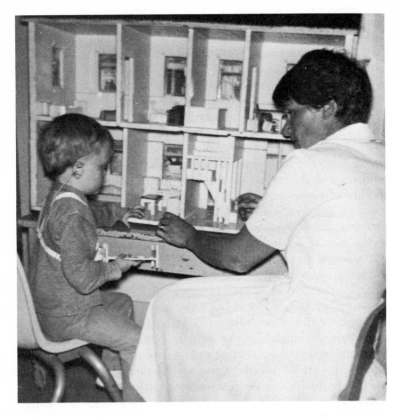

Plate VI. Three-year-old deaf child looking for a place for the toy bed in the dollhouse as her mother speaks to her about the bed and putting the bed in a bedroom. This activity (see #17 Appendix) lent itself naturally to both auditory and visual interpretation of spoken language.

The teacher would have snapshots of the child's home and his family, and the parent would have pictures at home of nursery school life. As the teacher and the parent talk to the child about things that happened at home, at school, or downtown, he is taking his first steps toward an understanding of the language relating to time and distance, abstractions which could present difficulties in later years if he has not been prepared for them.[166]

No attempt is made to "teach" the tenses of the verb, nor to make the child indicate an awareness of the use of certain phrases or other language forms, but the adult uses them naturally and casually just as she would in talking to the child who hears.

No good will come of creating a special language for the little deaf child. It is not easier for him. If a word such as *yesterday* or *again* would be used in a particular situation in talking to any child, the adult would use it in talking to the deaf child. Omitting it will not simplify understanding for the child, and may make the adult's speech and manner stilted and unnatural. The use of it does not necessarily entail an explanation of its meaning as a separate entity. The whole idea expressed in the sentence is what the child is interested in, and is what he must learn to understand.

Of course, there comes the time when the deaf child has become so conscious of spoken language, not only in terms of whole concepts, but of parts of sentences, that he will ask what something means. This may happen early or late depending on the individual child.[171] Although this is a highly acceptable development, it is often disconcerting for the parent and even the teacher who may feel "put on the spot," suddenly realizing the complications of our language, and the difficulties involved in "explaining" a word or expression which we use glibly day after day.

There are many single words which cannot be illustrated through pictures, and the adult is forced to use *situations* and *descriptive sentences* to *show* the child what is meant.

Take for example the case of the severely deaf five-year-old who was in her third year in nursery school, and whose parents had participated in her training from the time her deafness was discovered. During a play-house situation she was washing dishes used at a tea party. She began to take clean dishes and wash them after clearing away the ones that had been used. The teacher said, "That's not necessary, Beth. You don't have to wash the clean dishes."

Beth agreed, but, to the teacher's surprise, she responded with, " 'That's not necesary,' What's that?" The speech would not have been intelligible to a person who had not followed the events and conversation to that point. However, in the circumstances, it was understood by the teacher.

The teacher had to use as many objects and actions to which the expression might be applied as the facilities at hand would permit. And she used the expression in each instance. What she was able to do at that time did not cover every situation in which such an expression would be used, but it served for the time being to satisfy Beth's curiosity and to add to her understanding.

The explanation, limited as it had to be at the time, produced some interesting results. A few days later, Beth's mother asked the teacher if she had any idea where Beth might have learned to use an expression that sounded like, "That's not necessary." The teacher related the events of the previous situation.

The mother said that when she began washing some china that had not been in use for a while and which she intended using for some guests, Beth quickly informed her mother, "That's not necessary. Not dirty." The mother took the time to explain to Beth and to show her how dust collected, etc., so that in this case the dishes had to be washed.

Most five-year-old deaf children in all probability would not use the above expression, but they do adopt other expressions which are used casually in their respective environments. But they will not learn to use them if the adults try to establish a "special" language for them.

Every parent and every teacher, at some time, will encounter situations where they have to explain to the child. Since most such explanations have to be made by getting across the whole idea, it is important that from the first the child be exposed to "language that lives." Imagine the predicament of the adult if she attempted to explain each word in the expression, "That's not necessary"!

Parents and teachers give the child the language of society, make him feel understood when he tries to use that language, and give him explanations as concrete and as comprehensive as possible in the given circumstances.[162]

The basis of general lipreading might well be: Concept first, the whole before the part.

Chapter 6

Specific Speech Reading

The deaf child needs words. He must learn to use them in speaking, but before he reaches that stage, he must learn to understand them through lipreading. General lipreading experiences provide him with a familiarity with many words, and out of these experiences the parent and the teacher make a conscious effort to build a lipreading vocabulary. The so-called lipreading "lesson" has been designed for this purpose.

It has been stated that the child first appears to understand through physical clues. Then he gets a general concept of spoken language through a combination of what he sees on the lips with the physical clues which the situation provides. These stages are important since they develop naturally out of the child's everyday life. (Plate VII)

There is a need, however, to go beyond this point. The child must learn to recognize verbal clues as well as physical ones. The verbal clue may be a particular word in the whole sentence, one which he lipreads easily and which helps to make his interpretation and response faster and more accurate.

Because of the characteristics of the language, the child is certain to miss or misinterpret some words in sentences, in spite of all the vocabulary building that may be done. Since not all spoken language is visible to the lipreader, and auditory intake

Plate VII. Very young deaf child, under two years of age, learning to identify "eating" with "fruits," through experience and interaction with her mother who speaks very specifically to her about what is occurring.

for some conversational situations can be quite limited, he will always, to some extent in some instances, be dependent upon physical or situational clues. However, the more words he can recognize, the fewer he will miss or misinterpret, and the less dependent he will be upon physical clues.

Guided by the parent and the teacher in understanding words related to specific objects or actions, the child learns to lipread exact words spoken. If he is given enough of the "right kind" of practice, he may develop an impressive ability to point out pictures or objects, or perform actions at command.

It must be remembered, however, that an impressive list of words is quite useless in the total educational accomplishment unless the child understands their relation to other words and to his everyday life. For example, a young deaf child may be able to give an outstanding performance in lipreading in the schoolroom, but, once away from that environment, none of the words may mean anything to him.

Specific lipreading training will be effective only to the degree that it is made an outgrowth of general lipreading and the accompanying real experiences are related to casual spoken language. This does not imply that general lipreading stops when the specific is begun, nor that specific lipreading must be delayed until a defined period of time has been devoted to general lipreading. It does imply, however, that the rate at which the child can assimilate and understand isolated words will depend on the extent to which he has been exposed to spoken language in the home. Also, the choice of words for specific lipreading will derive in some degree from the child's past experiences and from his preferences for certain objects, activities, etc., which have been observed earlier.

Parents and teachers are constantly advised against regarding the vocabulary acquired by a certain child at a certain age as the norm in guiding other children of that age in specific lipreading. Differences in home environment, individual interests, and differences in personality will have some effect on the content and extent of each vocabulary.[125, 175]

Some children learn to lipread and understand number concepts earlier than other children. Some find colors easy to understand, while others who may be able to match colors easily take twice or three times as long to learn to lipread the names of colors. A child's attitude toward colors or numbers or actions could have some bearing on the time required for him to learn to lipread them.

Such considerations must influence our guidance of the young deaf child in the building of a lipreading vocabulary.

THE "RIGHT" WORDS

The person who is to guide the child may ask, "Where shall I start? What are the right words" One has only to watch the child in the midst of various situations—with toys, with puzzles, with pictures, with other children, with his parents and other adults—to get some idea of his preferences and so establish a starting point for specific lipreading.

Of course, one might say that all children like to play, that all children like toys, and that all children must learn this word or that word. Although it is unwise to be over-cautious, it is also unwise to make sweeping generalizations under which one might minimize the importance of the child's individuality.

The adult must consider what the child appears to enjoy most, to enjoy least, to be frustrated by, to be challenged by, to give most attention to. One might say that such investigations could go on for months, and delay the necesary training. They not only could go on, they should go on. This should not, however, cause any serious delay in beginning specific lipreading.

Everyone at some time or other has heard the parent of a hearing child remark that Billy is "just crazy" about cars, airplanes, and all kinds of machinery. In all probability, that parent didn't have to sit and take notes on her child every day of his three years to discover this interest. She accepted his interest, encouraged it, and continued to expose him to other activities and objects. A special interest does not indicate that the people in the child's environment must cease talking about other objects and activities, nor that the child will fail to acquire other interests and the corresponding words. The interest, however, should be used as a starting point.

The parent who has been *with* her child all the way should not have any difficulty in knowing *what words* to use in beginning specific lipreading. The teacher who has been trained in the observation of children as well as in the special requirements of the young deaf child, will discover in a relatively short time *where* to start.

If cars and airplanes seem to be the chief interest, *car* and *airplane* would be chosen for the first lipreading lesson. They may be in the form of toys, form boards, or, if the child is older, in pictured form also. Several toy cars and toy airplanes might be used. Each time the adult holds up a car, points to it, or gives it to the child, she talks about it in a pleasant way, permitting child and object to remain the center of interest while spoken language is used.

Generally speaking, to make use of the familiar and interesting object saves time in getting the "lesson" under way. If a disliked object is used, the child may react negatively or lose interest quickly—more quickly than his age-level would indicate. If an *unfamiliar* attractive object is used, the adult may have more than an "average" difficulty in getting the child's attention. He will want to play and experiment with the toy. This desire should be fulfilled.

Once this "new" object has become a familiar part of the child's life, he is more apt to cooperate in the lipreading situation. Probably he still likes the object, already knows a lot about it, and what the teacher or parent is doing with it now will tell him more about it. His previous satisfactions and his ever-present curiosity promote cooperation.[6]

In the first lipreading lessons, only two or three objects are used at one time. Much repetition of each word is required. However, the same objects should not be used day after day, week after week. If possible, the teacher and the parent would use many different kinds of toy cars, varying in size and color, and would improvise activities with the cars, to maintain interest while the child is being given the necessary repetition in lipreading *car*. If he begins to lose interest in a particular toy, it may be put aside for a few days and brought back later. Usually the child accepts it with renewed interest.[149]

TALK IN SENTENCES

Although certain words are made the core of the specific lipreading period, single words do not make good lipreading material. Each word should be presented in sentences so the child may get an early start in making the necessary associations between two words or more.

"This is a *ball,* Jimmy. It's a *big ball.* It rolls. See, the *ball* rolls like this. Now you have the *ball,* Jimmy. Roll the *ball* to me. Oh, you rolled the *ball!*"

The whole word in the whole sentence not only puts across the word, but prepares the child for lipreading of specific phrases such as *a big ball, a red ball,* etc. In the process of teaching lipreading, specific or general, teacher and parent are concerned with the development of meaningful language for broadening thought and for understanding ideas.

LANGUAGE FORMS

Specific lipreading periods must include exercises that will help to establish as many of the language forms common and necessary to every child as the little child is able to absorb.

The teacher and the parent cannot continue to "teach" only nouns. Verbs, adjectives, and other parts of speech must be given attention.

They would be presented, specifically, to the deaf child in an order paralleling that in which they are learned by the hearing child. Children are interested in objects; therefore, nouns tend to be the first language form presented. Action verbs might be presented about the same time. Part of the "lesson" might be devoted to nouns, part to action verbs, and in some cases to a combination.

It is not uncommon to find that some deaf children learn to lipread action verbs such as *jump, run, walk,* etc., before learning to lipread as many nouns.[1]

Adjectives, including color, number, and contrasting adjectives such as *big* and *small, hot* and *cold,* follow nouns and action verbs, and sometimes overlap.

As learning to lipread each new word is in progress, for example, a name word or noun, it is presented with other words such as color, size, etc., to allow for a growing, well-rounded language concept of each word. Thus, as understanding of spoken language with visual interpretation broadens, understood words can be used more and more in order to recognize and understand new words and expressions. The child gradually becomes less dependent upon external illustrations such as pictures and begins to use understood words and concepts to interpret broader or new concepts of language.[159]

A few minutes of each day would be devoted to the establishment of such language forms, according to the child's attention span, his interests, his readiness. All lessons would be short, interesting, and a form of play. Whenever possible, specific lipreading would be combined with speech preparation and auditory training. Every lesson should be supplemented in other situations, in and out of school and home, by exposure to general lipreading situations, so that lipreading goes on throughout each day.

THE "DIFFICULT" CHILD

In any group of families where there are deaf children, and in almost any nursery school for deaf children, there will be a child, or some children, who need special attention, and who may be referred to as "difficult."[7] Not infrequently, the specific lesson situation supplies the spark that starts the fire.

If many restrictions have been placed on the deaf child from a very early age, whether those restrictions have centered upon his behavior, eating, toilet training, or some matter related to the deafness, and if, at the age of three, four, or five, the child finds himself in an environment where freedom within limits and concerned guidance exist for the first time in his life, it is only natural that he try to make up for all the fun he has missed and seize upon outlets for expression of which he has been wrongfully deprived.[9] On the other hand, parents may have overcompensated for the handicapped child by "giving" him unlimited "freedom" to the extent that he really is not experiencing freedom at all.[41] This child may begin to act as though under pressure from within himself to find something to do that will give him inner satisfaction and comfort.[89, 95]

His actions may be so extreme, so negative, so aggressive, so "abnormal," that neither he nor the adult makes any progress in a lesson.[135] The causes of such exceptional behavior must be found and removed, but both teacher and parent must realize that pressure on the child will not solve the problem in any sense.[146]

Whenever possible, the parents of that child must be reached and helped, and the child must be given better guidance, more respect as an individual, and more understanding.[6]

TRAVEL AT THE CHILD'S RATE

The little deaf child, in specific lipreading as in any other learning situation, can travel only at his own rate, and he should be encouraged and stimulated to develop at full capacity. If the situations at home and at school are enjoyable, he will feel that his effort is worthwhile in itself, and he will develop a persistence, through pleasant experiences related to lipreading which will drive through to success.[16, 124]

Chapter 7

Speech—Language

Just as speech in the hearing person has been taken for granted, so has the lack of it in the deaf person been taken for granted by many people. A child is born, he is cared for, he eats, he sleeps, laughs, cries, and eventually walks and talks. The earlier he talks the prouder are his parents and the more admiring are their friends and neighbors. In spite of the premium that is placed on the child's ability to talk at an early age, few persons give thought to what is involved in the development of that highly prized tool for intercourse.

Speech does not appear miraculously from nowhere for no reason, in any person, and an understanding of its development in the young deaf child demands some understanding of its development in the hearing child.

THE HEARING CHILD—THE DEAF CHILD

Normal speech development in the hearing child follows approximately one general order: (1) birth cry, (2) cries that express needs and desires, (3) laughing, (4) babbling (vowel sounds first), (5) understanding of spoken language, (6) imitation of speech, (7) invented words, (8) speech to achieve something, (9)

one-word sentences—nouns and verbs first; prepositions, pronouns, conjunctions, etc., much later, (10) sentences and phrases
in haphazard order, (11) correct sentences.[46, 107]

The hearing child progresses from stage to stage as he hears
spoken language day after day, and eventually he gives back what
he hears in the manner and in the situations in which he heard it.
The deaf child goes through the first stages of laughing, crying,
and babbling in a relatively normal way. Like the hearing baby,
he enjoys the bodily sensations which occur in laughing and
babbling. However, he cannot go on to the next stage, understanding of spoken language, development of receptive language,
without special training. Auditory stimulation and awareness
must develop as this can in most cases, but, in addition to auditory intake, particularly in the case of the late-starting preschooler, additional special efforts must be made to render the
child more aware of language as expressed through speech.

UNDERSTANDING BEFORE SPEECH

Speech develops through the understanding of language—
not only an understanding of articulated language (speech), but
also through an understanding of the language of feelings,
thought, and experience.[127, 126]

The hearing child *hears* speech consciously and unconsciously from the day he is born. He hears speech in relation to
everything about him—to the feelings of his parents, to their actions, and to many experiences directly and indirectly associated
with his life. And just as he gives back the love, the hate, the
resentment, the frustration, the security, the happiness, or the
anxieties, which he has absorbed from his environment, he also
gives back the speech to which he has been exposed.

The deaf child absorbs all the influences that have to do
with feelings and experiences except the influence of speech, and
he reflects these influences in his behavior but not through
speech. He must be trained to understand speech in order that
he may use it. His feelings, attitudes, interests, and experiences

must not be impoverished or limited by depriving him of this training.

The parent of the young deaf child—as, later, the teacher—begins to make optimum use of the normal senses of sight, touch, smell, and taste. And special auditory training is begun also, to develop any residual hearing which the child may have. Parent and teacher must employ methods designed to develop a speech that is as normal as possible; hence, the pattern of speech development in the hearing child is followed as closely as possible.

The hearing child is exposed to speech that has meaning—not to isolated vowels and consonants, but to whole words, phrases, and sentences that express ideas.[52, 54] The same principle must be applied in the training of the young deaf child. Adherence to this principle will result not only in the child's developing a broad understanding of spoken language, but in his wanting to talk and in his having something to talk about. This understanding of verbalized ideas and words, which must come before speech, grows out of the general and specific lipreading which has been discussed.

People talk to the child about everything that is a part of his daily life. He learns to watch speakers, and to realize that he can do with his mouth what they do with theirs. He learns that, when he uses his voice in a certain way, he gets a more satisfying and prompt response.

As the child becomes more aware of speech and its meaning for him, he begins to imitate and to go through many of the stages of speech development that the hearing child experiences.

A GENERAL APPROACH

The child's use of his voice, in babbling and in imitating, must be encouraged. Every time the child babbles, chatters, or tries to imitate, even though the utterance is unintelligible, the adult should respond orally and accept the child's attempts at communication. This might be called a general approach to speech, an approach in which everyone may participate.

The deaf baby may wave his fist in a vague, general direction and say, "Ba!" The parent would not ignore this. The increased volume of his voice and his persistence in saying "Ba" may indicate that the baby wants something which he is as yet unable to go and get.

The mother responds with, "Ba? You want Ba? What's Ba?" The baby may continue in a demanding tone of voice, "Bababa!" The mother proceeds to find out what the baby wants, and talks about it. "Do you want the block?" and holds up a block. The baby may yell louder than ever, "Ba! Ba! Ba!" The mother looks around, sees a ball, holds it up, and says, "Do you want the ball?"

The baby may stretch out his arms eagerly and excitedly say, "Bababa," indicating that his desire has at last been fulfilled.

Incidents like this provide a simple, natural source for language understanding through lipreading and for speech development. Speech in similar situations can be especially effective when it is made a part of a response to a need.[17]

The adult's sincere attempts to understand the young deaf child when he wants something, wants to do something, or is seeking for an explanation, are of great importance in the general speech preparation. The child's spontaneous "remarks," during play or his participation in creative and other developmental activities, receive attention whether they are intelligible, partly intelligible, or unintelligible. The adult gives the child the correct words and spoken language, but the child's attempts at imitation should be accepted without the situation being turned into a painful, formal, corrective speech "lesson." [52]

For example, if a three-year-old deaf child comes to his mother with an "I want" look on his face and says, "Uppa," the mother quickly tries to understand what he wants. It may be his toy airplane. So she responds with, "You want your *airplane*?" He may nod quickly and say, "Uhuh, aipai," or some such approximation, and he is told or shown where his airplane may be found. The mother's response results in the child's more accurate pronunciation of the word. In all the probability, he could do an even better job, but the particular situation does not lend itself to more specific speech work. Instead, the parent makes a mental note of the word and will provide for further practice in both general and specific speech situations.

SPECIFIC APPROACH

Specific terms are used in reference to the development of each sense which enters into speech development. These are: visual, tactile, auditory, rhythmic, kinesthetic.

The *visual* aspects of the training has been discussed under Lipreading (page 39). The child learns to use his eyes in detecting differences and similarities in lip movements, in things and people around him, in actions and interactions. Development of the sense of sight takes place through living experiences of childhood, through sense training exercises, through developmental activities such as painting, block building, experiences with books, etc., and through the incorporation of all other aspects of the training. Adequate training of the sense of sight results in better lipreading and better speech.

The *tactile* refers to the sense of touch. The child learns a great deal through feeling and touching objects and people. He can also be made more aware of his own voice and the voices of others by feeling his own face, and the faces and bodies of others, during speech and speech play. Development of the sense of touch in every possible respect makes the use of the other senses more effective.

From the earliest possible moment the deaf baby, or the deaf child should be exposed to experiences in touching and feeling. It must be done playfully and happily so the baby or the child will accept the activity as part of his normal existence.[70]

Most babies touch and pat their parents' faces, and like to cuddle close to the parents' bodies, and deaf babies do the same. Every time it happens, the parent should sing, hum, talk, laugh, —use the voice in some pleasant manner. An awareness of the "feel" of voice and other sounds need not be forced upon the child, it should develop with him. In time, he notices that when the mouth moves he feels something, and gradually he thinks of these as a unit.[123]

The *auditory* involves stimulation of the hearing mechanism as a means of making the visual and the tactile more effective and of making the deaf child more conscious of sound for better speech.[88] (See Auditory Training—Language, page 87.)

The *rhythmic* includes every type of exercise or play that could arouse in the child an awareness of the flowing movements of the body and of the relationship between such movements and speech, music, and singing. Rhythm experiences help to lay the foundation for more fluent, more normal speech.[121]

The *kinesthetic* is concerned with developing the sense of timing and of feeling in the muscles involved in speech production. The baby and the young deaf child engage in speech play as they babble, etc. The child enjoys the sensations produced as he uses his voice experimentally. Babbling and speech play should be permitted and encouraged as giving the speech muscles a chance to perform in a relaxed way, as a sort of rehearsal for later performance in learning speech production.[74, 109]

These trends toward meaningful speech should be coordinated as much as possible and blended into the child's development as a whole. Techniques are necessary to speech development in the deaf child, but they must never become a bugaboo.

The teacher and the parent adapt methods to the child, letting one method predominate over others according to the child's enjoyment of and responses to various elements of the training.

If the adult finds that the child enjoys "listening" more than any other part of the training, she would make auditory training the center of most activities, and would use it as a wedge for the introduction, incorporation, and acceptance of other necessary elements such as lipreading, rhythm, sense training, speech imitation, etc. If the child prefers games, as much as possible should be accomplished through the medium of active play.[31, 179]

THE PARENTS' CONCERNS

The parent, understandably desirous of speech and understanding for her deaf child, may become far too concerned about the problems and difficulties that must arise, even to the degree that every real problem may be magnified. The anxieties, sometimes the nature of the guidance provided for parent and child, may force the parent unwittingly to subject the child to boring, fatiguing, technical methods that inevitably do more harm than good.

There is the parent who is disturbed because her child of three or four years doesn't have a *k* sound. She has struggled—perhaps the teacher has also—and all to no avail. Further investigation shows that relatively little, if any, attention has been given to language understanding through lipreading and experiences, or to the encouragement of spontaneous speech.

The young deaf child who has been exposed to fluent natural speech in his environment and who has been encouraged to use, spontaneously and in his own way, whole words, even phrases and sentences, has a far better chance of developing the highly prized *k,* or any other speech element.

The teacher knows that the development of separate vowels and consonants is necessary to intelligible speech, but she is also aware of the fact that many vowels and consonants develop easily and spontaneously by the use of whole words that have meaning to the child, through his own imitation of those words.

Mastery of any vowels and consonants and their many combinations by the use of whole words, phrases, and sentences, makes the acquisition of those still to be mastered a much simpler process for teacher, child, and parent.

Any speech work with isolated consonants and vowels should be in the form of speech play with emphasis on the whole idea and on the child.[111]

By the time the child is ready for more specific speech work, his speech muscles will have had much experience operating in a relaxed manner, he will have had sufficient time to acquire some understanding of language and a better idea of where speech fits into his scheme of things, and his degree of maturity will permit him to accept the more specific training which certain speech elements require.[147]

The little deaf child who has had some training in the home or in the school, or in both, may attempt words only when he can imitate a speaker. This may discourage his parents, who think that he will never talk because he doesn't do it of his own volition. The parent must be informed that many a hearing child does this, or—a parallel tendency—often has a jargon or language of his own. As the father of a little hearing child said, "Once in a while he talks English; most of the time it's some other language."

After the young deaf child learns to say one or two words well and spontaneously, he may attach one or both of them to everything he sees. This, too, is common among hearing children in the earlier stages of speech development. As the child learns to use other words spontaneously, this "improper" use of words gradually disappears.[117]

There are times when the deaf child will stop using words he has known and used at an earlier age, and the parent may become alarmed. This occurs also in the early speech development of the hearing child, although many people are not aware of it since they are not concerned so specifically with speech development as is the parent of the deaf child. The child simply has become more interested in "new" words and prefers them to the "old" ones.

The first words are not forgotten. Adults in the child's environment continue to use them as usual, and even though the child himself sees less reason for his using them at present, the words have not ceased to be a part of his environment and of him. In time, he learns to coordinate his whole vocabulary in expressing himself.

When the deaf child begins to use sentences, he, like the hearing child, uses nouns or verbs or both and usually omits prepositions, conjunctions, and pronouns. To any child, the important parts of a sentence are those words which indicate things and people and the actions revolving about both.

A complete understanding and the consistent, proper use of prepositions, conjunctions, and some pronouns demand a much longer period of training for the deaf child than the preschool years provide. The child should be exposed to all commonly used language forms in casual situations and in "lesson" periods, and as his understanding indicates a readiness, his attention might be brought to his omission of this word or that, depending on the occasion. However, drills on such words as *to* and *it* are not advised and seldom are helpful.

It is far more indicative of progress if the child says, "Go store," for "I want to go to the store," than if he could imitate the word *to* and couldn't understand the sentence in which it would be used.

If parents can be brought to understand that much of their concern is without foundation and that the so-called problems they see are frequently not real problems but positive signs of speech development, there will be fewer "errors" in their guidance of the deaf child.

The parent must also understand that the deaf child cannot acquire all the language and speech skills which are necessary to the adult while that child is still at the preschool level.[2]

SPEECH DEVELOPMENT—NOT SPEECH CORRECTION

It is important that the parent and the teacher be speech conscious, be aware of developments in speech as related to the whole child and of irregularities in the development which need extra attention. However, whether the adult is taking a general or specific approach to speech, the emphasis is on *speech development* and *speech preparation,* not on *speech correction.* It is imperative that persons who are training young deaf children understand that speech development is not the same as speech correction. *What isn't there can't be corrected!*

The young deaf child's first attempts at speech, regardless of how unintelligible they may be, should be considered neither "incorrect" nor speech defects. He is learning to use his voice for specific purposes and should be encouraged to do so. He must be given time to realize that he has a voice which he may use for a purpose.

If he is exposed to well-articulated, meaningful speech, and is himself happy and relaxed, speech correction should not enter the picture until he indicates that he understands what speech is for and how to use it. And, the amount of speech correction necessary will depend on how much attention and what kind of attention was given to *speech preparation* at the preschool level.[32]

PERSONALITY AND SPEECH

The personality factor is one of the first considerations in the development of meaningful speech in the young deaf child. Speech is only a part of the whole, and its quality and its use will be commensurate with the quality of the whole child. The teacher and the parent are not merely trying to induce the child to "say words"; they wish to train him to communicate orally, so that whatever qualities, aptitudes, and intelligence he possesses may be more effective in his relation to society.[76]

Both teacher and parent must understand the influence of family life and social surroundings on the total personality of the child, and that the coordination of the vocal mechanism with the mental processes is related to developmental growth and emotional stability.[87]

There must be an understanding of the child, his limitations, his possibilities, and a respect for his individuality. Emotional reactions of the parents and the teacher which could affect the child emotionally, could also affect speech production.[43] There must be relaxation, acceptance of the child, and provision for his fundamental needs, if speech is to develop as normally as possible.[58]

The child himself should always remain more important than speech. If he meets with approval only when he says something "well," he will come to feel that speech is more important to his parents and his teacher than he is, and he may refuse to talk or cooperate in speech situations. If the pressure has been so great that he develops fear, and tries to cooperate for fear of punishment, his voice may be strained and tense, and poor speech habits may be permanently established.[21]

Speech responses will be slow as compared with responses to sense training, lipreading, and those parts of the training closer to the child's normal senses. Speech is a great part of the objective that teachers and parents hold for the child, and the desire for it must not entail any attitudes or pressures upon the child which would retard speech.[57] The child will not accept speech nor use it as well as he is able, if he has been subjected to strain, unreasonable demands, and rejection from earliest child-hood.[87]

At its best, the speech of the very deaf child, even after years of training, cannot be described as "normal" in every respect.[116] Imperfections and deviations from the normal are bound to exist, but they may be minimized by making speech enjoyable to the child from the beginning.[113]

During the first months, parent and teacher strive to lay the foundation for the development of habits of attention, concentration, and cooperation which lead to social adjustment, emotional stability, and a healthful approach to speech.[117]

The child must be made to feel that he is a part of the world and that he has something useful to contribute. He must learn to understand and to feel understood. These are factors more essential in his development of meaningful speech than dry speech "lessons" involving techniques that he is not prepared to understand or accept.

The understanding he encounters and acquires in the first months through happy experiences within the family group and with others continues to grow until he exhibits a desire to speak. To accomplish this end, every adult who takes it upon himself or herself to guide the deaf child must remember that he or she is working with the child for the child, and the choice of methods and techniques will be made on that basis.

The essentials of speech development demand the removal of all unnecessary restrictions.[165] There has been considerable discussion and some disagreement about giving the deaf child of nursery years as much freedom as is the rule in some centers. Unfortunately, there still exist those persons who think that freedom in play is valuable, but that when it comes to the "lesson" a child should be strictly disciplined. It is also unfortunate that the same individuals cannot or will not see that unreasonable restrictions in one situation influence every other situation.[89]

There must be a consistency about child guidance.[101] The child who feels free in every situation, and at the same time feels secure in the knowledge that he is being guided by strong people who love him as he is, will be responsive in all situations, will

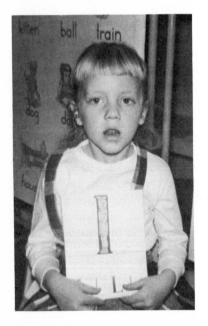

Plate VIII. This five-year-old child, with moderate hearing loss, is pictured saying words containing sounds in various positions in those words. Her language, receptive and expressive, was sufficiently well-established that she could profit from speech therapy. Pictures such as these, enlarged, can be a motivating factor in training procedures.

want to communicate with others, will be eager to obtain and retain information, and will have a sound foundation on which favorable speech skills can be built.[140]

The synthetic approach to speech development—that is, an approach that envelopes the whole child, the whole word, and the whole idea, in the whole scheme of living—leads to more normal speech with fewer "deafisms" in the speech and in the personality. And when the child is ready emotionally and intellectually for the analytical approach—that is, more technical training on *parts* of speech—he will be more accepting and cooperative, and the results will be more lasting and effective.[73] (Plate VIII)

Deaf children develop speech at different ages just as hearing children do. One deaf child should not be compared with another for his advancement in speech skills, nor judged on the basis of his large or small vocabulary. The child's achievements of this year would be compared with his own of a year ago, and his own progress from time to time would be the measuring stick for his growth.

The teacher and the parent must remember that speech is not the *all* in the life of the deaf child. The attitudes and habits necessary to the development of social skills, the understanding of language, and clear, usable speech, are established in the nursery years. Great responsibility rests upon parents and teachers.[83]

Chapter 8

Reading Readiness—Language

Reading skills are vital to the deaf person throughout life. The ability to read well puts him in touch with his world, helps him to develop his personality, and gives him an unfailing sense of recreation. Before he can understand the language of the printed page, he must have learned to understand language in its other forms—spoken language, the language of experience through play and activity in everyday life—and to have some conception of the role of language in society, and its place in his life.

This preparation or readiness for reading begins in the nursery years, long before the child has any awareness of the printed word. Every experience that the child has had from birth comes with him to his first true reading experiences in the schoolroom, and the nature and number of those experiences will have a definite bearing on the ease or difficulty with which he attempts the printed page.

The educator knows, and the parent must be brought to know, that reading is a basic tool subject throughout the school years. Difficulties in reading will retard the child in every other subject. The deaf child's progress in reading tends to be much slower than that of the hearing child, and accordingly his progress in other areas is held back. His progress may be accelerated by laying a good *foundation for reading,* early.[93], [109]

It would be unfortunate if, in the attempt to develop reading skills, the young deaf child were forced into the formal reading situation at too early an age. The child cannot be developed into a better adult, nor made to mature more rapidly, by making him behave as an adult; nor will he be made a better reader by "teaching reading" to him before he is ready, simply because he is a deaf child.

Reading difficulties are based to a large degree on language difficulties. The deaf child in the grades may be able to say certain words in a passage, may recognize them as meaning a particular object or activity, but he is not reading unless he can get the whole idea from the passage well enough to answer and ask questions regarding the content. If he cannot perform at this level, the teacher, even in the literature or social studies lesson, must turn the lesson into one on language, and the child will probably take two years to cover the work of one level.

There is no royal road to reading skills for the deaf child, and problems certainly do arise for even the best prepared. However, if a better language background is laid in the nursery years and if consideration has been given to all factors contributing to reading readiness, the difficulties in the grades should be fewer and more easily dealt with, and the whole progress of the deaf child could be speeded up.[83]

The hearing child has approximately six years in which to assimilate knowledge and experiences through living, before he is exposed to a reading program. He has learned to understand what people are talking about, to recognize the relationship between spoken words and activities and people, to observe actions and reactions among people, to use spoken language himself, and to express himself in many ways. His parents read books to him, give him the names of things and people about him, and expose him to all the experiences that his environment permits. These are all essential reading experiences which must precede experiences with printed words.

Studies have shown that mental alertness, good health, social adjustments, and emotional stability, ability to "perceive sequence" and to reorganize ideas, good work habits, ability to concentrate, sensory ability, adequate motor control, and a keen interest in learning, as well as an ability to understand in oral situations any words that might appear in the first reading books, are all important requisites for reading. "In general, a child is ready for reading when his total development is sufficient to enable him to engage effectively in the various activities involved in learning to read. However, it should be understood that lack of ability in any of the elements that comprise reading readiness may tend to retard the *rate of progress* in learning to read." [157]

Proficiency in these fields must be attained before the young deaf child can be expected to read. The fact that the child is deaf cannot justify the teacher's nor the parent's attempts to "teach reading" before the child is equipped with the tools that will make reading possible. Such attempts are at best superficial and harmful.

The deaf child must be physically ready before reading is introduced to him. His eyes, which are of such special importance to him, must not be overtaxed, and the eyes of a very young child are not able to make the visual discrimination necessary for word recognition and the reading of phrases and sentences.

Emotional readiness and maturity are equally important. The deaf child has to make adjustments beyond those of the hearing child, and further pressures, such as being expected to read while he is still at the preschool level, will increase his adjustment problems. Early reading, before the child is ready, may cause tensions that produce confusion in reading, defective focusing of the eyes, and a general retardation which may not appear until the child is past the preschool years, when both reading and emotional problems are much more difficult to resolve.

Although no formal reading program for the preschool deaf child should be pursued, the wise teacher and parent must recognize the need for an adequate reading readiness program. When the printed word enters of necessity into such a program, the adult in charge must employ it with due regard to the distinction between reading and reading readiness. The deaf child cannot be expected to read younger than the hearing child, but he should be, as early as possible, exposed to a reading readiness program that is directed toward his understanding the spoken language associated with all his experiences—lipreading, speech, sense training, auditory training, creative activities, free play, and activities with the people he encounters at home, in nursery school, and in the community.

Reading cannot become a social and intellectual tool skill until receptive language is developed.[75] The idea that the reading process is unrelated to an understanding use [158] of a syntactic language is misleading.[44]

Before he is introduced to the printed word, the child should have a working knowledge of that word in relation to everyday life. As the child is led from the known to the unknown and is taught to use the familiar (visual-auditory interpretation and experiences) to help him interpret the unfamiliar (the printed word), he is being soundly *prepared* for reading.

The word "reading" is frequently misused, especially in respect to deaf children. One must not get the impression that being able to recognize a number of isolated words is "reading," nor that the child who can recognize a number of words in a particular situation is able to read. Word recognition is merely a part of the reading readiness program. Furthermore, the degree to which the child understands that word and the contribution such recognition will make to his future reading skills will depend on how well he is able to understand it by lipreading and listening in the situations of everyday life, and how broad a concept of that word he possessed before he encountered it in printed form.[44]

The child who understands the printed word before him will not only be able to connect it with the corresponding picture or object in the immediate situation, but, consciously or unconsciously, will remember other experiences which he has had with that word. The teacher and the parent aim for this kind of recognition. The more experience the child is able to take to the printed page, the faster he will interpret the printed words, he will feel more secure about the new situation, he will be stimulated to learn more words in this way, and he will be getting another and a broader concept of language.

The language understanding that makes for good reading is developed by experiences with language through lipreading and listening in real situations and from developmental growth, not from printed words. (Plate IX)

Plate IX. Deaf children in their sixth years tracing over lines from left to right, part of a reading readiness program and preparation for later reading and writing.

WHEN AND WHERE TO START

The parent often wonders when the child should be exposed to printed words. Actually he is exposed to them from the time he is first read to from books. He may become interested in them before the adult thinks of introducing them. This interest of his, however, must not be interpreted as a signal to begin "reading" in the schoolroom sense.

There are three-year-olds and four-year-olds who have gone to their parents and teachers with printed pages, wanting to know "what they say." Certainly no teacher or parent will deprive the child of an explanation. Indeed, this situation offers an excellent opportunity for constructive talking to the child and for encouraging his interests. But the adult must not immediately go about setting up a program that centers around word-recognition. Most three- and four-year-olds are not ready to understand printed words, and although printed words may begin to appear for him in more and more places, no emphasis should be placed on those words. The child is merely being exposed to them as a means of making him conscious of their existence. Later he will become aware of their relationship to things in his life, and still later will be able to interpret them in the light of those relationships. If the deaf child of three or four is forced to spend a large part of the daily training in the superficial performance of identifying certain words, then other activities that are much more necessary to his total development, and in particular to his future reading ability, are being neglected.

In the event of a three- or four-year-old exhibiting a desire to find out about a printed word, the teacher and the parent should try to satisfy the child's curiosity through familiar channels. The child may be curious about the word printed below the picture of the boy. The adult would tell the child that it says *John,* and that the boy's name is *John.* "You are *Billy.* That is *John.* This is *John,* and that says *John."* If the child is still attentive and interested, the adult might get a pencil and two carboard strips, and print *John* on one strip and *Billy* on the other. "This says *Billy.* That says *John."* The adult might get a snapshot of Billy and clip the name to the picture, and place the other strip on the page of the book.

In such an instance the child is getting more practice in listening and lipreading, in matching a printed form to a picture, and, although his understanding of the printed form itself is at a minimum and is entirely dependent upon his understanding of spoken language, another concept of language is taking root.

Other simple printed words may be introduced gradually in connection with lipreading, speech, and auditory training. But they should be introduced as casually as a new picture would be hung upon the wall, with the emphasis on the lipreading, the pictures, and the activities that revolve about the word, not on any attempt to get the child to interpret the printed form.

Action verbs are frequently used by teachers in the early word recognition periods, especially with those children who are interested in activity and have therefore easily learned to lipread such words. In the lesson where such words are being used for lipreading and speech practice, the printed form of two or three might be introduced. The child has already learned to watch the speaker's face, and as the adult says, "Run," and holds up the printed word on a card, the child, although probably interested in this new approach, is still getting the idea through speech reading and listening. And he should be permitted to do so.

The adult must not expect the child to stand and study the word for minutes, to become frustrated, and even insecure and frightened, when he could be led to understand the printed word through his already established language skills. Once more, parent and teacher are reminded of the principle of leading the child from the familiar to the less familiar.

In time, as the child encounters a few printed words in connection with other lessons, he begins to realize that there are differences in printed forms just as there are differences in spoken forms, and in colors and forms used in sense training. And he begins to notice that, when a certain word is said, a particular printed form appears at the same time. The deaf child must be given time to make such identifications for himself without any force from the adult.

Usually, by elementary school entrance, the well-prepared deaf child associates the printed word as identifiable with some object, action, person or event. He may also realize that actions and activities may not only be spoken of, but may be printed about. This realization is a great stride toward reading, even though the child is as yet able to interpret but few printed words. Reading readiness has been established in his total development through the preschool years as one more experience by which to enrich other experiences, one more way of expressing himself— not a "subject" apart from living.

In the presentation and use of printed words, phrases, and short sentences, the adult is once more reminded that the symbols on the little strips of paper must not stand alone, as abstractions. Every printed form used is related to conversation, books, pictures, and other interesting activities, even to the five-year-old. There is a constant attempt to broaden the concept of any language form presented, and for this reason lipreading, speech, auditory training, reading readiness, and other means of language development must be combined as much as possible.

Printed forms must make their appearance as whole words rather than as single letters of the alphabet, just as whole words must be used in beginning lipreading and speech. The whole word, spoken or printed, can be illustrated, while a letter of the alphabet cannot, and in reading readiness, as in other phases of the training, the deaf child must be given a concept which can be made as concrete as possible and which he can understand in relation to living.[143]

Words are matched to objects and pictures, and to corresponding words, just as in sense training identical pictures and objects were matched. The parent and teacher will find that the child who has had ample experience with sense training activities will learn to recognize much more easily the similarities and differences among printed words. (Plate X)

Later on, simple phrases, such as *a big ball, a red house,* and others with which the child has become familiar, are introduced in printed form. In time, the child learns to match them to corresponding pictures and to corresponding printed phrases. Later still, short, simple sentences are used in a like manner.

Some deaf children, by the time they are ready for Grade I, recognize a number of words, phrases, and sentences; others may recognize very few or none. Differences among even the most intelligent children will be noted. The progress of the deaf child and his readiness for Grade I should not be measured by the number of printed words he is able to recognize, but rather by the requisite preliminaries to reading which he has acquired through the previous reading readiness program set up and followed by his parents and teacher.

The value of reading readiness at the preschool level should not be vitiated by making printed forms the core of the training. The deaf child at the preschool level can be *prepared* for reading; he will not read.

Plate X. Deaf children, approaching their sixth birthdays, identifying, upon request from a teacher, pictures in books or mounted on cards which correspond with seasons and seasonal activities. Children learn to tell a two or three sentence story about each season. Follow-up printed sentences, well-understood as to language content, may then be identified with each painting on the wall, and with others in books.

The printed form, introduced at the "right" time for the individual child, can be a source of stimulation and interest in learning, and although communicative language, person-to-person, takes priority, this new experience with words can be an accelerating factor in the total language development.

In setting up a reading readiness program for the young deaf child, parent and teacher will adhere to the basic principles of learning and teaching: to proceed from attitudes to habits to skills, to establish impression before expression, and to adapt techniques to the individual personality. They will not make the error of molding the child to a reading program that is far beyond his capacity to comprehend.

The parent and the teacher who can establish language understanding through lipreading and experiences which the deaf child must have will know how to prepare the child for future reading skills without destroying the developmental values that a reading readiness program should have.[179]

Chapter 9

Developmental Activities—Language

Developmental activities include all those activities which help the child develop himself through living. Whether the child is deaf or not, the avenue of learning for him, along which he makes his way from childhood to adulthood, is through play and other experience.[26] Since the problems of deafness could make this progress more difficult and complex, play and experiences that especially provide impressions and expression would be particularly relevant to the young deaf child's development.[60]

Observation of the child in all situations—play, games, painting, etc.—gives the parent and the teacher a better understanding of the child—his aptitudes, his problems, how far along in his development he may be, in what direction he appears to be going—and suggest what may be done to direct and redirect his energies for healthier and more positive growth.[71] Developmental activities, serving as a means of revealing problems, also serve as one means in resolving them.[99]

The fact that the deaf child during the first years is deprived of one outlet for expression—speech—could indicate an especially urgent need for more expression through the other means at his disposal. Provision for more interests, and outlets that are well-chosen in relation to his needs and personality, could help to alleviate frustration, as a "stop-gap" until the time when the child is able to express himself through speech.

As the child is exposed to many activities, he learns to participate with others, to achieve some measure of success in each activity, and to develop the special aptitude to the greatest possible degree.[133] This helps to lay the foundation for a more versatile adolescence and maturity. The child discovers not only what he can do best, but that he can do many things.[29] He does not stop painting because Johnny's pictures are more acceptable to the teacher, nor does he scorn Johnny's attempts at woodworking because his own are more acceptable to teacher and parent. The adult must not be responsible for adopting these destructive attitudes and imposing them upon the child.[122] Teacher and parent guide the child and measure his success both by the amount of effort he puts into an activity and by the amount of enjoyment he gets out of it, not by comparing his work with that of some other child.[54]

Language is related to these activities, and, although the value of the exercise of language should not be destroyed nor lessened by being turned into a speech or lipreading lesson in the formal sense, there are many times when the situation lends itself naturally to talking to the child. Teachers and parents discover that the deaf child's interest in the activities stimulates his desire to watch lips and to attempt further expression through his own speech.

Language grows through dramatic play, games, excursions, creative activities, music and rhythm, and experiences with books.[51] Such developmental activities are adapted to the child in the home, in the neighborhood, in the hearing nursery, or in the nursery school for deaf children. They are the need of all children, a common bond between the deaf child and the hearing child. (Plate XI)

The teacher and the parent with vision, who make the child's world rich in experience and opportunity for expression, determine to a great degree the nature of the child's future.[148]

"We define the child in development by Goethe's word as 'a stamped form, developing itself through living.' In other words, a personality nucleus is supposedly inborn, but life directs the development of this nucleus, stimulating certain parts, suppressing others.

Plate XI. This very young deaf beginner is finding opportunity to satisfy his curiosity at the same time someone nearby is talking to him about things in the barn, which may be pulled out one at a time through the larger door on opposite side, and named for him.

The educator with this viewpoint must first become very familiar with the nucleus of the child's personality. If the child shows extreme motor activities, it will go against the child's nucleus always to keep him quiet. But, on the other hand, the motor activities the child can be directed; they can be realized in sports emphasizing the child's feeling of his own body; they can be realized in games emphasizing the child's social relationships; they can be realized in the child's creative activities. The educator has the task of bringing into accord dispositions and aims, the 'what' and the 'for what.' The 'what' of the child's dispositions has to be explored carefully, observing his thought and expression. The 'for what' should be a mixture of the educator's ideals and the child's possibilities." [179]

Part 2

Activities
for Language
Development

Chapter 10

Auditory Training Activities
for Language Development

The activities suggested in this section are some of those which have been helpful in guiding and training deaf children toward language learning with an emphasis on hearing, listening, and auditory interpretation.

The born "deaf" baby, who within his first year of life is able to wear hearing aids,[70] sometimes night and day, and for whom essential provisions are made and maintained, has been known to benefit from appropriate auditory stimulation to the extent that his pattern of language development, with little time difference, has been very similar to that of the "normal," hearing child of the same age. He usually continues to vocalize, has fewer long periods of silence or yelling at unusual pitches, holds rather than drops the early "k" and "g" sounds as in the so-called "gooing" and "cooing," and begins to vocalize with a variety of sounds which are optional, depending on what response he wants from his parents. He is immediately reinforced by family members when his vocalizations resemble words unknown to him by their saying the words in association with something in the immediate surroundings. He is treated as, and therefore spoken to as a person. What the baby does during his waking hours, what others do in his presence, is put into spoken language near him.

The baby begins to drop some earlier sounds he made but which are not in the English language, sounds to which he is never exposed. The language with which he will receive his education is the one to which he must be exposed from the beginning of his training. Only training, with an emphasis on the aural aspects, will allow the little deaf child to drop unnecessary sounds, such as sharp tongue clicks, gutteral utterances, etc., which are very difficult to eliminate when the child is of school age. Sounds in the spoken language of the culture in which the child will probably spend most of his growing years must be emphasized, and all other sounds dropped. The little deaf child cannot cope with bilingualism at a speaking level.

The baby's prime interest in the expressive human face, over and above all other forms, including bright colors, allows parents to relate to him specifically and warmly with spoken language. As he becomes more capable physically—rolling, sitting, climbing, walking, etc.—his attempts and successes are accompanied by the spoken language of approving and pleased parents. During his second year, he begins identifying similarities in toys and other objects, working at one-piece puzzles, and looking for, sometimes calling, "Daddy," and "Mommy." By his second birthday, he may have a few words he uses for known purposes. In short time, he may have a few expressions and phrases which he uses meaningfully. Language for learning has been allowed to come into being early through needed experiences with auditory stimulation and training.[174]

TRAINING MUST BE CONTINUED

Deaf children, whose development approximates the aforementioned pattern, upon admission to highly language-oriented nursery schools, appear to function at a relatively "normal" and desirable level of behavior and response. There tend to be few separation problems and fears of the unknown, such as those demonstrated by older, beginning preschoolers, and these are short-lived if they exist at all. Nevertheless, such children still have a long way to go. Adequate total training, with emphasis on auditory training, has, up to this time when he is between

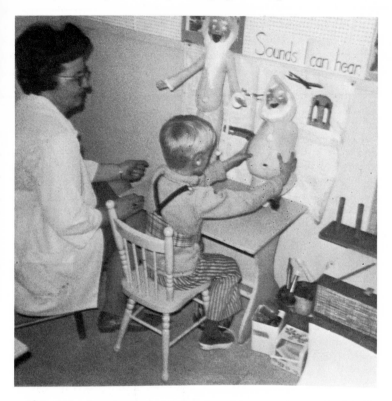

Plate XII. Preschooler in his fourth and last year in preschool, with profound hearing loss, bilaterally, identifying, through hearing only, the correct figure, described as: *the tall man, the fat man, the thin man, the short man, the tall, thin man, the short fat man, both men, the man with the long beard,* etc.

two and three years of age, given him an irreplaceable beginning. No educator and no parent can assume that the child will go on to build in needed language skills just through "normal" exposure to speaking and happily active children and adults.[45]

This implies that these motivated and well-reinforced early starters must be guided skillfully toward becoming as aware as possible, auditorially, of more and more language expressions, and the variations appropriate to every experience. (Plate XII)

Abstract forms which cannot be associated in isolation with real objects or with action, sequence of events in storytelling through pictures, acting out and spoken language, asking questions and not always in the answering role, concepts of one and more than one as in singulars and plurals, collective nouns and pronouns, plus all other needed expressive language of childhood, require training through childhood experiences. Where auditory responses have been well established, and where well-planned and thorough guidance is available at home and in the preschool, these early beginners should be able to establish (before school entrance) all the required language concepts, be able to understand them with relative ease, and use them spontaneously.[56]

The deaf (severely or profoundly) child, who by age two or three years has demonstrated by performance that aural emphasis in his guidance program as a child and as a hearing handicapped child really works for him, must have responsible parents and teachers to provide ongoing auditory learning opportunity for him. Under those circumstances, almost all language activities outlined in this book can be used with the child, and without depriving him of the opportunity to develop all sensorimotor skills, they can be carried out with emphasis on auditory intake for internalizing language. (Plate XIII)

OTHER DEAF PRESCHOOLERS

There are some extremely deaf preschoolers who may be late starters, some who are multihandicapped [118] or who have secondary handicaps, some with learning deficiencies, and those who suffer environmental deprivation.[130] The latter ones are possibly the most difficult to help in lasting ways, including the reinforcement that auditory training in a preschool center might provide. Sometimes, the nature of guidance provided in the center, particularly by the social worker, can arouse the interest of parents to some degree of constructive involvement. The least that auditory training can do for any of these children is to help them develop a greater awareness of environments and selves.[76] On that basis alone, each child should have the opportunity of profiting, if possible, from such training, at least until such time

Plate XIII. Severely hearing impaired preschool child, five-and-a-half years old, in her fourth and last year in preschool, responding to teacher's questions, such as: "Where is the picture of the boy kicking a ball?" "Which is the picture of the girl sitting on the floor?" "Find pictures of a girl eating and of a boy washing his face." "What is the boy with the yellow sweater doing?" Expected responses would include, for example, "There," "There it is," "Those" or "These," "He's drinking milk."

that it seems to be of no appreciable value to him, and perhaps could become a hardship.

These children, all of whom before special training, have been or have become handicapped beyond deafness alone.[105] Such children can easily be the forgotten ones, even in today's world. Yet there are deaf adults, successful by today's standards, who were late starters, had little preschool training, who were able to achieve all along the educational continuum and are quite capable of communicating with their neighbors. Each of these children should have a chance to profit from expert auditory training in conjunction with early childhood education. Late starters are becoming less numerous, but the others are with us in larger number at earlier ages. Where concerned, continuous parental involvement exists, the suggested activities in the following pages may be used with varying degrees of success. They have all been found useful in some way with most deaf preschoolers, including early starters.

In print, of course, the procedures may look so structured that the inexperienced may interpret the required training as "structuring the child." Many young deaf children need a very clearly channeled pathway toward learning, and the well-managed auditory guidance sessions in one-to-one situations, which most children with handicaps need, can be extremely enjoyable, supportive, and profitable for them. There are deaf children for whom immediate wearing of a body style hearing aid is not advisable, for whom use of earphones with auditory trainers must be managed with unusual care and skill, with whom one must work doggedly and with perseverance to the extent that some parents and teachers do not continue. The step-by-step auditory program, where selection of a particular activity is not left to the young child, wholly unprepared, to make, may become the most effective inroad to human interaction with the child. Attention and persistence may then start to evolve.

There are little deaf children, particularly those with additional difficulties, who will never achieve in fact unless training is highly structured. This pertains to aural aspects of training as well.

TALKING AND SINGING

Among the first things that the parent and the teacher may do in training the young deaf child are to sing and talk near his ear.[106] This is done, to the child's advantage, from the time his deafness is discovered and before he is ready for earphones or a wearable aid. And much later on, after specific training has been started, every opportunity should be used to utter near his ear a word, a phrase, a tune, etc. This technique, which is as simple as it is effective, may be carried out while the child is lying down, while he is looking at books and pictures, during the speech and lipreading lessons, and on many other incidental occasions during the day. If the child doesn't respond, the adult does not make an issue of it, nor try to make him respond.

This method is very helpful in encouraging some children to "use voice." A child may try to imitate a word he sees on the lips of a speaker, but in doing so may not use his voice. Sometimes, if the child's hand is placed on the speaker's cheek as the word is said near his ear, and then again while he watches, he will repeat the word using voice.

Talking and singing are usually natural and pleasant experiences for any child, and for the deaf child can be just as pleasant.

Earphones may be attached to the radio, or if the child is learning to use a wearable aid, he might put it on, and he would have an opportunity to listen to music and to people talking. The child may prefer listening to music rather than to talking, and this preference should be recognized and encouraged.

If he is listening to music, the adult should have pictures of the various instruments on hand, and when a particular instrument is being played, the corresponding picture would be displayed.

One parent constructed a scrapbook of musical instruments and kept it in the record cabinet. When the child "listened" to the music, with earphones, with a wearable aid, or just by touching the radio with his hands and placing his ear against the side of the cabinet, he and his mother would look through the scrapbook for the picture of the particular instrument he was "hearing."

If the child will listen to people talking over the radio, he should have an opportunity to become familiar with the speech of a man, of a woman, or of a child, and pictures of these people should be available for such occasions.

GROSS SOUNDS

Using gross sounds provides another way of testing the child's hearing and of helping to make him conscious of different sounds such as those produced by a bass drum, a toy drum, a toy whistle, a police whistle, a dinner bell, a cow bell, a bicycle bell, a toy cricket, a cymbal, a motor horn, and various pitch pipes.[33]

The adult should be cautioned against over-using this exercise. In many cases, the adult, finding that the child responds to a certain sound, from then on plagues the child with the sound until he gives up any hope of relief from it and decides that he doesn't want to hear it or anything else.

While it is quite important that the child be exposed to as much sound as possible, since the use of sounds may promote speech and lipreading responses, it is also important that the adult realize how annoying to a young deaf child the constant ringing of bells and banging of drums can become, especially since the persistent ringer of the bell usually insists upon some response over and over again. Such persistence can result in auditory training losing all its value. A child may even get into the habit of saying that he "hears" everything in the auditory training and testing situation, because he has come to believe that is all the adult wants of him.

When the child is able to respond to two or three of the gross sounds, the adult begins to use those responses systematically in training the child to indicate which of the two sounds he heard. For example, after the child has listened to a drum and a pitch pipe, in game and other play situations, frequently enough to be able to respond and to know that those sounds came from those toys, both toys might be placed before the child. The adult would strike the drum while the child watches and listens, then blow the pitch pipe while the child watches and listens. Then the child is turned around, one of the sounds would be produced, and the child would turn back to the adult and indicate which of the toys was the source of the sound. The child may need assistance for some time in learning what to do, and in learning to differentiate between two sounds.

The next exercise might consist of learning to discriminate, by hearing, between the drum and the cymbal; the next, between the pitch 'pipe and the cymbal; and so on until he has had a great deal of experience in differentiating between two sounds.

The next step would include work with three gross sounds, in which the child is trained to indicate which of the three toys in front of him was the source of the sound he "heard."

In accordance with the child's readiness and his capacity to "hear" the sounds, more and more gross sounds would be used in each lesson. There are three-year-olds who have learned to discriminate among a number of gross sounds, while some children will need all the preschool years to learn to discriminate between two or three.

The names of the toys used may be given to the child, and although the training with the sound of a drum need not imply that the child will say the word "drum" more intelligibly, there is a possibility that it will help in this respect, and certainly the child's understanding the word is broadened through this experience that has taken place in connection with it.

These exercises may be carried out with and without amplification. If amplification is employed, it should not be so great that the sound would reach the child in blasts, even for a child who is suspected of being severely deaf and who, at the time, appears to have very little if any residual hearing. The amplification should be increased gradually to avoid discomfort and shock.

VOWEL SOUNDS

From the time the child was first exposed to spoken language, he was also, in a general way, exposed to vowel sounds as they occur in words. Vowel sounds are usually the first sounds uttered by the child when he begins to imitate speech. In order to encourage the use of these vowels, in words, babbling, and speech play, to make the child acquainted with "how they sound," and because some of them are relatively easy to imitate and to see on the lips, vowels are incorporated into the auditory training exercises. This work appears to be more effective for the young child when the vowels are presented in animal sounds, such as *bow-wow, moo, baa,* etc.

The child must be given considerable practice in listening to these sounds as related to the toy animals and to the pictures of the animals as they are used in sense training, lipreading, and speech activities. Later, when he shows some understanding of the relationship between the animal and the sound, he may begin to differentiate between two of the sounds.

The adult might place a toy dog and a toy cow on a table before the child. A mirror might be hung behind the table, directly before the child. The adult would point to the dog and would say, as the child listens, places his hand on her face, and watches in the mirror, "The dog says, 'Bow-wow,' 'Bow-wow,' 'Bow-wow.' " As the child imitates *bow-wow,* he and the adult would clap, once for *Bow* and once for *wow,* in the same rhythm as the spoken word. The same procedure would be followed for a cow and the sound *moo.*

Then the child would be turned away from the mirror and the adult, and as he listens, the adult says one of the sounds near his ear, or into the microphone. The child turns back to the table and indicates which sound he "heard," by pointing to the animal and repeating the sound.

It must be understood that, although these exercises may provide a lot of fun for the deaf child, reliable responses may be very slow in developing. The child is given support in these exercises by the adult's acceptance of his attempts and responses, and by using two sounds that differ in number of syllables, for example, *Bow-wow,* two syllables, *Moo,* one.

There are instances where a child, after months or even a year or two of daily training, does not differentiate between two such sounds with any reliability. But the same child, through the constant practice he has had, has learned to say the sounds intelligibly, and has learned to say sentences such as, "The dog says, 'Bow-wow,' " with some intelligibility and much understanding, and is able to answer questions such as, "What says, 'Bow-wow'?"

The child sometimes enjoys looking through magazines to find and cut out, with the adult's help, advertisements illustrating people using such sounds as $\overline{oo}$, $\overline{o}$, etc., and the pictures may be used with such remarks as, "The woman is saying, '$\overline{Oo}$, the coffee is good!'" "I can say $\overline{oo}$ just the way the woman says it. Let me hear you say $\overline{oo}$." The child might watch himself in the mirror as he tries to match his lip formations with those of the woman in the picture.[162]

Drills on single vowels are not recommended. They are meaningless to the child, and there are so many interesting ways of using vowels that such drills are not necessary.

PIANO

When the parent and the teacher have access to a piano or organ, they should use it in the training of the young deaf child.[172] Some of the deafest children, after daily experience in watching, feeling, and "listening" with earphones, have learned to recognize differences between high and low chords, fast music and slow, loud and soft. They enjoy listening and feeling music that represents running, falling, jumping, and other actions, and have learned to recognize the music that goes with a particular action.

The young deaf child should have regular practice in counting chords played, clapping in time to the music. As three chords are played, he claps his hands three times, once for each chord. As he progresses, he learns to say the numbers as he claps. Since counting and clapping involve considerable preparation, the child should not be expected to master these activities in a short time. It would be an error to sacrifice the rhythm in the child's attempts at keeping time to the music, whether he uses his voice or claps his hands, either for the sake of articulation in saying the numbers or for the sake of clapping his hands in perfect time.

Some children enjoy knocking over blocks to music. If one chord is played, he knocks over one block, two chords, two blocks, and so on. He needs direction and a great deal of time to accomplish this exercise, which may appear relatively simple to the adult.

The deaf child has enjoyed babbling to piano music, matching his babbling to the tempo of the music, or babbling softly to soft music and loud to loud music. Piano work, along with the tactile and auditory techniques, has been effective in training deaf children to vary the pitch of their voices in using words, and has helped the child to use words with more normal inflection.

Speech work involving whole words, phrases, and sentences may be effectively pursued in conjunction with the piano and the hearing aid. From the adult's using spoken language as she plays the piano, the child gets an excellent experience of "listening" to the rhythm of speech in conjunction with the rhythm of music.

The degree of response will depend a great deal on the age, the hearing deficiency, the maturity, the personality, and the previous training of each child. The adult should be much more concerned with what daily exposure to these exercises, as a whole, do for the child than with the precision or promptness, or specific nature of his responses to them. The very fact that the child is deaf will limit him in his responses to piano work, especially as to clapping, counting, talking, etc., *in time* to the piano music. At the preschool level, the sensory experiences he gains from the piano work are extremely valuable. A rigid, technical approach to it could be harmful.

RECORD PLAYER

The record player is used by teachers and parents to give the child practice in listening to different kinds of music, to train him to know when the music is "on" or "off," and to train him to recognize one instrument from another in so far as this is possible.

Whenever possible, the child should have the opportunity of seeing the real instruments he hears through the record player, and of feeling them as they are being played. Then, while listening to the recording, the real or the pictured instrument or both would be displayed.[168]

After the child has had much practice and experience in listening to two of the instruments, he may be able to indicate which of the two is being played.

Some deaf children have learned to identify four or five instruments; others only one or two, even after a few years of training. But almost every child can learn that the music is "on" or "off," can be made aware of sound in another way, and therefore more conscious of his environment as a whole.

Records and tapes of musical, neighborhood, household, school, and farmyard sounds, and of the spoken language of the children themselves, are invaluable in further building of auditory awareness and perception. In association with illustrations, they can be used extensively from differentiation to word discrimination.

WORDS

In training the child to differentiate between and interpret words through listening, the same words would be used as have been used from the beginning in the combined speech, lipreading, and auditory training lessons. The more familiar a child is with a word, the faster he will learn to understand it in new situations. (Plate XIV)

The first two words chosen might be those which differ as to number of syllables in each, for example, *shoe* and *airplane*.

The chosen words would be repeated several times, as the child watches and listens and imitates. He would be guided in clapping to each word—once for the one-syllable word, twice for the two-syllable word—and where one syllable in a word is accented, he would clap loudly, the unaccented syllable being accompanied by a light clap. The more differences he is able to recognize in the two words, the better.

The next step would be to let the child listen without the help of lipreading or the tactile expression. Immediately after saying the word under these conditions, the adult permits the child to see her face as she repeats the word. The second word would be treated in a like manner. Then, covering her whole

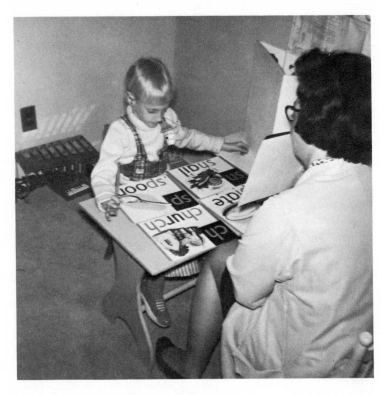

Plate XIV. This child, after almost four years of preschool training in aural training, is becoming aware of words and sounds more difficult to hear, more difficult to interpret visually, and more difficult to say clearly. Here he is seen working on words beginning with blends, such as "sp," "sn," etc., and applies himself well in taking up the challenge.

face, or just her mouth, the adult would say one of the words into the microphone, and the child would try to tell her, by indicating the corresponding picture and repeating the word himself, what was said.

This exercise requires concentration on the part of the child, and patience and ingenuity on the part of the adult, in order to keep the child interested. The exercise is valuable, regardless of how inexpert the child may remain at differentiating between words by auditory means alone. He is being exposed to spoken language every time the lesson occurs, he gets more practice with the particular language forms used, in listening to others speak, and in listening to his own voice.

Several different pairs of words may be introduced as the child begins to understand what is expected of him and as his skill increases in differentiating between the words of the one pair used in the first lessons. Some deaf children never get beyond differentiating between two words at one time. Others learn to identify any one of several words through listening alone. (Plate XV)

SENTENCES

The child is exposed to simple sentences from the beginning days of his training. As soon as he will wear earphones, he listens to these sentences as he lipreads, tries to imitate them and to match them to corresponding pictures. After he has had a great deal of experience in lipreading, in imitating, and in listening to sentences, two sentences which he understands very well, and which differ as to length and number of accented and unaccented syllables, would be used in training him to differentiate between sentences through listening alone.

This type of exercise requires concentration and undivided attention on the part of the child. He will continue to try only if he feels that the adult is helping him and is not forcing him to "do it or else."

In differentiating between sentences, the procedure is similar to that in differentiating between words. If the sentences (with corresponding pictures) are, *The woman has some flowers,* and *The boy is crying,* each sentence would be repeated several times by the adult, while the child watches, lipreads, indicates the corresponding picture, and then imitates. The child may be made more aware of the differences in the sentences if he watches the adult clap as she says each sentence, and claps along with her.

Plate XV. This five-year-old, profoundly deaf by measurement without his hearing aids, interprets quickly and accurately a number of spondaic words through listening with the use of two hearing aids.

The sentences should be spoken with normal fluency, not in artificial, chappy style: one word—a pause—another word.

Then the adult would cover her face, or just her mouth in the first stages, as she says one of the sentences into the microphone, and the child would try to indicate the correct picture and to repeat the sentence.

A short time devoted each day to this exercise, in conjunction with speech and lipreading, is more valuable to the preschool child than long lessons that are only empty drills, which the child forgets as fast as he can.

After the child has learned to differentiate between the sentences in several pairs, he may be able to differentiate among three familiar sentences. There are deaf children who have learned to indicate which one of several pictures was described, just through listening. And although such children were far too deaf to use hearing as a means of understanding people in their environments, there was a definite improvement in their speech and lipreading. There was also an outstanding improvement in the articulation of those sentences which were used for auditory training. The more sentences that can be used in such exercises, and the more practice the child gets in saying them, the more his articulation will improve—as well as his accent and fluency— without articulation having to be specifically worked on in those lessons. (Plate XVI)

This work with sentences at the preschool level has value that lasts far into the later years. However, for highest effectiveness, it should be continued well past the preschool level.

NURSERY RHYMES AND JINGLES

Deaf children should be exposed to the rhymes and jingles which hearing children enjoy. Hearing children have at first relatively little understanding of the rhymes and stories they hear, but they enjoy them anyway and want to hear them over and over again. If they are made interesting, the deaf child feels the same about them.

The adult tries to put across the *idea* of the rhyme while she gives the child some experience with the rhythm of the language of the rhyme. In time, the child learns the names of the people and things in the rhymes, and to "talk" with the adult into the microphone as the whole rhyme is repeated.

The deaf child enjoys recordings of the nursery rhymes, likes to have pictures of them to go with the recordings, and will clap and try to sing with the adult as the recording is being played.

Plate XVI. In this instance, the child speaks, the teacher listens, and identifies the corresponding picture. The child knows the teacher will not respond if he doesn't speak as clearly as he can. Being in a "lead" position motivates the child, and helps the teacher identify areas requiring more specific attention.

FILM STRIPS, SLIDES, LEARNING LOOPS, etc.

Slides, film strips, and other visual aids such as "Loops To Learn By," [132] as well as selected audio-visual aids, can be profitably used with preschool deaf children at various ages and levels of development. Although some of these aids are not accompanied by sound from machine source, they can be used effectively for auditory training. Where the group is small, or where tutoring of the individual child ensues, use of the slides and other aids, under conditions where lights are dimmed or off, can accompany the teacher's narration of what is seen. Indeed, as few other arrangements for training allow, these facilities allow emphasis to be placed on aural learning at the same time other sensory experiences are involved.

As the teacher speaks clearly near the child in a darkened room, the slides and other aids can help accelerate development of: (1) sustained visual attention and visual perception skills, (2) awareness of any memory for sequence of events which with similar props can later be carried out by the children, (3) ability to track a moving figure through a crowd, (4) understanding of parts to wholes, (5) perception of things and figures in space, and better understanding of background-foreground relationship, (6) more accurate and rapid recognition of the color, shape, form, texture, and use of objects, (7) language skills as the children respond spontaneously to what they view.

Some teachers have made up slides of the various activities in which the children may be involved in familiar environments, and of specific objects and sense training materials arranged in ways conducive to essential learning. The slides have been used in tutoring and small group situations for the improvement of auditory interpretation. The child's happy involvement in watching the picture in a different dimension has brought forth spontaneous, voluntary, correct responses with spoken language to a question asked by the teacher sitting back of the child. Visual and audio-visual aids, selected and well used, provide variety and enjoyment for the child as the necessary repetition for learning language auditorially is carried out.[160]

Chapter 11

Sense Training Activities
for Language Development

Teacher and parent must present the sense training exercises suggested here in whatever order seems best for the individual child, taking into consideration the child's age, what the "average" child of that age might be expected to do, the child's muscular coordination, and his attention span. Both teacher and parent aim at helping the child to develop skills in every part of the sense training program. However, through observation of the child during play, creative activities, and during free play with sense training materials at other times, the adult will discover the child's aptitudes and preferences—whether the child appears to be most interested in color, form, or other element—and will guide the child sensibly and naturally from the more interesting to the less interesting, from the simple to the more difficult.

The success attained in sense training will depend to a large extent on the adult's willingness to respect the child's individuality and to recognize his preferences and his requirements as more important than any arbitrary set of standards which the adult may have in mind.

SENSE OF SIGHT

A. Matching

1. Match Objects
    a. Match objects identical in every respect.
    b. Match objects of different size.
    c. Match objects of different color.
    d. Match objects of different size and color.
    e. Match objects (any of above) using tactile method.

The matching of objects usually comes first, since the child tends to be more interested in a form that he can hold and manipulate. The simplest exercise involves the matching of two objects that are identical in every respect. Two bright blue balls and two bright red airplanes might be used, or pairs of other objects which would be of interest to the child. (Plate XVII)

With a child who seems to be confused by colors, the adult would use objects all of one color; that is, every object used in the first exercises might be blue, later on another set of red ones might be used, and so on until the child has had more experience with colors and colored objects.

The primary aim is that the child learn to match the objects, and in most instances the same color helps the child to match pairs of objects more quickly.

When the exercise is presented for the first time, or even for the first few times, the child may want to feel the objects, to roll or push them, or even taste them. If he has had experience with similar objects in play situations, he may not wish to spend time experimenting with them. When materials are very new to a child, the parent and the teacher must be prepared to allow him to explore and experiment.

The adult might place a ball and an airplane on a surface near the child (on the floor, on the table, or elsewhere) and the corresponding objects in her lap. She might take the ball from her lap, hold it up, and say, "This is a ball, Johnny. It's a ball. Let's find the other ball."

The child may pick up the other ball, or he might choose the airplane. If he chooses the latter (and this is quite probable),

chair chair bird b

bacon bacon cat

picture to picture

size to size

object to object

shape to shape

object to picture

color to color

Plate XVII. Sense training materials.

the teacher will show the child what she means by indicating or picking up the other ball. Then she would put both balls together and say, "This is a ball, and this is a ball." A similar procedure would be used with the airplanes.

Johnny may not watch for long and, at first, may watch the objects rather than the speaker. The adult must be prepared for this reaction and be willing to accept it as the natural thing for the child to do. After all, the deaf child of two or three can understand what to do with a toy, if only to handle it, while as yet he cannot understand why he should watch the adult. Furthermore, at this stage, learning to match the objects is of the first importance.

The exercise may be repeated, and the second attempt may result in Johnny's handing the adult the correct object. The number of identical objects used in a lesson is increased as the child grasps the idea of matching.

Before long, objects that differ in size only may be introduced. Two balls, one large and one small, two airplanes, one large and one small, two shoes, one large and one small, and other familiar objects would be presented in a manner similar to that described for identical objects. (Plate XVIII)

As pairs of objects are matched, the child is confronted with more and more differences. In the first stages, it is preferable to use objects that differ in one respect only. If the two balls differ in size, they should remain the same in color or design, if the colors differ, then the sizes would be the same. This is not so imperative with the child of four or five years, but with the younger child, it makes the transitions easier, and he can be guided gradually to observe small differences in objects, an observation that has a bearing on lipreading development. (Plate XIX)

Whenever possible, without annoying the child or interfering with his execution of the exercise, the teacher and parent talk about the objects. The name of the object is repeated frequently. It doesn't matter if it is described as a big ball, a red airplane, or just as a ball, or an airplane, so long as it is spoken of in short, simple sentences or phrases.

Sometimes it is wiser to refrain from talking, as when the

Plate XVIII. Two two-year-olds playing with a number of objects, two of each varying in color, size, and shape. The objects may be paired according to *big* and *little,* or they may be grouped with all small toys together, and all large ones together. As these children went about their play, a teacher sitting across the table from them talked to them about their activity, making use of opportunity for aural stimulation and learning.

attempt to talk entails too much movement in order to get the child's attention, with the undesirable results of an annoyed child and an irritable, fatigued adult. The child, if given the opportunity of doing the job he sets out to do, will get the idea of watching the speaker more and more consistently when an object is presented.

Plate XIX. This sense training activity, with use of paired objects differing as to color, size, and shape, is being used in this instance for opportunity to learn meanings of "another ---," "one more ---," "the other one," and eventual use of such language by the child, herself.

When the child becomes accustomed to matching, after a good relationship has been established between him and the adult, the tactile approach may be introduced. Occasionally, as the adult presents an object, she places the child's hand on her cheek and talks about the object. This helps to draw more attention to the speaker's face and lips and is a step in speech preparation. This should be done as casually as holding up an object.

f. Lipread name of object using tactile; match object to corresponding object.
g. Lipread object without tactile; match to corresponding object.
h. Lipread object using tactile and auditory; match to corresponding object.
i. Lipread object using auditory, no tactile; match to corresponding object.

As the child enjoys numerous experiences in matching objects in incidental and more formal situations, and gets practice in placing his hand on the speaker's face, the habit of lipreading is taking root. Imitation of speech may have begun also. The tactile and the auditory may be introduced into the activities connected with lipreading and matching, but only at the rate at which the child can accept such variations.

The adult holds up one ball, places the child's hand on her cheek, and says, "This is a ball, Jimmy," and pointing to the other ball says, "This is another ball." Then, using the tactile again, she would talk about the ball she has, asking, "Where is the other ball?" or saying, "Give me the other ball." If the child doesn't respond, she might hold out her hand and repeat, "Give me the other ball."

This rudimentary preparation of the child for lipreading through matching should be pursued both with and without the tactile approach. Although the tactile approach is of tremendous value to the child and an essential part of his training, he also needs experience without it, and there is danger that its overuse might cause the child to reject it.

The matching exercise might be varied again by placing the child's hand on the speaker's cheek, talking about the object while he watches, and then repeating the word or phrase near his ear. When earphones are used, then tactile, auditory, and visual approaches may be combined. The child may watch for lipreading, may feel the speaker's face for speech, and listen as the adult speaks into the microphone.

Occasionally, the adult might hold up an object, and while the child listens in his earphones, could cover her mouth and say the word into the microphone. Since he is a deaf child, he should have the experience of listening for speech patterns.

Since the child is able to see the object in the adult's hand, he will be able, in all probability, to get the corresponding object immediately, regardless of how much he "heard." But the exercise still has value in furnishing him practice in listening in relation to something which *he* can do.

Whenever this variant of the exercise is used, it should be followed up immediately by the speaker repeating the words as the child watches the speaker's whole face.

2. Matching Object to Picture
   j. Match object to picture (added differences).

Matching objects to pictures increases the child's understanding of the relationships between pictured objects and real ones. It is common to see a very young child try to pick a pictured object from a page or card. He expects to pick it up just as he picked up the real object. Matching of objects to pictures helps the child to understand more about his environment.

The first exercise would involve the use of a few objects and identical pictured ones to correspond with the real objects. In later exercises, more pictures and objects would be matched, with gradual changes in color, size, and possibly in contour, according to the objects.

The child learns to connect a big ball with the small one in the picture, a red chair in the room with the green one in the picture, the pictured door of the doll house with the door in his home, the three-dimensional object in his hand with the flat one on the paper.

Lipreading and the use of the tactile and auditory approaches would be incorporated into the lessons according to the readiness of the child, and in a manner similar to that prescribed for the matching of objects.

Parents are encouraged to supplement the nursery school training, or whatever specific training the child is getting, by exposing the child to pictures and objects at home. Pictures of his toothbrush, facecloth, soap, towel, etc., would be pinned or pasted in the bathroom below each of those articles. Pictures of the clothing in each of his drawers might be tacked to the outside of the drawer or near by so the child can match each piece of clothing he or his mother takes out of the drawer to the pictured article. Pictures of food might be put up somewhere in the kitchen.

The more he practices matching picture to object in such situations, the more success he will have in the lesson situation.

   3. Matching Picture to Picture
      k. Match pictures that are identical.
      l. Match pictures that illustrate objects of different size.
     m. Match pictures of objects that differ in color.
      n. Match pictures that differ in color and size.
     o. Match pictures that are increasingly more detailed and complicated.

The first pictures matched are simple, clearly defined, and identical. There should be just a single object illustrated on each card. Gradually, the child learns to match more complicated pictures that include several objects and people.

If the first pictures presented to the young deaf child for matching purposes included many people, many activities, and a wealth of detail, he would tend to spend time investigating each of the objects or people illustrated instead of matching the identical pictures, or he would be completely confused about what is wanted of him when the adult tries to have him match such pictures. The child should have plenty of opportunity to explore pictures in books at other times during the day, but in the specific training situations he needs to be guided systematically from the simple to the more complicated, and should not be expected to match just *any* pictures which the adult may have on hand.

These matching exercises should include some activity that will lend interest and variety. The child might enjoy matching pictures to corresponding ones which have been placed across the room, he might enjoy searching through a pile of pictures for the right one, or he might like to "find" corresponding pictures in boxes or drawers. It is worth the time involved in the child's having to go and get a picture, or to look for a picture, if the activity helps to maintain his interest.

4. Lipreading with Picture Matching
   p. Lipread name of object illustrated, use tactile; match to corresponding picture.
   q. Lipread, using tactile and auditory; match picture to picture.
   r. Lipread, without tactile or auditory; match.
   s. Lipread, using auditory; match.

Lipreading as it is introduced in these matching exercises would appear to render error on the child's part almost impossible. This is as it should be, and is important in the transitory stage. The child is being introduced gradually to lipreading, is getting an unconscious grasp of language through lipreading at the same time that he is enjoying experiences with colorful, interesting materials. He must not be expected to lipread nor imitate the names of objects at once.

So much repetition is required that the teacher and the parent find themselves constantly thinking up new and different ways of putting across the same idea. Some children take much longer than others to understand that they must watch the speaker in these matching situations. Since the child must not be forced to watch nor to conform to adult standards of behavior, the whole situation must be made so stimulating and interesting that the child will naturally accept the techniques devised by the adult for the promotion of language development.

Sometimes the use of "suspense" or "mystery" in the lesson results in more attention to the speaker's face. A few pictures might be placed on the table, the corresponding ones on the adult's lap. The adult might take one in hand, pretending to hide a very special picture from the child, and say, with playful expressions, before showing the picture to the child, "I have a ball, Johnny. A pretty ball." Then she would flash the picture quickly and match it quickly to the one on the table. She would use a similar procedure with the other pictures, talking about each before showing it to the child. If he wants to match them at once, he should be permitted to do so.

When this has been done, the adult might ask the child for each picture, sometimes using the tactile method, sometimes without it. When the child selects the correct picture, with or without help, he might place it in a box which the teacher or parent has given to him.

Simple game situations do a great deal to hold the attention and interest, especially if they are not overdone. The child quickly catches on to the fact that an adult is going through this or that action or "antic," not because she is enjoying it with him, but because she is trying to place emphasis on something else, outside and beyond him and the sheer enjoyment of the game. If he realizes this, much of the value of the picture matching and the game is lost. Unfortunately, often the adult doesn't perceive as quickly as she should the child's understanding of these situations. In that case, the matching just goes on as a task from day to day, and becomes more and more boring to the child.

Since picture matching can become so boring and devoid of interest for the child who has to have some work in it day after day, the adult must not only be on the alert for new ways of presenting picture matching for language growth but also must be able to enjoy the child and herself in whatever approach she may choose.

Lotto games, where individual pictures of objects are to be matched to corresponding pictures on a cardboard chart, furnish another variation in picture matching. Teacher and parent may make their own charts and cards to include objects that are not included in the lotto games available in stores.

B. Color

The child's interest in color must be developed before he is introduced to the lipreading of color names, or prepared to say the colors and to recognize the beauty of color in daily surroundings.

The little child finds enjoyment in going from room to room or from object to object within one room, matching a color in his clothing, or in a favorite toy that he holds, to a corresponding color in the furniture, the walls, the dishes, the curtains, etc. He likes to do this when out walking, while looking at picture books, and at other times.

Colorful toys can be used to advantage. Three or four toy cups, each a different color, might be placed before the child. Bows of colored yarn or ribbon would be handed to the child, one at a time. The blue bow would be placed in the blue cup, the red bow in the red cup, etc. The child has to be shown what is expected of him, and, according to the individual child, more or less time will be required to master the operation. The child may not be interested in little bows, and in that case the adult will find it necessary to get the color matching idea across in another way. The child should not be forced to use bows if he doesn't like them.

The exercise may be varied by using colored beads or colored blocks, which could be dropped into boxes of corresponding color. Sometimes the child likes to pour colored water into painted tin cans of corresponding color.

If the child's coordination permits it, beads might be strung on colored laces. The child would be given three laces, a red one, a blue one, and a yellow one. There would be three beads from which to choose—a red one, a yellow one, and a blue one. The child would be guided in putting the red lace through the red bead, the yellow lace through the yellow bead, etc.

Tops of matchboxes might be painted or covered with colored paper. Then toy cars of corresponding color might be rolled into each cover as a car into a garage. Or toy cars and toy airplanes might be rolled onto pieces of colored cardboard on the floor.

The adult might outline and color a network of "roads" on a large piece of cardboard, and the child could play at "driving the car" on the road which is colored to correspond with the car.

There are color boards which resemble puzzles and which may be bought or made. The simple form board might have one section lined with blue, into which the blue pieces would be fitted; the section lined with red would be filled with the red pieces of the puzzle.

Form boards that have a single object insert for each base

may be used in color matching exercises. For example, a blue ball cut-out would fit into the board with the blue base and the round cut-out. In this case, the child is matching not only color but also shape.

Fortunately, these little form boards are easily made, since the parent and the teacher usually find that there are not enough simple ones available in stores to give the deaf child the repetition he needs. The object may be drawn on a piece of plywood about 4 inches square, and cut out with a coping saw. Then a piece of stiff cardboard would be glued firmly to the base of the plywood square. Both square and cut-out would be painted the required color. When completed, the cut-out fits easily into the base from which it was originally cut.

Throughout the color matching, the adult gives the child opportunity to use his hands, to observe, to finish what he has started, and to study and concentrate on the activity. She talks to him as much as possible, and encourages him to watch her as she talks about each color. The tactile and auditory methods are combined with lipreading and matching as they were in the matching of pictures and objects. (Plate XX)

C. Shape

The type of form board just described under *Color* may be used for practice and experience with various shapes. Form boards and puzzles composed of a single object or shape per board should come first, more difficult and complicated ones being introduced gradually. Some parents who have attempted this work have made the error of presenting puzzles far beyond the comprehension, coordination, and attention span of their respective children.

There are available in stores many colorful puzzles, ranging from single object inserts to more complicated ones depicting children's activities and nursery rhymes. The adult usually finds it necessary to supplement those available in stores. The proper use of puzzles and form boards gives the child an early and enjoyable start in sense training, lipreading, and other aspects of language.(Plate XXI)

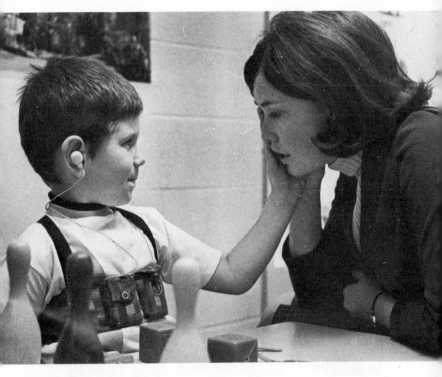

Plate XX. This activity is set up for practice in the child's use of colors, red, yellow, and blue, as they occur in phrases, in questions, answers, and comments. This child is being helped in saying more clearly the blend "bl" as it occurred in the question he asked the teacher, "Where is the blue block?"

Geometric shapes cut from colored paper and pasted on cards are attractive to most children and serve as material for matching shapes. From a sheet of red paper, the adult might cut out two squares, two circles, two diamonds, two rectangles, two triangles, two polygons, etc. Each shape would be mounted on an individual card. For variety, one set of shapes might be mounted on cards and the other set on a large chart.

The child who gets sufficient practice with these shapes, and

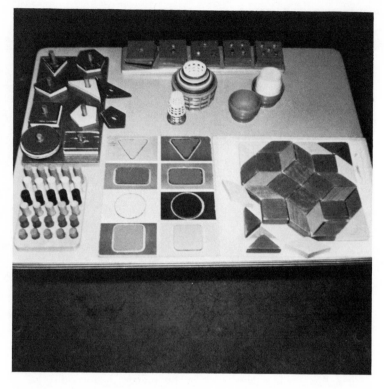

Plate XXI. Sense training materials for use in learning more about color, shape and form, size (breadth and height), number and quantity, and relationships of the foregoing in constructing a form and completing a task successfully.

continues to show interest, learns that circles match each other, that triangles go together, regardless of what color they may be or whether they are large or small.

At first, the two circles would be identical as to color and size, the triangles identical in the same respects, and likewise for other shapes used. Gradually, the colors are changed so that the child finds himself matching a blue triangle to a purple triangle. In some cases, there may be some sign of conflict about the situation. The child may offer resistance to the problem of whether to match color or shape. He may start out by matching the blue triangle to the blue circle. Patience and continued direction on the part of the teacher and parent result in the child's learning to match the shapes rather than the colors in the appropriate situation.

As the child becomes more adept at matching shapes, assorted colors and sizes are introduced, and the child learns to place all the triangles in one row regardless of size or color, all the squares in another row, etc.

Geometric solids made of natural wood, unpainted, are useful in learning to match shapes. Every parent and teacher should provide a set of these for the children. The adult may use them as identical objects were used in matching. She would take a few in a box and give them to the child, while keeping the matching ones in her lap. She would hold up one and the child would find the corresponding one in the box. The number of different shapes from which the child would have to choose would be increased as his understanding of the situation and his attention span would permit.

D. Memory

Stick designs made of kindergarten splints offer a means of developing the memory. The child watches the teacher or parent make a very simple design with two or three sticks. She may repeat the process two or three times. Then, the teacher's design being left on the table for the child to see, he is given the required number of sticks with which to copy the design.

If the child has difficulty, the adult might place one stick on the table, and have the child do the same, place another stick near the first, and have the child copy, and so on until the design is completed.

The very young child may not want to follow the example set by the adult. He may want to pile the sticks in a heap or line them up on the table. In this case, the adult might copy what the child has done, to help put across the idea of imitating.

If the child prefers to place the sticks in a row, the adult might use a number of red sticks for one row, blue ones for another row, and continue until the child remembers the order of colors. As the adult continues to accept the child's way of using the sticks, the child will gradually tend to reciprocate, and will eventually cooperate by following her way of using them.

Once the child has learned to copy some simple designs—squares, triangles, diamonds, houses, tables, chairs, and others—he may begin to construct designs from memory. The adult would make a design as the child watches, then remove the design, whereupon the child would try to remember how it was made and reconstruct it. In time, the child makes the transition from copying to *remembering*.

Objects may be used in memory exercises. Two or three objects may be placed in specific positions on a table—possibly one in each corner. The adult would remove them and put each back in the original position as the child watches. Then the objects would be removed from the table. Each object would be handed to the child who places it in the appropriate corner. Considerable practice may be required before the child masters this exercise. The number of objects and corresponding positions which would be included in the exercise will increase as the child's ability to remember develops.

Objects might be placed in various positions in a room as the child watches. Then they would be removed, and the child would put each back in its former place. This memory exercise may be combined with lipreading and speech preparation.

Objects might be placed about the room as the child watches. The adult would hold up a corresponding object and ask the child to find the other ball, airplane, etc. The child's memory in this instance would be measured by the speed and accuracy of response. Later, when the child has some grasp of lipreading, he would be asked to find the hidden objects without the aid of a corresponding object.

SENSE OF TOUCH

The geometric solids mentioned under *Shape* are convenient in developing the sense of touch. The adult might place two or three of these solids in a paper bag while the child watches. She would pick up one of the corresponding shapes from the table, feel it, and then reach into the bag without looking into it, feel around, and pull out the solid that matches the one from the table.

The child would be given a solid to feel, then permitted to put his hand into the bag, feel the few solids in it until he touches the one which he thinks feels the same as the one on the table, and then pull it out.

The first shapes used in this way should be quite different in shape to facilitate the child's task of matching through touch alone. The number of shapes placed in the bag would be increased as the child's skill increases.

Toys may be placed in the "grab-bag" and used in a manner similar to that described above.

The cylinder board has been widely used in developing the sense of touch. After the child has mastered the matching of pegs to the corresponding holes in the cylinder board, he might be blindfolded and expected to do this from touch. Sometimes, it is necessary for the adult to perform this operation to show the child what is expected. Some children object to being blindfolded but will allow the adult to place her hands over their eyes. In the case of a child who objects strenuously to having his eyes covered, it would be advisable to eliminate the exercise until he is ready to accept it.

Children enjoy feeling materials and matching them. Two pieces of satin, two pieces of woolen fabric, two of cotton print, and other materials may be used. One set of fabrics might be sewn to a hoop or to a short stick to add interest. Some children enjoy having the materials pinned to a clothesline with clothespins. The child is given an opportunity to match the materials through *touch and sight*. When the child is able to match the materials in this way with ease, the exercise is made more exacting by introducing more colors and designs in the same materials. When the child has begun to show ability in matching materials through touch and sight, a few samples might be placed in a bag and chosen by touch only to match a particular material which the adult presents.

Children usually enjoy learning to match hard materials to

hard ones, soft materials to other soft ones. Through feeling many objects and materials, the child learns that some are hard to the touch, some are soft, and he learns to group hard materials together, and soft materials together. Exercises with soft and hard materials offer practice in the lipreading of adjectives as well as in learning to identify materials through touch.

The importance of sense training in the early guidance of the deaf child has already been emphasized. It is advisable to combine lipreading, speech preparation, and auditory training with the sense training activities, but the parent and the teacher must be ever mindful that the value of the sense training activity can be nullified very easily by "improper" handling.

The activity, the child's effort and enjoyment, are more important than the adult's desire for responses in lipreading and speech. Through the use of sense training activities, the young deaf child may begin lipreading, and even imitation of speech, in a few weeks after the training is begun, or he may not show signs of lipreading nor any interest in imitating speech after months of sense training activities.

If measures are taken to force him to lipread before he is ready to do so, he will not only reject lipreading and its necessary allied activities, but will reject the sense training activity itself. These activities are extremely important in themselves, apart from lipreading and speech, and overanxiety by the parent or teacher for the development of those skills could retard the child in the development of sensory skills, which in turn retard the development of other skills that the deaf child needs.

The experience with sense training achieves its real purpose when the child begins to express himself with language, and subsequently, with *creative* use of the materials. He is able to go beyond mere manipulation of materials and successful completion of form puzzles, however complicated the piece-by-piece assembling may appear to the adult. The child is able to progress from limited performance levels as he transfers learned language concepts to imaginative and creative play within which order and organization are seen emerging.[180]

Chapter 12

Speech Reading
and Speech Activities
for Language Development

The activities described in this section are designed to build speech and lipreading vocabularies. The teacher and the parent consciously construct lessons around words that will be useful to the child in everyday life. Systematic planning is necessary in order that every lesson will have some value, even when changes "on the spot" become necessary to meet the needs of the individual child.

The person who is guiding the child will find that a small amount of specific training each day is more effective than a long period once or twice a week, especially in the case of the younger children—two- and three-year-olds.

Lipreading, speech, and auditory training are so closely combined that it would be difficult to say where one leaves off and the other begins. This is especially true of lipreading and speech with the very young child, and is the reason for presenting lipreading and speech activities as a unit in the pages that follow.

The adult will find that, as the child is exposed to more and more training, he reaches a stage where he is able to accept more intensified specific training. Then, adult and child may concentrate on either auditory training, lipreading, or speech preparation, to the exclusion of the others, for short periods. Throughout the preschool training, however, success in lipreading, in speech, in auditory training, will greatly depend on the degree to which the combined approach has been used.[133]

If the child is being trained to lipread a particular word, the adult would not only say that word as frequently as possible during the lesson, but would also grasp every opportunity to place the child's hand on her cheek as she says the word, would encourage the child to use his voice and to imitate, and would say the word within best known pick-up by his hearing aid(s) or, if the situation permits the wearing of earphones, into a microphone. (Plate XXII)

The parent or teacher of the young deaf child never endangers the potential success of a technique by sacrificing the child's comfort or mental health. Each child must be given time to adjust to any technique that might be introduced, and all lessons must be short. Five or ten minutes of keen enjoyment and interest produce better and longer-lasting results than half an hour of drudgery.

For purposes of discussion, the desirable exercises are grouped here under nouns, verbs, adjectives, etc. In practice, however, no one word is ever presented as a separate entity, but only as a word in relation to a real object, and to other words, so that whole phrases and sentences must necessarily enter each lesson.

Parent and teacher should become very familiar with the sense training exercises, as these overlap almost constantly the lipreading and speech preparation of the earlier stages.

THE PARTS OF SPEECH

Nouns

The young deaf child's first introduction to lipreading generally comes through sense training exercises, primary of which are those connected with the matching of objects. Hence, the first words in lipreading are most naturally nouns—the names of these objects.

The teacher or the parent will find herself frequently revert-

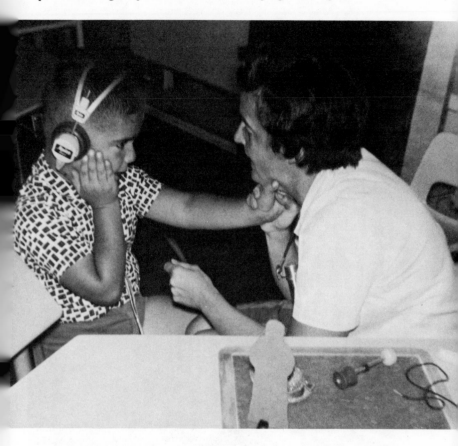

Plate XXII. This severely deaf child, a late starter at five years of age, responded most happily, consistently, in the one-to-one situation with a teacher, where auditory-visual intake-output of language with use of tactile-touch technique were combined. Here, he is having language experience opportunity with objects, *Blackboard, lamp, hat,* and *man,* all words having the common vowel, short *a.*

ing to these early matching exercises to facilitate the child's lipreading and speech training. As the child's interest in watching the lips and desire to understand through lipreading grow, he will become more and more independent of matching objects for

Plate XXIII. A deaf four-year old saying, "That's a dog." Would you know that he is saying "dog" at this point if you had no clue such as the picture? This is all he is able to see of the spoken word.

purposes of lipreading. This serves to point out the importance of early identification and diagnosis, with immediate and continuous aural stimulation and training for easier interpretation and spoken language. (Plate XXIII)

But in the early lipreading and speech work, especially with the two- and three-year-olds, objects rather than pictures should be used, and only objects until the child has had an opportunity to make the transition from objects to pictures.

Parents have found that the children often want to pick the pictures from the pages or even to throw the pictures—reactions that are perfectly normal for the child who doesn't understand that the ball in the picture can't be picked up or thrown, as can the ball from the box of toys. But while objects are being used in the early specific lipreading and speech work, the object-picture relationship is being developed and clarified through sense training.

A group of three objects is sufficient for the first lessons, and the words would be those which do not look alike on the lips. *Car, ball,* and *airplane* might be the first words chosen for a lesson. After the child becomes familiar with the words, the one which he appears to lipread most easily might be omitted for a while and another object, such as a shoe, might be used with ball and airplane. At a later date, *car, shoe,* and *ball* might be used at one time, then *airplane, car,* and *shoe* in a group, and so on, in order that the number of words included in one lesson remains small. Variety is added to each lesson by making slight changes that do not cause confusion. Only one new word at a time is added to the familiar ones, providing for both challenge and success at once.

The adult would pick up each object and tell the child what it is as she holds his hand to her cheek. "This is a *ball*. This is a *car*. This is an *airplane*." The ball might be given to the child and as his free hand is placed on the speaker's face, sentences such as, "You have the *ball*," and "Put the *ball* into the box," would be used. The child must be shown what is meant by putting the ball into the box. Whenever possible, the child's hand would be placed on his own cheek and he would be encouraged to imitate what the adult is saying.

A similar procedure is used when speaking of the other objects. Parent and teacher should not be afraid to talk about the objects in different ways. The same expressions need not be used time and again so long as the special words are repeated.[149]

After the three objects have been put into the box, the adult might say, holding out her hand if necessary, "Find the *ball* and give it to me," or "Give me the *ball*. Yes, the *ball*."

The adult must be prepared for inaccurate responses, and be ready to help prevent the child's feeling insecure and inadequate in the situation. If the child picks up the car instead of the ball, the adult merely says, "That's not a ball. It's a car. I want the ball." She replaces the car in the box, and asks again for the ball. When the right object is selected, it is not replaced in the box but is kept by the adult. If the child continues to have difficulty in spite of many repetitions of the spoken word, the adult might get another ball and say, "This is a *ball*. Now, give me the other ball."

When all three objects have been taken from the box, the adult might place them about the room—the ball in a corner, the car on the window sill, the airplane behind the door. As this is done, the child goes along and watches the adult as she speaks about each object. Child and adult return to their original positions and the adult asks for each object, using the tactile, visual, and auditory approaches. The child runs for each object and brings it back to the adult. Any failure on the part of the child should be treated very casually, and assistance be forthcoming.

Paper bags may be used for further practice of these words. Three bags might be placed on the table along with the objects. The adult might say, "Show me the *ball*," and after the child indicates the ball—with or without help—the adult would open one bag, hold it before the child, and say, "Put the *ball* in the bag." The same procedure would be followed using *car* and *airplane*.

The adult would place the child's hand on her cheek, cover her mouth or place her hand over the child's eyes (if he will permit it), and say one of the words; for example, "*Car.*" Immediately following this, the child would be permitted to see the speaker's lips as the word is repeated, and he would be shown that that object is in a certain bag. The same procedure follows for airplane and ball. The next time this operation is carried out, the child is given an opportunity to find the particular object by himself.

Over a period of time, the young child becomes relatively skillful at finding objects by the tactile means alone. Although he should be allowed to lipread along with the tactile means, he should also be given regular experience with "feeling speech," sometimes with lipreading and the auditory, sometimes without either lipreading or auditory.

Parent and teacher will find that the use of boxes and paper bags helps to maintain interest, especially in the case of the two- and three-year-olds who enjoy finding things, like to take objects out of things, or put them into something. One parent discovered that she got best results in lipreading and imitation of speech from her three-year-old when they sat on the floor by the bottom drawer of his bureau in the bedroom and hid toys under his clothing. Gradually, he became interested in working with the same objects in other situations, but his interest was first stimulated successfully through the child's desire to hide things in his drawer of clothing.

The three-year-old may enter into a number of activities revolving about a few objects in one lesson, without tiring and with interest, or he may remain attentive for just one activity. If his attention span is very short for such training, the lesson should be short and continued either later in the day or on the next day. Teacher and parent are advised to have several sets of the objects, in different colors and sizes, so the child will feel a new interest while he is getting the necessary repetitive practice in the same words.

The four-year-old who has had previous training for a year or two can be expected to do "more advanced" work with nouns. He may perform through lipreading many more actions involving objects and *pictures* of objects, and will use more speech as he imitates the adult.

Some four- and five-year-olds who have had earlier training enjoy working in groups of two or three, especially in playing "school," with one child as teacher and the rest as pupils. This situation has been especially successful with five-year-olds. The "teacher" asks a child for a specific object, another child for another object, etc., and then another child takes a turn as "teacher." This exercise gives the children practice in lipreading one another, an experience which should begin at the preschool level.

The child of four or five, depending on previous training

and present skills, is likely to enjoy the following game. He is given a few picture cards, and he and the adult review the names of them. Then the adult turns her back, the child says a word, and the teacher or parent turns around and indicates the corresponding picture. If the word is not said as well as the adult feels the child could say it, she pretends she does not understand, thus getting him to repeat it. This technique must be put over with discretion so that the child will not at any time feel that he is a failure, and that he cannot be understood.

The teacher and the parent construct lessons carefully around nouns that enable the child to become familiar with speech elements as they occur in whole words. There is no need for the use of printed forms to accomplish this. A small group of words, in which a specific sound is common to all, would be selected and used as were *airplane, car,* and *ball* in the previous examples of activities.

Since *b* is easily seen on the lips, the words *boy, baby,* and *ball,* with corresponding objects or pictures, might constitute material for a series of lessons in lipreading and speech preparation. Such lessons tend to have more value over a period of time if auditory training is included in each one. It is important that the child *not* be exposed to *b* or any other speech element alone, but only as it occurs in words. The element *b* alone means nothing to the child, and constant drill on the isolated form may result in the child's saying, "bu-aby," for "baby."

Other lessons may consist of words for practice in the use of *d,* such as *doll, daddy,* and *door,* of *fish, foot,* and *flower,* for practice in the use of *f,* and so on. As the child's experience, training, and total readiness develop, the words in the lipreading lessons may be grouped according to the initial consonant, so that words beginning with *p* would be used in one lesson or in one part of a lesson, those beginning with *th* in another, and so on. Later, words which end in the same consonant might be grouped together, and those with a common central consonant together, for example, *drum* and *gum* might be used in the same lesson, *paper* and *supper* in another.

It must be kept in mind that, although such groupings are designed to familiarize the young child with specific speech elements, he cannot at once imitate them. The child needs considerable practice in seeing them on the lips as they occur in whole words before he should be expected to try them himself. The daily lipreading practice in relation to interesting objects and activities gradually impresses him with the formation of those sounds, and little by little he learns to recognize similarities and differences in the sounds and to imitate them with increasing success, as he tries out a whole word, or as much of each word as he is able to manage.

As the child's ability to lipread nouns progresses, those nouns should be grouped not only according to initial, medial, and final consonants, but may also be grouped according to such classifications as food, furniture, toys, transportation, animals, dishes, things outdoors, clothing, parts of the body, family, friends, etc. In time, the nouns which he must learn for lipreading and speech are included in charts of many varieties which add interest to the training he must have.

A wealth of materials is necessary for this preparatory speech and lipreading training, and the parent and teacher find that many individual pictures, individual table-size charts, and larger wall charts must be prepared, to keep the child interested and to provide acceptably for the repetition he requires. (Plate XXIV)

One need not be an artist to make attractive speech and lipreading cards, charts, and books. There is no point in spending hours laboriously coloring outline pictures when they may be cut out quickly from current magazines. When a required picture is not immediately available in a magazine or picture book, the parent and teacher may find it necessary to draw and color one, but this occasional necessity need not be made a grueling task.

Each word to which the child is exposed for lipreading and speech preparation should be illustrated on its own separate card. Each child should have small charts which fit easily on his table or desk and which he can manipulate with ease. There should also be larger charts which can be hung on the wall or stood on the floor. The child also enjoys having his own book of words he has learned to lipread, and of words he can say with some intelligibility.

Plate XXIV. Two very deaf children, each wearing two hearing aids, are identifying singulars and plurals of pictured objects requested by the teacher out of their line of vision. Isolated words such as *mouse* versus *mice,* and *goose* versus *geese* are much more easily understood through hearing, as well as through speech reading, than are words such as *potato* versus *potatoes.* The final "s" is difficult, often impossible, to hear or to see as it occurs naturally in spoken language. The children discover this, must learn to interpret the whole spoken concept, as in, "That's *a* big potato," and "Mother bought a bag of potato*s*," "This *is* a potato," "Those *are* potato*s.*"

The parent and the teacher are advised against putting too many pictures on one page or one chart. It is more effective to have three charts for food, where the pictures are clear-cut and well-spaced, than to have all the pictures of the food on one chart

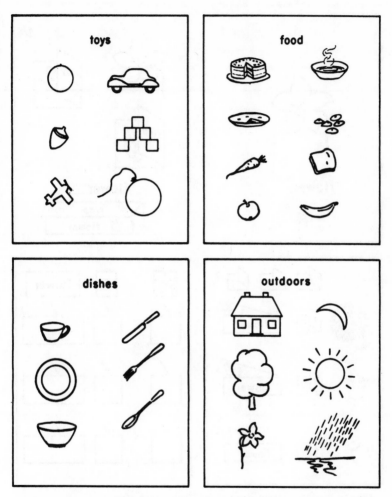

Fig 1. Suggested charts for lipreading; others for animals, clothing, people, parts of the body, etc. Mounted or drawn. The five-year-old could use these charts with the printed word beside each picture.

and so closely spaced that the child has difficulty in recognizing any one picture quickly.

Figure 1 shows examples of charts or pages in the individual child's book which may be used for lipreading practice of nouns.

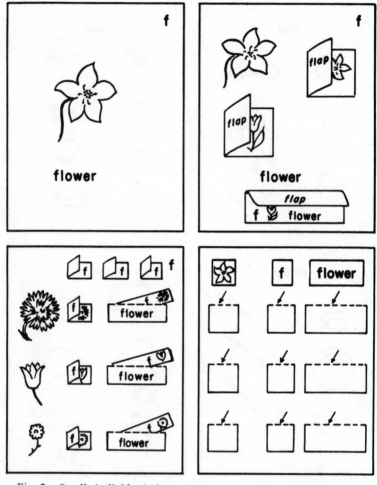

Fig. 2. Small, individual charts for speech and lipreading and auditory training for four- and five-year-olds. Same ideas omitting the printed forms are excellent for three-year-olds, and some two- and two-and-a-half-year-olds.

As the child's vocabulary grows, he may make one little book of toys, another of food, etc.

Figures 2 and 3 show charts which may be used in familiarizing the child with speech elements.

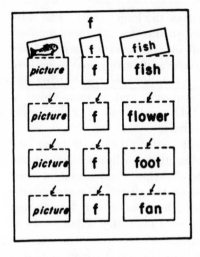

Column 1: Picture of object beginning with *f* sound would be pasted on outside of pocket—child inserts matching picture after lipreading it and saying it. *Column 2:* Sound is printed on outside of pocket for four- and five-year-olds. Child says sound, finds corresponding card on table and inserts opposite word he has used in column one. *Column 3:* Printed word is placed on outside of pocket for five-year-olds; child finds corresponding flash card on table, says the word, and inserts card in pocket.

1. Same object *on* different objects

Fig. 3. A chart made of cardboard on which paper pockets or envelopes are pasted serve as interesting practice material for lipreading, imitation of speech, spontaneous speech, and may be used with ease in auditory training. Similar charts may be made for each vowel and consonant. The sections involving printed forms would not be applicable to three-year-olds or younger. Printed forms may be included with four- and five-year-olds, as long as interest is centered in speech and lipreading, and emphasis is *not* placed on the printed words.

In the training situations, the large chart may be used one day, the table-size chart on another day, and the child's individual book or books on another, and there may be situations when a combination of these may be used.

When the child is learning to indicate certain objects through lipreading, he might be given a little wooden pointer with which to indicate the specific words on the larger charts. Using such a gadget or plaything makes the process somewhat more acceptable to the child.

The small charts are useful in auditory training along with lipreading and speech preparation since they require less tablespace than a series of single cards or the larger chart. The child lipreads the adult, points to the picture on the chart, imitates the word as he places one hand on the speaker's face and one on his own cheek, and listens to the adult's and then to his own voice as each speaks into the microphone of the hearing aid. Later, the earphones may be removed, and as each object is spoken of by the adult, the child would find it on his small chart and also on the larger wall chart.

Four- and five-year-olds with some previous training and progress in language understanding through lipreading, will find printed words appearing beside or below the pictures in their speech and lipreading books and on the charts. The same charts or similar ones may be used with five-year-olds in lessons that combine lipreading, speech, and word matching. Figure 4 shows charts that may be used for such purposes.

Teacher and parent will find envelopes very useful in adding variety to the lessons. These envelopes may be kept separate or they may be pasted, flap-side out, to large pieces of cardboard. One envelope may be used as a container for pictures of toys, another for pictures of clothing; or each envelope might contain pictures of objects whose names begin with a common sound. Each time a child finds a picture from lipreading, he may say the word, and place the picture in the envelope. Any procedure that includes some action on the part of the child seems to be more effective than mere lipreading and speech with the same words in the same way, day in and day out. (Plate XXV)

The blackboard, cut-outs of paper or felt, hand puppets, black silhouettes of objects, lotto games, dolls, peep-shows, and other such devices help to make the lessons more enjoyable for adult and child.

Objects may be traced on felt and the design cut out. Then, as the child lipreads and says each word, the corresponding object may be placed on its slightly larger piece of felt, to which it will stick without pasting. This process seems to fascinate every child.

Hand puppets and paper dolls are very helpful in learning the names of clothing and parts of the body. Dolls are sometimes useful in encouraging children to place the hand on the speaker's

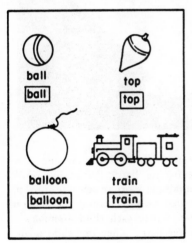

Fig. 4. Suggested charts for combining lipreading, speech and word matching. The words in the squares represent separate strips of paper or cardboard on which the word is printed. These charts might be made about note-book size, so that each child could have a set. Larger wall charts of the same type are effective for five-year-olds in group teaching.

face, and many a deaf child has played at "talking" to her doll, placing the doll's hand on her own cheek. Surprise situations, games, color, variety, mystery, etc., all aid in developing attention span, deeper interest, better cooperation and understanding.

Colorful classrooms and training areas, where pictures and objects, well-chosen to be within the range and interest of each child, are tastefully arranged, are themselves stimulating. Noth-

Plate XXV. These "sort and sound" picture cards are used for practice in listening for, speech reading (or both), and saying (individually and in sentences), words containing short vowels a, e, i, o, u, and for learning to group the illustrated words according to common vowel. These may be used as a game where each child assembles a set of five pictures, each picture in three parts. Then one child might ask the other for a word to go with "cup," upon which the picture of the "bus," would be handed over to be placed with that of "cup." This activity blends well into reading readiness activities also.

ing can be more boring and uninviting than a bare room where lipreading and speech are carried on over a little table, with mere routine talking by the adult and parroting by the child. The imaginative, ingenious, interested, and courageous adult, whether teacher or parent, finds no more satisfaction under those conditions than does the child.

The young child, who, in the middle of a lesson, will pull off the earphones, run to a shelf for a picture or to a book or chart to find a picture or object that is related to the lesson, is a much happier and more interested child than the one who just sits and does "as he is told" day after day, month in and month out, in fear of moving. The adult may be reasonably certain that such a child is escaping from the situation in some way, if only in imagination, and everything possible must be done to prevent this. Deviation from the planned lesson often promotes lipreading and speech, and will certainly produce a much healthier situation than one in which the child must find relief in his own imaginary situations.[123]

Verbs

Action verbs such as *bow, run, fall, jump, walk,* etc., are used in the first lipreading and speech lessons on verbs. As in the case of nouns, many charts and pictures are required. The teacher and the parent will have on hand a collection of separate pictures of each verb. Charts needed for the study of each verb are very easily made. The *run* chart would include pictures of a dog running, a man running, a girl running, a cat running, and a boy running. This type of chart helps to put across the idea that the action of running may be performed by different people and animals, and also gives practice in the use of nouns with the verb.

Pictures in silhouette cut from black paper may be used as well as colored, more detailed pictures. Stick figures, made of straight lines, may also be used. Figure 5 shows the detailed picture, the silhouette, and the stick figure, all on one chart.

The young child enjoys finding the colored picture and matching it to the silhouette and the stick figure, and each picture offers an opportunity for using speech.

If the verb *bow* is being practiced, the following procedure might be used. The teacher shows the child a colored picture of a girl bowing and says, "The girl is *bowing*. I can *bow*." Teacher

Fig. 5. Verb chart.

bows "You bow, Jean. *Bow*." Child bows. "I bowed and you bowed."

The child is asked to find on one of the charts another picture of a girl bowing. After indicating the correct picture, the child's hand is placed on the adult's cheek and the child is encouraged to speak with the adult and to imitate afterwords, "The girl is bowing," and "Bow." The child is given practice in clapping for accent as the sentence is used.

The child might be asked to bow again, and then assisted in saying, "I bowed."

This work with action verbs must involve variety and activity. A child can become so weary of bowing and hopping day after day, in the same place and for no apparent reason, that the practice can lose all its value.

Four-and five-year-olds who have had an early start in this work often enjoy practicing action verbs in small groups where they have an opportunity of telling one another what action to perform. The adult who is doing the guiding must not only provide opportunity for lipreading these verbs but for the use of them by the child, both separately and in short sentences. This frequently requires the adult's acting as the pupil while the child plays teacher, especially where group work is not yet possible.

Additional verbs are introduced into the lessons as the child's age and learning capacity permit. The verbs would be those which arise in conversational situations, which will occur later in reading readiness books, and which may be illustrated; for example, *laugh, cry, buy, give, dig, make, draw, paste, cut, eat, sleep,* and others.

Children at the nursery and kindergarten levels enjoy owning their own series of little verb books. These are easily made by the parent and teacher. One book might consist of many pictures illustrating the verb *run,* another for *walk,* until the child has a book for each verb learned for lipreading.

Each child might also have a book of verbs which he has learned to use in speaking. One page in this speech book might illustrate a few verbs which begin with *p,* such as *pull, push,* and *play.* Another page might illustrate the verbs, *burn, buy,* and *bow.* These speech books may be used in some of the lessons as another way of practice in saying the verbs, using the tactile, visual, and auditory techniques. The single verb would be spoken as well as whole sentences using the verb. For example, the child should have practice in using *sleep:* "The boy is sleeping," "I slept; *run:* "The dog is running," "I ran"; and others, in appropriate situations.

There has been some question regarding the advisability of using verbs in the present progressive form with young deaf children, and yet the parents are strongly advised to talk to the child as they would to a hearing child. If a hearing child sees another child running and if he were to comment on what he sees, he would say, "Bobby's running," since that is the form he has heard from the adults in his environment. The very young hearing child might say just "Run," and the adult would probably follow this up with, "Yes, Bobby's running." The deaf child must have the opportunity of becoming conscious of the various forms in which a verb may be used, even though he is not yet able to use the right form for every situation.[2]

Five-year-olds who will work in small groups, and occasionally two or three four-year-olds who have had previous training and who will work together in a group for a very short period, may enjoy the following verb game. The adult might say to one child, "Billy, let me see you *walk*." While Billy walks, the adult says to the other children, "Billy is walking." When Billy comes back and sits down, the teacher or parent goes to him, places his hand on her cheek and says, pointing to him, using his finger to point to himself, and encouraging him to imitate, "I walked." Then she might point to herself and each other child in turn, and say, "I didn't walk, Jimmy didn't walk, Doris didn't walk, *Billy walked*." Then each of the other children would be assisted in saying, "Billy walked."

Each of the other children would be given an opportunity to participate by acting out the same or another verb, and of using it as well as he is able, and the appropriate form would be used by the adult.

Exercises of this type where "correct"—that is, normal—verb forms are used, help to lay the foundation for future language work involving tenses. Certainly the child will not be expected to use all the tenses of verbs, to which he has been exposed at the preschool level, on his entrance to Grade I. He would be a very exceptional deaf child if he did. The most that can be expected is that he will be aware to some degree of different ways of saying things at certain times, of an action taking place here and now, of an action that has been completed, and of an action that may take place later on.

Even after he has entered Grade I and has had further specific training, he will probably need prompting by the teacher and the parent. However, an early experience of this sort with verbs should help him to cope with tenses in the grades, to get the meaning of a statement where the particular tense has significance, and to feel secure since this language is not entirely unfamiliar to him. Impressions received, even unconsciously, while the child is still at the most impressionable stages definitely increase his ability to recall related experiences and use them to interpret new ones.

Games that revolve about the store, the post office, the playhouse, the farm, the zoo, the beach, etc., are easily improvised by the adult and interesting to the child, and are helpful in verb study. Make-believe situations should be similar to real ones which the child has experienced. For example, the play-store situation will mean much more to the child in every respect if he has had experience in going to the store with his mother.

Empty wooden crates provide shelf and counter space for play-store activities. Canned goods, empty cartons, and paper boxes with the original pictures on them serve as materials to be purchased. Paper money may be used, although many children like to pretend that they are handling money without using either the real or substitute variety. (Plate XXVI)

The child should get practice in using such expressions as, "Milk, please," "Thank you," "I bought some milk."

Activities throughout the day provide for practice in lipreading such commands as, "Close the door," "Bring me the ball," "Open the door," "Give Betty the flower," etc. Occasionally they may be included in a lesson. However, unless they can be incorporated into the lesson in interesting, meaningful ways, it is advisable to spend very little time in specific situations in the lipreading of such expressions. They are, of course, important, but unless the adult uses discretion in presenting them, the situations may become boring and superficial.

Printed forms of the verbs begin to appear below the illustrations of verbs when the child is at the four-year-old level, and the single verbs and sentences with the verbs *may appear* with illustrations when the child is at the five-year level. Please note that these words only *appear,* since the printed form is not stressed at this time. The child at the preschool level must become familiar with printed forms, although understanding the verbs and learning to use them in speaking *must* come first. Placing stress on the printed form of the verb, prematurely, can retard the understanding and use of it in speech, since the preschool years are not long enough for everything. If wisely used, the printed word may add to the child's language experiences even at this level.

Each time that the printed word or sentence is attached correctly to the illustration of a specific verb, the child is being given another opportunity to lipread and to talk.

Forms of "to have" and "to be" as they should be used

Plate XXVI. This colorful puppet theatre, made of heavy cardboard, is sometimes used for "one man" shows with spoken language by the child, for pantomimes when the audience must guess what is being acted out, and as a store where canned and packaged foods, books, and at times, toys and "dress-up" clothing, are sold.

within spoken concepts may be missed by the deaf child, or there may be various substitutions or approximations when put to use. Early attempts at use of tense of verbs are heard among deaf children as with young hearing children, such as "havdud" for "had." [1] There is less tendency if any for the very early starting deaf child to use, when ready, forms of "to have" for forms of "to be," as is frequently found among deaf children who have no internalized language upon school entrance and who are known to say, "I have tall," instead of "I am tall." Words such as "have," "has," "had," etc., cannot help but come within the young child's experiences as related to possession, and opportunity for learning appropriate use within the total concept is very frequent.

Forms of "to be" must be learned within the total concept, such as in "It's raining." "Mother's here today." "There it is." "That's mine." "Are you and Mother going shopping after school?" "Were you at the zoo yesterday?" Since some of the forms are difficult to see as well as to hear in connected spoken language, the child will need reminding to include them in his own speaking until use of the whole concept is habitual.

In all the work with verbs, the "correct" forms of each must be used in relation to activities that are meaningful and enjoyable for the child. Drills that are exacting and often meaningless to the child are not advisable, and are not necessary in building the kind of foundation most essential to future language skills.

Adjectives

The young child's interest in *things* provides many opportunities for practice in learning to lipread and use adjectives. When the child sees an object, he usually has some feeling about it. He may be attracted or repelled by its color, its size, its shape, the use to which it may be put, or some other characteristic. The characteristics of each object may be described by the use of adjectives together with familiar nouns and verbs.

The child should be exposed to the many adjectives which would be used day after day in describing objects that enter into the child's experiences. However, in the specific lesson situations, it is advisable to work within a limited sphere, giving the child a great deal of repetition in the use of very few adjectives until they are fairly well-established.

Color—Adjectives

Colors attract most children, but their names may or may not be easy for the children to lipread. Teacher and parent must be ready to accept this situation if it arises. Too often, young deaf children have been expected to learn to lipread colors easily, just because of their apparent interest in colors.

The child has already had some experience with matching colors in his sense training activities, and probably has made a start in lipreading a few color-names at that time. He has probably learned to recognize similarities and differences in colors.

The first colors chosen for lipreading would depend somewhat on the child's preferences but more upon which color-names look different in speech. *Blue* and *yellow* might be the first ones chosen.

Since only two colors are to be used in the first lessons for specific lipreading and speech, several objects of each of these colors are needed to hold the child's interest. The same blue object and the same yellow one, day after day, may lose all attraction for the child and such a situation would certainly do little to broaden his concept of the colors and the words.

Although colors are used in phrases and sentences in real situations throughout each day, the specific lessons on color adjectives for the first few weeks, possibly months, would be concerned with individual words. This does *not* imply that the single word is repeated over and over, apart from other words, but that the color, itself, is to be emphasized. For example, if a series of blue and yellow objects were being used, the adult would indicate the yellow ball and say, "That's a *yellow* ball. It's yellow." Then, indicating other objects, she would say, "That's *yellow,* that's *yellow,* and that's *yellow.*" A similar procedure would apply to the blue objects.

Then, all objects, except one blue and one yellow, would be removed from the immediate area, and put in various places about the room. The adult would point to the yellow object near by, place the child's hand on her cheek and say, "That's *yellow.* It's *yellow.*" The child's other hand would be placed on his own cheek and he would be encouraged to repeat, both with and without the adult's assistance. "That's yellow," or "Yellow." The blue object would be used in a similar manner.

Practice would follow in lipreading the two color words, as the adult says, "Show me the *yellow* ball," and "Which is the *blue* ball?" Then looking about the room, she might say, "Find me something else that is *yellow*." "Find something *blue*," etc., until all the blue and yellow objects have been collected.

Day after day, for short periods, these color words would be practiced, using tactile, visual, and auditory means in connection with many objects, pictures, charts, and activities, until the child shows some indication of understanding through lipreading what is meant by *blue* and *yellow*.

The next lessons might consist of *red* and *yellow*, then *red* and *blue*, then *purple* and *yellow*, and occasionally three colors may be included in one lesson as the child becomes more adept at lipreading. The adult must not make the error of hurrying the child, of expecting him to learn to lipread all the color names within a few months, or even in a whole year, of training.

The *color phrase* composed of a color adjective and a noun has been presented to the child in many situations before specific work in this area is begun. His readiness for it will depend largely on his general language understanding, and ability to lipread isolated nouns and color adjectives. Some three-year-olds have been able to start this work; other children aren't ready until they are four or even five years old.

When specific lipreading and speech revolving about the color phrase are begun, it is wise to use in each lesson a series of phrases in which there is a constant, familiar word. For example, a lesson might include a group of phrases such as, *a red shoe, a red ball, a red house,* and *a red car.* Another group of phrases for a lesson might include *a blue shoe, a blue ball, a blue house, a blue car.* For variation, a group of phrases such as, *a yellow shoe, a red shoe, a blue shoe,* and *a pink shoe,* might be practiced. The use of a constant color throughout, *or* of a constant noun with different colors, provides the gradual building up of a vocabulary which so many deaf children need.

After the child has had a wealth of experiences in lipreading and saying such phrases, the exercises might be made considerably more difficult and challenging by including in one lesson separate phrases as *a red ball, a blue cup, a yellow hat,* etc. This demands more concentration on the part of the child.

The child who finds color less interesting, and who learns very slowly to lipread the colors, must be approached very patiently, and the lessons for him should be made especially interesting and appealing. The fact that he doesn't lipread the colors easily is no indication that he is not capable of eventually doing so, nor that he is retarded. One child may lipread colors, separately and in phrases at the three-year-old level, while another child who is quite as intelligent may need all the preschool years or even longer to accomplish the same end.

As the child learns to lipread each color, it would be illustrated in his little book designed for this purpose, and the colors which he learns to say with some intelligibility would be illustrated in his speech book of colors.

The printed form of each color name and each color phrase may be included when the child is ready for that. As in the case of other printed forms already discussed, the emphasis would be on understanding and speech preparation, rather than on the printed form.

Number—Adjectives

The child's first specific experience with numbers usually comes through sense training exercises when he learns to match cards illustrating a certain number of circles, squares, and other number pictures.

The child will not learn to lipread the numbers as quickly as he will learn to match the cards illustrating the number pictures, and this fact necessitates the use of many sets of number cards to provide interest and the required amount of repetition. Each time a number picture is presented, and the child matches it to another on charts and in number books, the adult talks about it. "That's *one,* that's *one,* and that's *one.*"

It takes time for the child to realize that two spots are equal in number to two shoes, and that two blue circles are equal in number to two green circles. Each difference in color and shape that enters into the number work presents another transition which the young child must make. For this reason, parents are particularly cautioned against moving ahead faster than the child is able to assimilate numbers.

The first number cards should be simple and identical. After the child learns to match one blue circle to one blue circle, he learns to match one blue to one green, two blue to two purple, two chairs to two chairs, two chairs to two tables, etc., and finally reaches the stage where he can place all number pictures of two together, all ones together, all threes together, regardless of whether the pictures show squares, circles, chairs, balls, or any other objects. Throughout this number experience, the tactile, visual, and auditory means are used to promote lipreading and speech.

Number charts similar to those in Figures 6 and 7 add interest to the child's daily training in number work. Number books also provide for greater interest and further practice.

Besides learning to recognize number pictures, the child should have some experience in learning to count. The events of each day usually provide some opportunity for counting, and once the child begins to count, he is often found counting his possessions for others, counting the blocks he plays with, and so on, even before he is able to count very far or to say the numbers intelligibly.

The teacher and the parent use a number of simple exercises, similar to the following one, to give the child a broader concept of numbers through counting. The adult might take a number of blocks from a shelf where many blocks are kept. She would take three blocks and place them in a row on the table. Then indicating the other blocks in her lap, she would ask the child for "three" more blocks, and would help him to find them. Then one block would be placed on each of the three already on the table. Taking the child's hand, she would count, *one, two, three,* moving the child's hand from block to block and from left to right.

The adult might place three blocks in front of her, and three in front of the child, and both adult and child would count (from left to right) *one, two, three.* The rhythm of the movement and of the speech should not be sacrificed for articulation during this operation.

The child should get a great deal of practice in counting many objects, from left to right and in rhythm. Following this counting experience, the adult might show the child a number

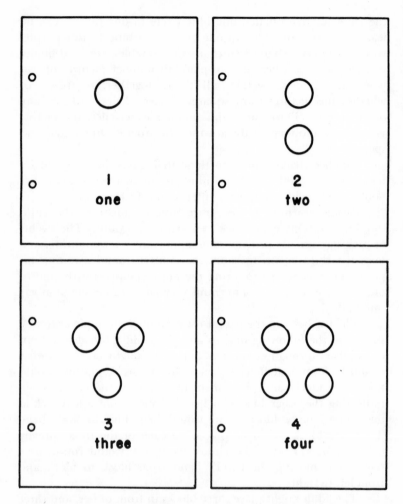

Fig. 6. Suggested number cards, or pages in scrapbook, for the five-year-olds. Similar cards to five or six. Additional cards illustrating cars, airplanes, apples, etc., would be used. These might also be used for word matching. Number symbols and words are added as the child's age and responses indicate a readiness.

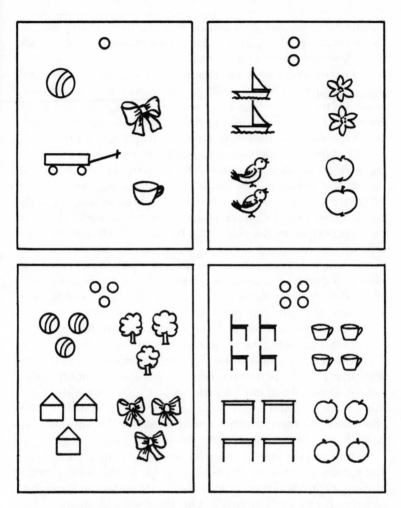

Fig. 7. Suggested number charts for lipreading and speech. Child learns to recognize immediately the number picture without counting. Large wall charts and smaller individual ones make this number work more effective.

picture of three, and demonstrate how the three blocks may be made into a number picture. This often means placing a block on each pictured object on the card.

The recognition of number pictures should be correlated with counting as often as possible. But it must be clearly understood by the adult doing the guiding that the child should be trained to recognize the number picture as whole, and *not* have to *count* the objects in the constructed picture. (Plate XXVII)

Counting is important, and usually of interest to the child, but it is not as simple as many adults seem to believe. The child may repeat numbers after the adult, and "count" just as far as he is "trained" to count, but this is no indication that the child has a well-rounded concept of each number named. It is far more important to the child that he have a well-rounded concept of each number, from one to five or six, by the time he enters Grade I, than that he be able to "count" to twenty, or even to a hundred, if he does not realize that *five* is more than *three,* that *five* may be in the form of a picture, a symbol, or a word, and that *five* may mean five chairs in his home.

It has been mentioned several times already that the pre-school years provide time for just so much training and no more. The child can't possibly learn everything about numbers during that time, and the person training the child—a parent especially —must be content to put "first things first." Of course, there are times when the child wants to count many objects and to be told how many are there, and his questions should be answered, as he perhaps counts with the adult from left to right.

However, the teacher must recognize the child's immaturity and remember that, on the basis of work in this subject with hearing children, every child's ability to understand number concepts is definitely limited. The three-year-old should have many, many experiences with numbers to three, the four-year-old with numbers to four, and so on. Thorough training with a few numbers results in faster progress in number work later on, when the demands on the child are greater. Each child should be permitted to progress as fast as he is able, but this principle must not be misinterpreted nor the child's natural curiosity about quantity exploited, to the detriment of present and future training.

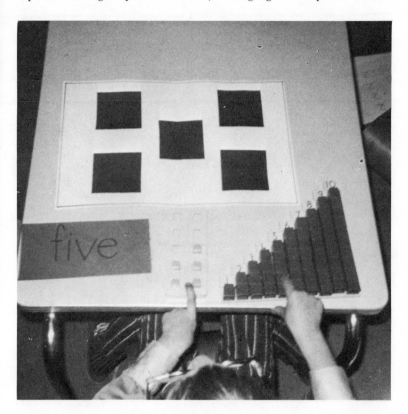

Plate XXVII. Some representations of *five*: (1) the large number picture on which an equal number of blocks or other objects may be placed; (2) another arrangement of five using small blocks inserted in the number tray; (3) interlocking blocks in the number stair with the corresponding figure; (4) the printed word "five."

The enriched number program within the child's comprehension may seem not too interesting to the adult and will surely involve a maximum ingenuity and imagination on his part, but it is the only kind of program that the child should have.

The procedure in presenting number phrases is similar to that described for color phrases. Although numbers should be used in phrases and sentences as much as possible, specific work

Plate XXVIII. Interlocking blocks and the number stair are being used here to give the *prepared* five-year-old some understanding of addition and subtraction, using all necessary spoken language.

with them must be gradual and well-planned for the individual child.

Number work is usually fun for the young child. It lends itself easily to many activities, such as hiding and finding, and other game-like situations. The child gets practice in lipreading the numbers in phrases, sentences, and stories as well as separately, and in using the numbers in speaking and in answering questions. (Plate XXVIII)

The question form *How many* is used over and over in many

situations of an adequate early training program, so that, by the time the child enters Grade I, he should seldom make an error in answering a simple question of *How many.* The importance of any child's being able to understand the principles of conversation of quantity *before* he can develop number concept is one more reason for emphasizing language meanings for deaf children within the language of quantity.[19] The order and value for continuing the number work which little deaf children seem in the beginning to enjoy and to cope with easily must be learned with language. Otherwise, later mathematical problem solving will not be possible.[126, 128]

Other Adjectives

The deaf child of three to five or six years of age may learn to lipread, and in some degree to say, such adjectives as *big* and *small* (or *little*), *soft* and *hard, pretty* and *funny, old* and *new, good* and *bad,* etc. Descriptive adjectives like these are used frequently in most environments and the parent should try to show the child through the use of pictures, objects, and real situations, what is meant by each. When the child is ready for specific work involving these adjectives, he seems to learn to lipread and use them most easily when they are presented in the comparative sense; for example, the *big* ball stands out because the one beside it is *small.* The obvious differences help to explain the adjectives.

The first work is in relation to matching objects and matching pictures illustrating such adjectives. Many pictures and charts are necessary for lipreading and speech practice, even long after the child has become less dependent on object matching and picture matching.

These adjectives would be used separately, in phrases, and in sentences, and the child would be encouraged to use them in the lesson situations and in spontaneous speech.

Prepositions

During the first year in nursery school, if the child is three years of age or under, no specific work is done with prepositions. The child will have some *incidental* experience with preposi-

Plate XXIX. In the process of vocabulary building—using for example "cup" and "spoon"—prepositions, numbers colors, size, verbs, and other language forms, are normally used. As illustrated here, there are cups and spoons of various colors and sizes in a number of positions: a spoon *in* a cup, a little cup *in* a big cup, a cup *on* the table, a cup *under* the chair, three spoons *between* two cups, etc.

tions at these early levels in relation to the work with nouns and verbs and in daily conversational situations. For example, when the child is asked to find a ball and put it *in* a box or *on* the table, when he is told to put his coat *in* the locker, and to carry out other requests, he is inevitably getting some valuable experience in the use of prepositions. (Plate XXIX)

When the adult says, "The ball is on the chair," the child eventually realizes that there is some connection between *ball* and *chair,* and even though he may be quite unaware of the word *on,* his understanding of the whole sentence is a very real achievement that will make special work with prepositions more meaningful for him later.

Some four-year-olds and most five-year-olds may begin specific work on prepositions. The amount and nature of such training will depend on the individual child and his general language background. It would be an error to impose such training upon the child who has not some understanding of language through lipreading and who hasn't established some lipreading and speech vocabulary. And, under no conditions, would any child at the preschool level be exposed to a purely technical consideration of the use of prepositions.

In so far as any preschool deaf child is able to understand any preposition, he will achieve that understanding through activities related to familiar words such as nouns and verbs.

Two prepositions such as *under* and *on,* which are easily illustrated and which do not look alike on the lips, might be used in the first lessons. The child might be given a number of objetcs and asked to put one *on* the table, another *under* the table, another *on* the table, another *under* the table, etc. Preposition charts that illustrate the objects (which correspond to the real ones) *on* and *under* tables might be used in connection with the game.

Figure 8 shows samples of charts which may be made for each preposition. In the charts is set forth a carefully devised sequence to be followed in simplifying for the child his understanding of the preposition through lipreading.

Preposition books are helpful and of interest to the child. He might have an *On* book consisting of many pictures of familiar objects *on* many familiar objects, another book for *Under,* etc.

The child is encouraged to imitate the whole phrase or sentence in which the particular preposition is used. In order to make it clearer to the child, the adult may stress the preposition without breaking the rhythm of the sentence; for example, "The ball is *on* the box," "The ball is *on* the floor," "The ball is *on* the table."

In spontaneous speech situations, most preschool deaf

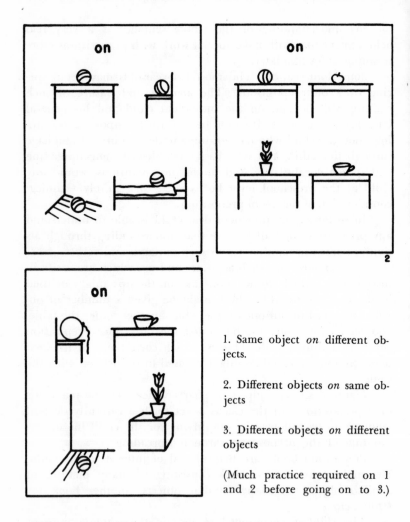

1. Same object *on* different objects.

2. Different objects *on* same objects

3. Different objects *on* different objects

(Much practice required on 1 and 2 before going on to 3.)

Fig. 8. Preposition charts. Pictures may be cut out and mounted, or drawn in outline and colored. Similar series for each preposition. Large wall charts of each type supplemented by individual ones for each child.

children will eliminate the preposition, and will continue to do so long after they have learned to understand it in sentences, and even to use it in the specific speech situations where they are prompted by the adult. In spite of all the excellent early training the child may have, he will probably have to be prompted more often than not, after entering Grade I.

The five-year-old who has had two or three years of previous language training may be reminded casually of his omission, and assisted in repeating the sentence using the preposition. These casual reminders, in addition to such specific exercises as those described above, constitute the extent to which the child may be trained in the understanding and use of prepositions. As a pre-school child, he is not ready for a more analytical approach to language, and if at the end of his preschool training he has acquired a relatively broad understanding of the use of the most commonly needed prepositions in childhood, such as, *to, at, on, in, under, for, with, before, after,* etc. to put across his ideas, he will have done well indeed.

Pronouns

The little deaf child should have been exposed to pronouns in simple language from the time people began to talk to him. In spite of this exposure in earlier stages, the three-year-old shows little if any understanding of any pronoun. As the child continues through the preschool years, his attention may be called to such pronouns as *I, me, you,* and *mine,* as they occur in sentences and other expressions. These pronouns may be more emphasized in working with the four-year-old, although he would not be expected to use them. In the lesson situation he might be encouraged to say, "I have a gun," instead of merely saying, "Gun." The adult responds with, "Yes, *you* have a gun. *I* have no gun."

When the child finally becomes conscious of these words he is often confused by the way *you* and *I* are used. He can't quite accept *you* calling him *you,* when he is supposed to refer to himself as *I.* And when he realizes that *I, me,* and *mine,* may all be used in relation to himself, he may use any one of them to the exclusion of others or may use all of them, usually in the "wrong" situation. However, he is using them, and with each occasion when he is reminded casually of the "correct" form, the confusion gradually passes and, sooner or later, the pronouns fall into place.

For the most part, right up to the end of the preschool training, the best practice in the use of pronouns is provided by general conversation. The specific work helps to make the child more conscious of pronouns and their respective meanings, but it is the casual practice that he gets from day to day which counts the most in the end. It is very difficult for either parent or teacher to determine what pronouns the child actually "knows," but they can be certain that constant exposure to pronouns during the preschool years, no matter what confusion the child may exhibit, will make his future language work much more meaningful and less difficult to master.

From the lipreader's standpoint, pronouns can be very elusive. While trying to understand the connected language of a speaker, many a child, or adult, will miss the whole sense of a remark through a misinterpretation of a pronoun. The parent and the teacher can help the child to obviate many difficult situations in the future by establishing some early foundation for understanding pronouns.[22]

Conjunctions

Conjunctions, like any other commonly used language form, occur very early in the child's general language training. The specific training, however, cannot be begun until the child's general language understanding, his vocabulary, and his attention span indicate his readiness. For example, a three-year-old who has learned to lipread the words *ball* and *shoe,* and who is asked to find the ball *and* the shoe, may dash off to get the ball without watching the speaker until she has completed the request.

When the child is ready to watch for longer spoken phrases and sentences, he usually enjoys being able to find more than one object, or performing more than one action, as would be required in exemplifying the conjunction *and.* Four-year-olds, after the necessary preparatory language training, are able to lipread such expressions as, "Show me a ball *and* an airplane." "A car *and* a truck," "A girl *and* a boy," etc. The five-year-old takes another step forward when he learns to lipread, "Show me a ball, a car, *and* an airplane.

Four- and five-year-olds learn to lipread and carry out such commands as, "Run *and* fall." "Walk to the door, turn around, *and* run to me," "Find the picture of the girl sleeping *and* the picture of the boy running," etc.

Attention is brought to the conjunction as the speaker uses the tactile, visual, and auditory techniques, and the child is encouraged to imitate the whole expression.

In the formal lesson, the child learns to use the word *and,* although in spontaneous speech situations he tends to omit it. At the five-year-old level, he may be remainded of his omission and encouraged to repeat the expression in full.

The conjunction *or* figures in daily situations in expressions such as, "Which do you want, the red socks *or* the blue ones?" "Do you want the wagon *or* the truck?" For some time, when the adult asks, "Do you want the red ball *or* the blue one?" the child, in all probability, will reach for both balls. Only constant practice in making choices, an experience which is often difficult and frustrating for the young child, can establish any concept of the conjunction *or,* and in spite of the maximum practice possible during the preschool years, the deaf child at the end of that time has little real understanding of *or.*

The conjunction *and* should be fairly well established at the end of the preschool training, and other conjunctions such as *or,* although not established to any noticeable degree, should have become a regular part of the language experiences.

PHRASES AND SENTENCES

Phrases have been mentioned several times in relation to adjectives, prepositions, and conjunctions. It is important that the child be exposed to the use of phrases from the beginning of his training. Gradually he is trained to lipread and to say simple phrases made up of familiar words he has learned.

The last year of preschool training should include some daily work in lipreading phrases, in saying them, and in listening to them. Any work with the printed forms must be done in conjunction with lipreading, speech, and auditory training.

Granted that the child has had the necessary preparatory training, he usually is able, by the time he enters Grade I, to lipread with relative ease such common phrases as *two cars, three big boys, a blue balloon, a pretty dress,* and others, using the colors, the numbers, and other adjectives with familiar nouns.

The child is also able to use some phrases in answering questions; for example, "Where is the basket?" *"On the table."* "Where did you go yesterday?" *"Down town."*

His speech may be quite intelligible, or it may be almost unintelligible. It is hoped that the child's speech will be sufficiently intelligible for the listener to distinguish what he means to say, since the most important accomplishment of the whole preschool time is that the child understand spoken language and begin to try to use the same language.[93]

Sentences are used in talking to the child throughout his early training, both before specific training is begun and while it is being carried on. They are used in connection with each language form which the child is trained to lipread and use. Specific training in lipreading sentences is also valuable in showing the child that a toy, an activity, or a picture may be described in a number of ways.

The first specific sentence work probably begins about the time the child is learning to match pictures illustrating activities which may be described in such sentences as, "The boy is running," "The man is driving a car," "The woman is carrying a baby," "The girl is playing with a dog," and others. He also learns to match, and eventually to lipread, simple sentences using *has* and *have;* for example, "The boy has a ball," "The woman has a baby," "The girl has a dog," and so on.

As the child progresses from the three-year-old level to the four, and then to the five, the sentences increase in number and in length, and become increasingly challenging, as his vocabulary expands and his experiences are spoken of in different ways.

Many colorful pictures and charts are needed for practice in sentence work. The adult finds it necessary to assemble a collection of useful, interesting pictures. Each picture may be mounted, or clipped to medium-weight paper of a neutral shade. The pictures should be catalogued in folders, or systematically numbered, so both child and adult are able to find a wanted picture quickly. There will be pictures that provide for practice in the use of each verb, each preposition, and other language forms in sentences. Pictures may be collected and catalogued according to whether they illustrate holiday activities, home activities of child and family, school activities, activities of community workers (the postman, the garageman, the storekeeper, the milkman, the policeman, etc.), special excursions and trips (to the zoo, to the beach, to the mountains, to the library, etc.), places of interest in the community (the post office, the docks, the fire-station, the city hall, the farm, the department store, the drugstore, etc.), and others.

As the child becomes more familiar with lipreading, the adult purposely changes the wording of a sentence so the child will be able to get the thought of the sentence whether it is constructed in one way or another.

The sentence work is planned and presented as a progression from the simple to the more difficult, and the adult must be constantly aware of the fact that the child is still very young. To present such a group of sentences as, "The boy is eating peas," "The boy is eating beans," "The boy is eating beets," in one lesson would be quite unreasonable. *Peas, beans,* and *beets,* look exactly alike on the lips, and even the most expert adult lipreader would have difficulty in understanding which of the three words was being used.

The five-year-old who has had two or three years of previous training often understands that certain words look alike on the lips, and there are some children who enjoy being given words which look alike, and who have fun in trying to guess which word is being said. However, since most children of this age are not so sophisticated about language, it is up to the adult to make each lesson in sentences interesting and challenging without being either fustrating or discouraging. It is possible for two sentences which sound different, and whose meanings are different, to look fairly similar on the lips. The child should learn to lipread such sentences, but should not be required to work in the most difficult manner.

Some deaf children at the preschool level have learned to lipread sentences by watching the side of the speaker's face. Four-year-olds have begun to do this. They have been exposed to the sentences as the adult allows them to watch the full face, the face at an angle of about 45 degrees, and then the side of the face.

Certainly, this elaboration of the usual lipreading is not a *must*. No child should have to strain to interpret spoken language in this way. However, if the matter is well-managed in an offhand way, the little deaf child can enjoy these variations. If he does, even though he is not expected to become expert at "lipreading from the side," the exercise helps to make him more aware of muscles, and of movements of other parts of the face besides the lips.

The child should have practice in lipreading sentences from other angles; for example, when the face of the speaker is above his eye level, and below his eye level. Such practice, of course, should take place only when the child has become familiar with lipreading when the adult's face is on a level with his.

Whenever sentences are used, the child should be encouraged to say them with the adult, or to imitate them. As he progresses in lipreading and imitation of speech, he should be encouraged to use sentences spontaneously in describing familiar pictures.

In the child's use of the sentence, the rhythm of the *whole sentence* is more important than the pronunciation of individual words in the sentence. As he gets more practice and encouragement in saying sentences rhythmically, his speech becomes even more intelligible.

As his speech improves and he becomes familiar with the speech pattern of the sentences, more attention may be given to certain words in the sentence. This part of the training of the young deaf child should be in the hands of an expert. A wrong move here may destroy much of the earlier, hard-earned progress. The skilled teacher will know how to strike a balance among articulation, fluency of speech, and the maintaining of a good voice quality (in so far as this is possible for a deaf child), these three elements in the right proportion being essential in developing intelligible speech. The skilled teacher never sacrifices fluency, meanings, or voice quality for articulation, for example—a regrettable misplacing of emphasis which could take place when the child is at the preschool levels.

Parents should be aware of such dangers, especially those who are determined to "do something" about speech development in their respective children. Some parents resent being told to restrict their speech work with their respective children to the imitation of speech, and often resent the fact that the teachers aren't "doing more about" *speech*. There are good reasons for the teacher's way of approaching speech. In spite of much authentic, well-founded advice, there have been parents who have unwisely taken things into their own hands, and then, when their children started to school, the teachers had to begin "at the bottom" to try to repair the damages done, and the parents were utterly bewildered by a situation which they themselves created.[139]

These matters are discussed here since the use of sentences—or misuse of them—by the children frequently disturbs the parents. They are struck by the realization that to give language and speech to the deaf child seems an almost hopeless, and certainly a tremendous, undertaking, and their anxiety may drive them on to what they call "action."

When a child uses a succession of nouns, or one or two-nouns and a verb, in attempting to make a sentence, to tell the parent something, to ask for something, the child should not be discouraged nor made to feel that no one is satisfied to try to understand him as he is and as he talks. He should not be subjected to extreme corrective measures, nor be forced to "say that word better." If the situation lends itself to casual correction, as many do, the parent may repeat what the child has tried to say, using the appropriate language. Then, if the child will repeat the sentence, he should be given approval and a response. The same principle applies in the more specific work which the parent may carry on in lipreading and use of sentences.

The value of the child's willingness to lipread and say a sentence *as a whole* must not be vitiated by stopping him in his effort, by manipulating his lips and tongue, by drilling on a particular word or consonant. This kind of meddling, aside from the harmful psychological effects, results in the stilted, "one-word-at-a-time," jerky speech, which so many parents react to in listening to some deaf children talking.

A great deal of sentence work may be done in conjunction with auditory training, and this is discussed at some length under the section on Auditory Training Activities for Language Development.

QUESTIONS AND ANSWERS

The ability to understand questions by lipreading, to answer, and to ask questions is a goal which parents and teachers hope the deaf child will reach as early as possible. The deaf child who has learned to ask and answer questions has come a long way. When he is able to use language in this manner, he is using speech as a social activity; and he is rapidly nearing the stage where he may use speech in "influencing the behavior of those about him," [144] a use to which speech is put by the majority in society.

Questions and answers cause confusion and frustration for many deaf children, especially when the need to use these language forms confronts them in social situations in and out of the home, and in lessons on almost every academic subject. A foundation should be laid in the preschool years which can help to obviate such problems. Preschool training in question and answer work will not eliminate all possibility of future language problems caused by questions and answers, but it should help child and adult in meeting those problems and resolving them more readily.

Parent and teacher begin asking the child questions from the time his training is begun. Needless to say, the adult has to do both the asking and the answering for some time. Simple questions such as, "Who is that?" or "Where is Mother?" arise many times during a child's day, and although the child cannot answer since he doesn't understand the significance of the question, the person who has asked the question should help the child to bridge the gap between question and answer by answering aloud as the child watches. In time, the child begins to see a relationship between the question and the answer.

The four-year-old who has had a year or two of previous training may begin to answer some simple questions. In the beginning, he may indicate an understanding of the question by some action rather than by speech, if he hasn't grasped the idea of responding with spontaneous speech. The adult will accept his means of response and at the same time will assist him to use the appropriate words.

After the child has had considerable experience in lipreading and in imitating speech, he may begin to repeat the question which the adult asks, and when she gives him the answer, he will repeat it, too.[158] If the child follows the "normal" channels of language development, he will go through this stage. Occasionally, the adult is more confused by this development than the child is. The adult who "fusses" about it and tries to clarify the situation by "logical" explanations, or by stopping the child in his imitating, will find the situation becoming more and more confusing for her and the child.

As the child is going through this stage of imitating both question and answer, he is taking note of other factors. He begins to notice that every time the speaker says, "What color," the word, "red," "blue," or some other color is used; that every time the speaker says, *"Who* is that?" a person is referred to, and so on. He must be given time to recognize these relationships through much daily practice in general and specific situations.

Later on, the adult will find that as soon as the child imitates the question she has asked, he quickly gives the answer without any assistance. At this point, question games are introduced, in which the child asks the questions and the adult gives the answers. Before long, the child realizes that one person asks the question and the other person responds.

It takes a long time for the child to acquire the knowledge and the language that enable him to answer and ask questions of the simplest variety, in spite of the many situations that lend themselves to such practice.

Number work furnishes practice in lipreading and using the

question form *How many;* color work offers opportunity to practice the question form *What color;* work with nouns provides for
the use of *What's that,* or *Who is that;* preposition work for
Where; activities bring forth questions such as *What happened,
Did you go down town, What did you do,* etc.

Question games provide an enjoyable way of learning to
lipread various question forms and to answer them. A child
might hide a few objects about the room while the adult covers
her eyes. Then the adult will ask, *"Where* did you hide the ball?"
or *"Where* is the airplane?" or *"Where* did you put the gun?"
and the child would answer, using the appropriate phrase.

In a group of children, each one might be given a toy which
he hides behind his back. The adult may ask, "Who has the
ball?" The child who has the ball would bring it into view and
say, "I have." Or, one child might be asked to guess who has the
ball, who has the book, who has the drum, etc., and would respond with the name of the child who has the particular object.

The child who has had adequate language experiences
should be given every opportunity to ask questions, and this
often means that the child becomes the teacher, and the teacher
the pupil who must answer. This technique is usually very
successful with five-year-olds.

THE TIME ELEMENT

The parent often finds herself faced with the problem of
explaining to the child that something will happen tomorrow, or
at some other time. The little deaf child often wonders why one
child has the pretty birthday cake with candles placed before
him, and when his turn will come. He may wonder why windows
in the stores display a big man in a red suit and what all this
will mean for him. He may have some understanding of Christmas in terms of Santa Clause and gifts, and as soon as he sees
Christmas decorations and pictures he may want his Santa Claus
gifts immediately.

Daily use of the calendar at home and at school (if the child
is in nursery school) helps to put across the idea of time, and the

child begins to understand that, even though he may not like it and regardless of anything he may do, he must wait until the special day arrives.

Large calendars should be used with ample white space around the numbers, so that, next to each printed date, a small drawing of a birthday cake, a Christmas tree, an Easter rabbit, may be inserted, to denote the *time* for special occasions.[39]

Each month usually offers a holiday or some festive occasion, and the child begins to notice that as each day is crossed off, the special day draws nearer. The adult uses terms such as *today, tomorrow, yesterday, in three days,* etc., and uses the calendar to explain what she means.

The preschool deaf child has very little understanding of the terms *today, tomorrow,* and *yesterday.* The preschool hearing child constantly confuses them. Nevertheless, the adult uses the terms without expecting the child to use them. The deaf child does begin to understand the difference between *a long time* and *in a little while.* Many a parent has discovered that the young deaf child—like the hearing child—becomes quite "skilled" in the use of such phrases as *after a while* or *in a minute* as means of putting off something which he has been asked to do. One five-year-old child who had been begging her mother and father to take her to the beach and who had been told many times, "After a while," instead of being given a definite answer, one day responded with, "After a while. All the time, after a while." The child soon learns that time terms may be used by both adults *and children* in delaying actions and activities.

Calendars may also be used for language work in connection with the weather from day to day. Four- and five-year-olds usually enjoy this. If the day is sunny, the adult, and later on, the child, might draw a picture of the sun beside the date; and the sentence, "The sun is shining," would be practiced for lip-reading and speech. If it is raining, a picture of rain and an umbrella might be drawn beside the number, and the sentence, "It is raining," would be practiced. Other weather language, such as *It is cloudy, It is hot, It is cold,* may be practiced in a similar manner.

The child's day follows a certain pattern—time for school,

time for lunch, time to go home, time to go to bed, etc.—and the child enjoys learning to identify these times with certain positions of the hands of the clock. The adult might make a large cardboard clock with movable hands. The hands might be set at lunch time, twelve o'clock, and when the hands of the real clock on the wall reach the same position, the child is shown that they are the same and that it is time for lunch.

If the child, impatient about going downtown, must wait another five minutes, the adult would tell him, "We'll leave in five minutes," and show him five minutes on the clock. In most cases, the child keeps an eye on the clock, and in five minutes is back to remind the adult that it's time to leave.

With the best of training, the preschool deaf child's understanding of time is limited, but he can acquire some understanding which makes life much more comfortable for him and his parents, and which makes future language work with time simpler and more interesting for him.

STORIES AND PICTURE DESCRIPTIONS

Specific work with stories and picture descriptions, which demands a background of general experience with language and storytelling, seldom begins before the child's last year in preschool when he is five or six years old. Up to this time, the child should have had many experiences with the common stories of childhood, and with pictures that have been described to him over and over again in various ways.

When the child is ready, specific steps may be taken through the use of familiar stories to impress upon the child that there is a *sequence* of events in each story. For example, the child doesn't understand the story of *Jack and Jill* if he thinks that Jack fell down the hill before he went up. Probably the child has had some experience in pantomiming the story and has established some notion of the sequence. In order to ensure a correct idea of sequence, the adult would have a series of pictures, each picture illustrating a specific step. The pictures would be presented to the child one at a time, described in a simple sentence, and placed side by side on a ledge or in a slot chart until the whole story is told in pictures.

After all the pitcures are in place, with the first picture on the left, the last on the right, each one is described. The child is encouraged to describe each picture, using the sentence which the adult has used. Then the pictures might be removed, mixed up, and handed to the child, who proceeds to put them back in the chart or on the ledge in the correct order. As he becomes more and more adept at doing this, he might be asked to talk about each picture as he places it.[97, 134]

The adult might collect a series of pictures that illustrate a trip to the store. One picture would be of the child being given money by his mother; the next picture might be of him walking toward the store; the next, of him walking into the store; the next, of him buying an article from the storekeeper and paying for it; the next, of him walking home; the last, of him giving it to his mother. Pictures of this sort may be drawn or may be found in the prereading books available in bookstores.

It must be made clear that stories should not be analyzed on the level of much older children. The training should be fun and can be fun. The story is told using colorful, attractive pictures, it is pantomimed and dramatized, and the individual pictures would be described and placed in proper sequence. After this has been done, questions on the story may be asked.

This work is extremely important. The child's understanding of the sequence of events, of the fact that one thing must happen before another event occurs, has a definite bearing on the quality of work he will do in the grades. He will be better equipped to get the thought of a whole story or paragraph, spoken or read, and to answer questions regarding it with greater ease.

Stories may be developed from the children's excursions, using blackboard drawings and sketches or pictures from magazines and children's books. The child should be encouarged to say anything he wants to say about the excursion or the picture. When all the interesting incidents of the excursion have been discussed informally, the adult reorganizes them into story form, and, using the illustration, talks to the child and encourages him in his attempts to tell a story.

The success attained through these story-games, which are designed to promote logical thought along with language skills, will depend on the skill with which the teacher or the parent guides the child. The child must be happy in the situation, and in addition, there must be guidance and an aim.

Chapter 13

Developmental Activities for Language Development

CREATIVE ACTIVITIES

The child's creative effort is part of the developmental processes of early childhood. Since the beginning level of creativity comes into being only when the child voluntarily places an oral label on his accomplishment, it is important that young deaf children be given the opportunity to reach this goal and to then proceed to higher levels of creativity.[94, 180]

As the child becomes more involved in experimentation with various media and materials, he becomes more expressive, productive, and inventive. Simultaneously, his activity should be used as a means of sponsoring language beginnings. Once the child has reached the beginning level of real creativity, his efforts begin to reveal more insight and deliberation. Using various media and materials, he begins to produce from within himself. If one accedes to the point of view that once a person has aspired to creativity he never returns to the commonplace, it becomes vital that opportunity beginning in the very early years be provided for the hearing handicapped child to achieve this goal.[120]

The activities provided for through busy hands and colorful media offer many opportunities for expression, and for casual training in lipreading, speech, and language understanding. If the activities are to be effective with the deaf child, the materials provided and the methods followed should parallel those employed in the guidance of the hearing child, and adult guidance of the deaf child should obey the laws of child growth rather than of deafness.

The following activities are among those which might be used to advantage by parent or teacher: (1) Easel painting, (2) finger painting, (3) paper cutting, (4) paper tearing, (5) pasting, (6) weaving, (7) paper folding, (8) lacing, (9) mural painting, (10) painting on felt, (11) crayon on felt, (12) crayon on paper, (13) clay manipulation and modeling, (14) construction with wood, (15) painting fences and large surfaces with large brush and water, (16) modeling houses and roads in sand, (17) building with blocks and planks, (18) visits to art centers, (19) excursions to see and appreciate the beauty of nature, as in flowers, the sky, trees, rain, pools of water, reflections in the water, etc., (20) room arrangement, flower arrangement, arrangement of toys on shelves.

Among the necessary materials and equipment for such activities are the following items: tables and chairs of right sizes for the respective children, easels of suitable height, and preferably adjustable; oilcloth covers for tables and easels; washable linoleum on floors; paint brushes with short thick handles and thick brushes; easel paper; crayons; pastels; drawing paper; pieces of felt, large and small; finger paint; finger painting paper; paint containers; water; painter's brushes for painting large surfaces with water; aprons; plasticine; clay; clay boards; clay pot; paste; small, blunt scissors; construction paper of various weights and colors; hammers and nails; planks of various sizes; sticks; log and chain; blocks of various sizes; folding and cutting paper; weaving paper; sewing cards and laces; sandbox and sand; materials for sewing and cutting. (Plate XXX)

In the presentation of materials for original and creative expression, the adult must remember the levels of development on which the child thinks and feels in regard to what he is doing. The child's efforts, pleasure, and interest in a specific activity are more important than the finished article. His use of the various

Plate XXX. These four- and five-year-old children are cutting out clothing forms freehand, without patterns, and pasting them on stick figures drawn on heavy paper. They print their own names, with felt pens, on the finished products. The children name the completed article of clothing as to *dress, suit, sweater,* etc., and parts of each such as *sleeve, button,* etc. Conversation among the children and with the teacher goes on intermittently while hands remain busy "doing."

materials gradually develops along the usual channels until he shows a conscious effort to create a definite form, although it may be at first unrecognizable to the adult and only later recognizable.[63]

This development is retarded if demands are made of the

child to draw "this or that," to hurry, or if the adult interferes to do the child's work for him. Whatever contribution the child makes is acceptable, whether it is merely a heap of pounded clay or a mass of one color on a sheet of easel paper.[12] His *efforts* are worthwhile, and the adult desires the child's voluntary expression entirely free of direct, adult influence. The principles of free expression should predominate.[20]

The adult who is guiding the child in expressive activities must remember that the child's world is not the same as the adult's. His drawings, paintings, modeling, in the earliest years are not recognizable, in most cases, to the adult. As his attempts take on a more "realistic" form, they are still out of proportion to the adult. To the child, that is not important; it is not out of proportion to him. If he draws a huge head on a miniature body, he probably sees it that way. To him, expression may seem to come from the face of a person, and is therefore more important than any other part of the body. He is concerned with expression as related to himself, and adult interference can be very frustrating for him. Freedom in such activities helps him to bridge the gap between his world and the adult's. The child is primarily concerned with the act as part of *himself* and *his* life.[179]

It is quite possible to follow these principles and make use of intervals here and there to talk to the child. The error made by so many people, especially over-conscientious parents, is that of "leaping at the child" when an opportunity to talk arises, and of destroying the value of the activity and the opportunity for language growth by making the whole situation unpleasant and annoying.[30] Then, there are those persons at the other extreme who, feeling that there is too much emphasis placed on communication, don't talk to the child at any time during the activity. Both groups are making the error of placing too much emphasis on the deafness; they talk too much in the situation, or not at all, and they forget that they are guiding *children*. No one should become so far removed from normal children that her guidance of the deaf child *as a child* is warped into taking some other direction. Teachers and parents of deaf children should take time regularly to stand back and "take stock" of their own actions, and ask themselves, "Do I talk too much in the 'wrong' situations?" and "Do I miss opportunities for talking to the child when it could be done easily for him and me?" "Do I really feel that these creative activities are valuable, or am I too concerned about making them one more means for attaining what *I* want for this child—speech?"

In all probability, if the adult is honest with herself, she will find that she does err in some way and can make the training better. If she is sincerely interested in the child's progress, she will continue to make every attempt to improve her methods before it is too late.

The adult never gestures to the deaf child when it is possible and plausible to talk. The preparation for each activity would include such expressions as, "Get your apron"; "The red paint is on the shelf"; "What color do you want?"; "John has the blue paint"; "Here is your brush"; "Let's wash our hands"; etc. When such expressions are used each day for a number of months, the child gradually learns to recognize the suggestion, the statement, the question, in association with the specific situation.

The three-year-old will show very few signs of proficiency in lipreading such phrases. He is still primarily concerned with expression and more expression. However, without special emphasis or imposition from the adult, a certain amount of "absorption" of language forms as related to himself and his interests is taking place.

Most three-year-olds cover pages quickly with paint, and want one page after another. The child may want to use just one color to a page, although he often begins to use more than one and intermixes them. When the colors are given to him, the adult might name them as they are placed in the box-shelf on the easel. When the painting period is over, the pages might be hung on a line to dry, and, later, be pinned on the wall. The adult might count the pages for the child, and, although number is irrelevant to the basic value of this activity, if the child is willing to give any attention to the situation, he may derive some value and some pleasure from watching the adult count his "works of art."

The three-year-old is concerned with his achievement as related to himself, and often indicates that he has made this or that, tapping his chest as he points to the finished pages. The adult follows up such actions with, "Yes, you made that, John. This is yours, too. This is a blue one, and this is a red one. I like them very much."

Some three-year-olds will make objects of clay and paint them. They may not be recognizable to the adult, but the child may attempt to name them by showing the adult a picture or an object in the room which it is meant to represent. The adult accepts what he has done, and makes no effort to change the form. She does, however, give the child the name of the object.

The little child sometimes enjoys having an adult sit with him and work with the clay. Even when the adult does this, the model should be well within the comprehension of the child, and should not be left in front of him alone to copy. He may learn something from watching the adult at work, but he should be permitted to take from the model what *he* desires, what *he* understands, and what *he* can do.

Throughout these activities, the three-year-old seldom reflects in speech and lipreading the language that has accompanied the activities. However, the value of both the activity and the language is revealed more clearly at the four-year level.

The three-year-old who has had experience with such activities—painting freely with brush and fingers,[145] learning to build with and balance blocks, manipulating and pounding clay until a form results, etc.—emerges as a four-year-old who is unafraid to tackle materials and media, who feels successful in his attempts, and is more persistent in working through a problem. He should have no fears of putting his fingers into clay and paint, nor of "getting dirty," and his improved muscular coordination and emotional stability help him to be neater and more proficient in handling materials. His progress has been a result of free expression, of experience, and observation, *not* of adult demands for neatness, cleanliness, and specific results.

The child who reaches the age of four years with *fears* about getting his hands soiled needs attention, and his parents need advice. It is indeed a very sad sight to watch a young child painfully struggling to stay within lines, to remain "clean" instead of plunging into an activity with sheer enjoyment. There are parents who point with pride to their children who "insist" upon being clean all the time, who cry if a spot of color accidentally finds its way to a part of the page beyond the "working area." Unfortunately, the insistence and the cry did not originate with the child, but with the parent, and probably in situations entirely removed from creative activities. The parent cannot expect the child to express himself creatively at full capacity if emphasis is placed first on cleanliness by adult standards, not only in the activity situation but in other more basic situations, such as toilet training and eating habits, etc.

It has been stated earlier in the text that developmental activities may be a means of revealing problems as well as of solving them, and the earlier these problems are revealed, the sooner they may be solved by the adult, the teacher, the psychologist.[153]

The growing maturity of the relatively well-adjusted four-year-old offers many more opportunities for language growth and for a wider variety of activities.[119] The child grows ever more capable of producing from a number of media a form that *resembles* a "real" object or person. Often, he voluntarily tells the adult what he has created. He may nail a piece of cloth to a stick, and call the result a flag. He may draw a face with a crayon, and indicate that it represents his playmate or one of his parents. He may use the paint and brush for the portrait of a favorite animal, or he may model a favorite toy from clay. When the child brings his achievement to the adult to tell her what it is, she gives him the appropriate language, encouraging the child to imitate her while she endeavors to share his feeling of pride and achievement regarding the particular object.

After drawing a face, or a figure with a predominant face, the deaf four-year-old has used words such as *eye, nose, mouth,* etc. The adult may respond with, "Yes, that's an eye. There are two eyes. You have two eyes," etc. If the child has drawn, painted, or constructed a car from blocks, and brings the adult's attention to it, adult and child may talk about its color, the fact that Daddy has a car, etc.

The experience of the child at this age usually causes him to prefer a color or colors, and he learns to ask for the specific colors. Although the adult should not spend time here on articulation, she does encourage the child to ask for any color, using appropriate language. If the child has derived pleasure and satisfaction from the activities, he begins to use the language of the activities more spontaneously and more frequently.

Some four-year-olds have exhibited their first conscious awareness of printed forms during creative activities. Occasionally, in the midst of a maze of lines and colors, letters have appeared, and the child has indicated not only that he did it, but that the letter or letters refer to him. In one case, the child printed *M* in a corner of a page, and pointed to himself. His name began with *M*, and of the whole word which he had seen printed on his drawings each day, that letter stood out. He recognized a connection between himself and the finished work, and between the marks on the paper (printed by the adult) and himself.

When the child printed *M* on the paper with his paint brush, the adult accepted the attempt with sincere approval, even though the letter was large and asymmetrical. She showed him a card with his name printed on it, said his name, and the child repeated it. The child pointed to the *M* he had printed and to the one at the beginning of his name on the card. No attempt was made to improve upon the child's contribution at this time. It remained on the front of the page as the sole indication of possession. Within a few months following, the child was printing his whole first name with the paint brush, so that it was recognizable, if not "perfect," with every letter in correct sequence, without copying, and without having been "taught" to print. Still later, but at the four-year-level, he also carved his name after a fashion in clay, with his finger or with a stick.

Four-year-olds enjoy work with felt. Crayons, paints, and pastels may be used effectively on felt. The pieces of felt should vary in size for experience in drawing on small and large surfaces, and for practice of the terms, *big* and *small*.

Paper work is also an enjoyable experience. The child learns to produce various shapes through folding, cutting, and tearing paper. The use of scissors should not be required until the small muscle coordination is sufficiently developed to manage manipulation of scissors and paper. The child might use them to cut paper at random, and *much later* he may be able to attempt cutting along lines to produce specific shapes.

Paper work involves intelligent adult guidance to prevent, in so far as it is possible, any frustration or a feeling of loss on the part of the child for having mutilated a piece of paper. The five-year-old handles scissors and paper much more efficiently than does the four-year-old. The younger child's evident interest in scissors and in cutting paper does not mean that he can use scissors and paper with the skill of an older child. Many four-year olds tend to "try anything" and to show off their skills in as many ways as posisble. This can be either advantageous or problematical for the child, depending to a large degree on the guidance of the adult.

The adult has to manage the activities in such a way that they are challenging and interesting but not potentially frustrating, beyond the four-year-old's capacity to adjust to possibly unacceptable or discouraging results. In woodworking, frustrating incidents can be overcome, partially at least, by the child's pounding out his feelings on the wood with a hammer, and very little damage is done to the finished article which has come to assume some importance for the child. However, in paper work, crushing and tearing in the face of frustration may satisfy an immediate feeling, but when the child views the results of his act, other feelings of frustration and failure may be aroused. Every child encounters frustrating experiences, which he must learn to face and overcome. However, there are situations which cause the destructive kind of frustration, neither necessary nor valuable from any viewpoint, and unfortunately, the activity situation has become too often the parade ground for such unhealthy developments. The adult who is guiding the child must be especially skilful in knowing what activities to present, how to guide the child, and when and where to step into the situation to support the child without weakening his sense of possession and achievement.[94]

The child of five is quite different from the four-year-old. The world has enlarged for him and he is more aware of it. He finds out that this broader and more interesting world makes more demands on him. He takes pride in his endeavors, and enjoys the sincere praise of adults. False praise he has learned to recognize, despise, and take advantage of, and if he has been the victim of this kind of adult response, his dissatisfaction may be reflected in his attitudes toward the achievements of other children.[113] The five-year-old who has been subjected in the earlier years to false praise, of bribes (there is little difference between the two), will have more difficulty in adjusting to the demands which his age place upon him. If he has been guided by adults who sincerely appreciate him and respect him, his adjustment to his world as a five-year-old will be easier.

The deaf child of five enjoys the activities which most children of kindergarten age enjoy.[171] There is a great need for creative endeavor at this level, as means of self-expression, emotional outlet, and language practice.[91, 94]

The deaf child of five, who has had earlier nursery school training featuring equipment and materials for creative expression, usually lipreads the names of those materials and the equipment. He has learned to understand through lipreading the language involved in the getting and putting away of materials.

Five-year-olds who have had previous training should have little difficulty in following directions such as: "Billy, you may get the red paint and the yellow paint." "Jimmy, you may get the paint brushes." "Bobby, would you like to help me put the paper on the easels?" etc. If the child doesn't understand immediately, the sentence is repeated for him, and if he still fails to understand, he *is shown* what is meant, just as he was shown at earlier levels in other, simpler situations.

The five-year-old draws, paints, and constructs objects and forms that are recognizable, at least to him, and usually to the adult. He will try to name them spontaneously, or will ask the adult how to say the word or words he wants to use. There tends to be an interchange of ideas among deaf children at this level, and, in a group of deaf children participating in creative activities, *conversation* takes place among them.

The child at this age has little difficulty in thinking of something to draw, to paint, or construct. He has learned to bring his home, school, and other experiences to the easel, to the paper, to the clay, or to the woodworking corner. He is learning to express himself in terms of what has impressed him.[60]

The five-year-old frequently demonstrates his developed sense of color, his awareness of space and form, and his ability to use colors dramatically and with originality in creating forms and designs.[120] Some deaf children are interested in making designs using squares, circles, triangles, and other shapes, and in filling in each space with a particular color. Some fill in the spaces with favorite animals, objects, or people whom they can name.

In one instance where a group of five deaf children were participating in creative activities, three of them filled pages with very effective designs entirely of their own making. The teacher hung them on the wall, which was papered. One of the children immediately noticed a connection between the wallpaper design and the designs on the paintings. The teacher agreed with her observation, for the first time was able to give the word *wallpaper* to the children in a meaningful situation, and went on to show the children that there were also pretty designs in the floor linoleum. Before long, every child in the group had tried his hand at creating original wallpaper and linoleum designs. It was interesting also, to note that the designs of the linoleum and wallpaper of the room were not copied.

Group activity at the five-year-old level frequently stimulates best efforts and a maximum of enjoyment and application. The children often show enthusiasm over group projects, such as the painting of murals depicting their joint experiences—an excursion to the park, free play in the yard, a visit to the zoo, etc. The deaf child may participate in such group activity with other deaf children, or with hearing children.

One group of five-year-olds completed a mural illustrating the nursery school yard. Each child took responsibility for the part for which he had a preference and which he tended to do best. The one who liked to cover large surfaces with paint, and who managed in a "free and easy" way to get interesting effects with paint, did the sky and the ground. Another did the cutting, another the pasting, another the painting of small objects, and so on. The completed mural served not only as a room decoration, but as a means of demonstrating to the children the attractive results of group participation, and also as a source of language practice. Such questions as, "What is this?" "Who drew the swing?" "Who painted the sky?" "What color is it?" "Where is the sandbox?" were asked of the children. The children also enjoyed playing teacher in turn, and asking simple questions of one another regarding the mural.

Each child attains a different degree of skill in the various activities. One child may cut out materials and even use a needle with ease, while another might have great difficulty in managing such activities. One child may turn out a very good piece of woodwork with ease and speed, another of the same age may not get beyond hammering a nail into a board. One child may appear quite talented in painting, and show little skill or interest in paper folding. An attempt should be made to permit each child to do what he likes to do, at the same time that he is offered the opportunity of observing and participating in all other activities. This encourages the child to develop his special interest to the extent of his five-year-old possibilities, and to experience all other activities in some degree.

MUSIC AND RHYTHM

Music is a language. Rhythm is a language. Music and rhythm are both means of expression. This holds true for the deaf child as for the hearing; but music and rhythm serve an additional purpose for the deaf child—they serve as outstanding means of developing more natural speech.

What are some of the characteristics of the speech of the deaf that make it so different from that of the hearing? Inflection is frequently lacking; breathing is not regulated to the utterances of the speaker, so that the speech is less intelligible to the listener; rhythm in speech is broken; muscles are tense; tone is monotonous; pitch is often abnormally high or low; resonance is frequently lacking; and rate of speaking is often slow and laborious. Music and rhythmic exercises can help to prevent such characteristics to some extent, if applied consistently to various phases of the child's experience at the preschool stage.

Music may be incorporated into the lessons in auditory training, lipreading, speech, and creative activities. There should be a short period each day devoted to music and rhythmic exercises where they are the center of interest, and where the other phases of the training are secondary to them.[94]

The adult should have some definite objectives in mind when guiding little deaf children in musical games and rhythmic activities. Objectives and the program should coincide as closely as possible with those for the hearing child. The adult has to be quite realistic about the deaf child's limitations in relation to music, and must remember that certain developments will, of necessity, be slow. However, the development should be limited only by the deafness and capacities of the individual child, not by the adult's possible negative attitude toward music for the deaf child.

Exposure to music stimulates spontaneity, individually and with the group. It encourages the child to express his feelings of joy, dramatic action, creative expression, and individual interpretations. It aids the child in developing more graceful movements and motor skills. He develops a sense of rhythm which carries over into his speech, since muscles of the body, including the speech muscles, learn to move more rhythmically. Activity with music develops the relaxation which is so essential to good speech. The child has an opportunity to coordinate music and bodily movements with the voice in a relaxed, spontaneous manner, in a situation where no demands are placed upon him for better articulation. The adult hopes to increase the child's ability to change pitch for expression as the rhythm, timing, and expression change in the music.

The adult hopes to develop in the deaf child an interest in the activities related to music.[65] To attain this end, he must be introduced to music through familiar channels that include pleasant activities and freedom in movement and expression; and the adult, herself, must enjoy the situation. In the beginning, the adult finds herself adapting the rhythm of the music to the child's movements, rather than expecting the child to adapt his movements to the music. No technical approach nor specific responses are necessary. Freedom and originality are the keynotes of the music periods.

The little child, deaf or hearing, enjoys random movements. It may be patting clay, beating on a toy drum, putting pegs in a pegboard, rocking a doll's cradle, or drawing strokes on paper with a paintbrush or crayon. The adult, whenever possible, would play a selection in time to what the child is doing. Gradually, as the child becomes aware of the vibration and rhythm of the music, he begins to recognize a connection between what he is doing and the music which the adult is playing. Eventually, he notices that each time he pats the clay, he "feels" a "beat" from the piano.

Sometimes, if the teacher and the parent, or two parents, are present, one may play the piano while the other guides the child. The following simple exercise worked out very effectively in a situation where parent and teacher were working together in the child's training program. While the teacher played the piano, parent and child stood beside the piano with a pegboard on top of the piano in front of them. The child was leaning on the piano while the parent placed one hand on it, and with the other hand took pegs out of the board in time to the music. The child had a choice of taking out some pegs or of just watching. In this case, he watched. After a few sessions, he began to do what the parent was doing. The parent began at one end of the board, and the child began at the other end, which was closer to him. Part of the rhythm of his movements was, of course, an echo of the parent's movements. This was considered quite acceptable and worthy of approval. The child was guided in keeping time to the music without having any adult pressure placed upon him to do so. Gradually, he became aware of the beat of the music in direct relation to his own movements, and he was able to do the exercise himself before his fourth birthday.

Some four-year-olds, who have had previous training with music, learn to do similar exercises combining them with speech play; for example, saying, "pum, pum, pum," in time to their movements and to the music.

It must be kept in mind that specific exercises related to music, if unwisely managed, are not helpful. In no one exercise should the child be *expected* to keep time to music.[112] He will learn to do it after a while, following the steps leading up to it which involve simple activities of interest to him. The most important preliminary is that the adult *take the music to the child* in a way that he can understand. Each child differs from others in coordination and individual interests, and his ability to "understand" what the adult is trying to put across to him is at a minimum. The young child is much more interested in experimenting with his body, in amusing himself with sounds *he* makes and feels, than he is in "following directions."

The young deaf child should have the opportunity of seeing various musical instruments, of touching them and feeling the vibration and rhythm as they are played. The adult may find that the child is developing an interest in the piano and the book of music, and in so far as it is possible he should be given a chance to understand the connection between the notes and the playing, the notes and singing.

The child of nursery and kindergarten years enjoys movements such as running, jumping, falling, and hopping. Enjoyable, rhythmic exercises involving such actions might be carried out in conjunction with stories, excursions, and animal pictures. The adult might play a selection that would suit the tempo and mode of walking of a particular animal. The elephant, for example, is pictured with big, heavy feet, and most children have seen a live one at the zoo. The accompanying music might be slow and emphatic, and the child might imitate the walk of the elephant in time to the music. One five-year-old who had been to the zoo many times and had liked the elephant, would thump along for a few steps in time to the music, then would stand on his "hind" legs and stamp heavily on the spot, then go on walking for a few more steps. Such spontaneous interpretations are encouraged, even though they aren't always as realistic as the adult might think they should be.

The child may learn the concepts *soft* and *loud, quiet* and *noisy,* through music. The adult might show the child a picture of a baby sleeping, and show him how we tiptoe, or walk quietly, to quiet music.

Some activity with music may follow the storytelling period. After the story of "The Three Bears," the child may touch the piano and the adult's cheek or throat, as he senses the high squeal of the little bear, the soft voice of the mother bear, and the low growl of the father bear, as suggested by chords on the piano.

Some five-year-olds like to use rhythm band instruments. If they have had earlier experiences with music, they may be able to keep relatively good time with the instruments and to co-ordinate the voice with the movements involved. Where there is a group of deaf children, the adult may find that among five-year-olds there are those who like to conduct and who should have the experience. Some five-year-olds have learned to check the rhythm of the other children, although this is neither required nor expected.

Deaf children discover that interesting stories may be sung. Deaf children, after having listened to the story of "Mary Had a Little Lamb," like to watch, clap, and sing with the adult as she plays to piano. The preschool child's desire for repetition—to listen to the same song over and over, and to play the same music game over and over—simplifies the adult's task of guiding him and provides naturally for the repetition necessary to language development, as well as for enjoyment and developmental growth. (Plate XXXI)

Music for three- and four-year-olds should be brought to them through what they happen to be doing, whereas the five-year-old often has ideas to contribute, and has less difficulty in coordinating movements, music, and voice. The five-year-old deaf child has learned to "sing" a word at different pitches, for example, "Run, run, run,"—the first high, the second medium, the third low.

Five-year-olds who have had previous training have learned to march to music, to say sentences to music, to make up dances, to participate in rhythm bands, and to maintain a certain rhythm throughout a selection.[121]

In spite of the trained five-year-old's growing ability to understand music in relation to other activities, the adult must bear in mind that even at this age the child is still limited, due to his deafness and his age, and that *technical* training should be at a minimum. The idea of the music program is to encourage spontaneity, free use of the voice in relation to music and activity, free use of the body, and emotional expression.

Many deaf children have used a better inflected speech in spontaneous situations after exercises with music than from spe-

Plate XXXI. As the teacher plays the piano, the little boy rocks the horse in time to the music, and the little girl, holding a corresponding picture, keeps time with her feet. Both children, having severe to profound hearing losses, vocalize with "lalala . . .," and as they relax in the fun-filled activity, voices becomes more resonant, tonal and pitch quality is more natural, breathing is better, and utterances are more fluent.

cific speech instruction, although the articulation may not have been as good. However, since pitch and breathing are so important to more normal speech for the deaf child, and since he has to breathe more freely while actively engaged in a rhythmic exercise which he enjoys for enjoyments sake, it is possible that his use of voice in such situations could effect a better coordination of speech and breathing. Young deaf children have developed better speech as a result of alternating and correlating the specific speech lesson and the spontaneous, free use of voice in the music and rhythmic exercises.

Neither teacher nor parent should expect the deaf child to become a musician or a singer; but they should like to see him develop an understanding of the role of music in society, and a feeling that he may join in with a singing group if he wishes to do so. He may be guided toward recognizing his limitations, but at the same time will feel less "different." Music will be one thing that he cannot manage as well as he does other things, and in that respect he is not unlike many hearing people. Music should not be something remote and unknown to him. The self-confidence and originality he developed through music and rhythmic activities as a child will supplement the confidence, assurance, and originality in other fields, in which he has become skilled. Music and rhythm help to improve speech and language, but most importantly, they help the child in socialization.[76, 136]

BOOKS, DRAMATIZATIONS, AND EXCURSIONS

The child learns through experience, and one way of ensuring his present and future enjoyment of living is to establish a pleasant familiarity with books. He must be permitted to spend time in the company of books, to look through them, to share and exchange them with his friends, and to bring them to adults for explanation and mutual enjoyment. This kind of experience helps him in learning to turn to a book for the definite purpose of obtaining information, or for pastime, and for a broadening of his experiences. He should be exposed to books in as many situations as possible, as a beginning step in reading readiness,

Plate XXXII. This three-year-old child has drawn the attention of the nearest adult to pictures of dogs in his selected book, and is attentively watching and listening to her talk about his special interest.

even before he is aware of printed words or their significance. (Plate XXXII)

Dramatization and excursions help to maintain and stimulate interest in books. The adult allows the child to become familiar with certain books. Then she tells him a story from one, showing pictures of each episode. The child learns to live through these experiences and to understand them more thoroughly by imitating the actions illustrated.

The child learns to recognize similar experiences and ideas in other books and stories, and to tie up his own experiences with what he sees in the books, what he has dramatized, and what he has seen on the lips of the storyteller.

Excursions are a necessity in the development of the child. The adult cannot take for granted that the child will understand what is seen in a picture if he has not had an experience of the real thing. This need is especially acute in the young deaf child whose lack of language understanding makes many verbal explanations futile. Along with the verbal explanations, he has to see or experience the situation in reality, before the adult can be sure that he understands it through pictures and stories. After having seen a series of pictures of a particular place or activity, the real situation which he encounters later will mean something to him, but the books and the stories have more meaning for him if he has already had similar, real experiences.

Every nursery school and home should have a library corner for the deaf child. Tables and chairs should be comfortable, and the height of the book cases or shelves should be suitable. Cushions and rugs sometimes add to the child's enjoyment of and interest in using the corner. A collection of plants, insects, and other objects that might be mentioned or pictured in the books, stimulates the child's interest in books and in exploration.

Books in the library should be suitable to the child's age-level and individual interests, and should be well illustrated. If the child has made any books, they should be included in the library. The books should be easy to handle, in strong attractive bindings, on good quality, unglazed paper, and by authors who offer something worthwhile to a child. If possible, there should be more than one book for each story. For example, "The Three Bears" is published in several different editions, each telling the same story, but in different language and with different pictures that put it across.

Experiences with books, dramatizations, and excursions develop interests in new experiences, in vocabulary building and language, and help in developing character.

OTHER ACTIVITIES

The young deaf child, in nursery school and at home, learns many language concepts as he prepares for and participates in routine activities such as eating, resting, toileting, free play, and exploring various parts of the building such as the kitchen, the living room, or the sitting rooms, the offices, etc. The conversations in conjunction with such activities are casual, and the child learns to understand the language concepts through association with real routines that go on every day.

Washing and toileting situations provide many opportunities for exposure to casual language. The child in nursery school and, if he has brothers and sisters, in his home often has to wait his turn; and, often, one child stands by and watches while another washes his hands. Occasionally, the adult may talk to the child who is waiting. "Johnny is washing his hands. When he has finished, you will wash yours. Dry your hands, Johnny. Billy is going to wash his hands now."

The child begins to notice that the adult cleans the washbowl after he has washed, and often takes responsibility for doing this himself.

Every deaf child should have some kitchen experience, for purposes of preventing many dangerous habits that the curious, inexperienced child may develop, of overcoming "fussy" eating habits, and of adding to his experiences. The feeling of accomplishment, of being important and "grown-up," makes the child's role in the kitchen very important to his total development. The smelling, tasting, feeling, and seeing which the child experiences in the kitchen activities are an essential part of his training.

The adult who takes the child into the kitchen must realize that there may be some waste, many mistakes, and even accidents, but in consideration of the value of the experiences, a broken dish or some spilled milk should not eliminate the "kitchen program."

The preschool deaf child has learned to prepare and cook vegetables, to make cookies, toast, salads, and other simple dishes under unforced, well-planned guidance. He may learn the names of the utensils, and their uses. He learns to understand such expressions as, "Get the flour," "Fill the cup," "Put the flour in the bowl," etc. He learns how and when the stove is used. Children who have had their curiosity regarding the use of stoves and matches satisfied are less likely to indulge in dangerous activities with stoves, burners, matches, etc.

In nursery school, four- and five-year-olds have made food dishes in groups. The children stood in a semicircle behind their tables, each with his or her set of utensils and ingredients, and as the teacher gave instructions, the children watched, lipread, and performed. The teacher had her own utensils and ingredients before her to show the children what she meant as she talked. Lipreading and activity were coordinated.

The casual conversations that take place in the midst of developmental activities are essential since they are usually composed of the language of everyday living. They are usually effective since the activity holds the center of interest rather than the lipreading or speech.

The adult who is guiding the young deaf child will not underestimate the value of developmental activities, and will use them to broaden the child's experiences, his understanding, and his means of expressing himself.

Chapter 14

Suggested Activities
for Language Training

The following outlines are presented for the purpose of giving the adult in charge additional guidance in the use of activities suggested in previous chapters. There is always some danger in presenting such outlines since they have been known to be misused. However, these suggestions should be helpful in concretizing for the adult the steps involved in various lessons for language development. All value is lost unless the guidance of the child is based on his own patterns of thinking and feeling. Any suggested procedure must be subject to change and used in accordance with the manifestations of the individual child.

SUGGESTION 1

Aim

To familiarize the child with consonants *p, b,* and *m,* in words beginning with these consonants, and in words presented as concepts. The tactile, visual, and auditory means would be employed for the promotion of lipreading, speech, and auditory responses.

Materials

Individual, colorful pictures of familiar words—a pie, a pig, a boy, a ball, milk, a man.

Pictures of activities revolving about the above nouns; for example, a picture of a boy with a ball, a picture of a man with a pig, etc.

A mirror and a hearing aid.

Procedure

1. Child and adult seated before a table of comfortable height for child, with mirror behind table and directly in front of adult and child.

2. Pictures of a pie and a pig placed on table.

3. Child's hand is placed on adult's cheek. Child watches in mirror while adult, holding up the picture of the pie, says, "That's a *pie*. A *pie*."

4. Adult repeats sentence and word near the child's ear, while he watches in mirror.

5. One of child's hands is placed on adult's cheek, the other on his own cheek, and he is encouraged to say the sentence and the word with the adult, as both watch the procedure in the mirror.

6. The same procedure is followed using the word *pig*.

7. Adult asks the child, "Where is the pig?" "Show me the pie." Child lipreads and indicates the appropriate picture. He is encouraged to say the word when he indicates the picture.

8. Same procedure followed, using words *boy* and *ball;* then *milk* and *man.*

9. Place on the table a picture of a *pie*, one of a *boy*, and one of a *man.* (*p, b,* and *m* all look alike on the lips, but do not sound alike.)

10. Adult uses the three words, as the child watches, feels, and listens.

11. Introduce activity pictures or those which illustrate the particular objects in relation to other objects or people. Place earphones on child and set volume control. Describe each picture simply as child watches, listens, and feels (visual, tactile,

auditory); for example, "The *b*oy has a *b*all." "The *b*oy has a *p*ie." "The *b*oy has a *p*ig." "The *b*oy has some *m*ilk." "The *m*an has a *p*ie." "The *m*an has a *b*all." "The *m*an has some *m*ilk." "The *m*an has a *p*ig." Pictures may be described in other ways; such as, "The *b*oy is *p*laying with a *b*all," etc.

12. Some or all of pictures may be described again while adult and child clap to the rhythm of the sentence, accenting key words; for example, "The *b*oy has a *b*all." Child is encouraged to speak as he claps. Movements and use of voice should by rhythmical.

Note.—The above exercise is meant to be general. More specific work with the consonants *p, b,* and *m* develops out of such a general approach. The very specific work with such sounds should be in the hands of a *trained* person.

SUGGESTION 2

Aim

To familiarize the child with consonants *t* and *d* in words and sentences and in babbling exercises. The tactile, visual, and auditory means would be combined wherever possible.

Materials

Objects such as a top, a toy table, a doll, and a toy dog. A hearing aid.

Procedure

1. Child places one hand on adult's cheek, one on his own cheek. Adult says the following babbling sounds and child repeats: dŭdŭdŭ, dŏdŏdŏ, dōōdōōdōō, dēēdēēdēē, tŏtŏtŏ, tēētēētēē, tātātā, tătătă.

2. Adult and child babble and say a word related to the babbling exercise; for example: dŏdŏdŏ—dŏg; dŏdŏdŏ—dŏll; tŏtŏtŏ —tŏp; tātātā—tāble, etc.

3. Incorporate some activity by having the child carry out instructions through lipreading; for example: "Put the *t*op on the *t*able." "Put the *d*oll on the *t*able," etc.

4. Place the four pictures on the table before the child. Adult points to each and asks, "What's that?" Child is guided in saying, "A top," "A table," "A dog," etc.

5. In the case of the child who has some language understanding, the adult might use the following: "What's that?" Child answers, with or without help, "A table." "Is that a dog?" (pointing to the top), and child answers "No, a top," etc.

SUGGESTION 3

Aim

To familiarize the child with the consonant *f* in whole words, phrases, and sentences using tactile, visual, and auditory means.

Materials

Objects (a fish, a flower).
Pictures (a fish, a flower).
A paper bag, a slot chart, and a box large enough to hold objects.
A hearing aid.

Procedure

1. Adult shows the toy fish to the child, places child's hand on her cheek, and says, "Here is a *f*ish. A *f*ish." Child places other hand on his own cheek and says the word. (Same procedure for *flower*.)

2. Both objects are placed on the table. Adult says, "Show me the *f*ish." Child indicates correct object, and says "Fish," with or without help from the adult. (Same procedure for *flower*.)

Lipreading—"Put the *fish* in the bag." "Put the *flower* in the bag." The bag may be held towards the child to help him in understanding what is meant, until he has had more practice with the activity and the language.

4. Child is asked to find each of the objects by reaching into the bag without looking (touch only). "Find the *fish*." Child feels the objects in the bag and pulls out the fish. After the adult asks, "What's that?" the child says, "A *fish*." (Same procedure for *flower*.)

5. Remove the paper bag and place the box on the table. Adult "hides" one of the objects with her hands, and says, "Guess what I have in my hands," or "What do I have, a fish or a flower?" Child "guesses"; when he "guesses" correctly and says the word, the adult says, "Put the *fish* in the box," and "Put the *flower* in the box." The child may be allowed to "hide" the objects, for the adult to "guess."

6. Pictures of the flower and the fish would be introduced and the child would lipread, "Show me the picture of the *flower*." He indicates the correct picture and says, "*Flower*," or "That's a *flower*." (Similar procedure for *fish*.)

7. Pictures and objects would be placed on table, and the child would lipread, "Show me a *flower*." "Show me another flower." "Show me a fish." "Show me another fish." . . . "Yes, that's a *flower*, and that's a *flower*. That's a *fish* and that's a *fish*." (Adult might point to the flower and say, "Is that a *fish*?" Child would be guided in saying, "No, a *flower*.")

8. Pictures of a fish and a flower are placed in a slot chart hanging near child. The child might play "teacher." The adult would turn her back to the child and he would say one of the words, or, if he has had more training, might be able to use a simple sentence such as "show me the fish." If the speech is relatively intelligible, the adult turns and points to the picture of the fish in the chart, and says, "That's the fish." The child may take the adult's hand, place it on his cheek, and "help" the adult in saying, "*Fish*," or "That's a *fish*." As he supposedly helps the adult, the adult is taking advantage of the game situation to help him. (Occasionally, the adult makes "a mistake" in order

to give the child another opportunity of saying the word more intelligibly if possible, and of using expressions such as, "No, a flower," etc.)

SUGGESTION 4

Aim

To give the child more experience with numbers in relation to lipreading, speech, and auditory training.

Materials

Lightweight box with slot to represent a mail-box; peaked cap for child; ten or twelve envelopes; numerous, small, cardboard circles (penny size), preferably of a bright color.

Procedure

1. Child puts on cap.
2. Adult places cardboard circles on table, and gives the child an envelope. Adult takes an envelope, counts out two circles as the child watches, and puts *two* in the envelope. (If child has had sufficient number work, *three,* and then *four,* circles would be used in a like manner.) Time should be taken at this stage to show what is expected of him.
3. Child watches as adult says, *"Find two."* Child picks up two circles. Adult asks, *"How many* do you have?" Child counts the circles and says, "Two," Any assistance the child may need in getting the "right" number should be readily forthcoming and casual.
4. Adult tells child to put *two* in the envelope.   •
5. Child is given a second envelope. He is asked to find another number of circles, one, two, three or other number commensurate with his training and age.
6. This procedure is followed until the child has put a specific number of circles in each of a number of envelopes.

7. Throughout each activity, expressions such as "How many," "Count," "Put them in the envelope," "Put three in the envelope," etc., are used by the adult; and the child is encouraged and assisted in using spoken language corresponding to what he is doing.

8. When a number of envelopes have been filled, the adult draws a number picture on each of the envelopes to indicate the number of circles in each, and places the envelopes on the table or on the floor.

9. The adult points to each number picture and asks the child *"how many"* there are in that envelope. The child answers; and then opens the envelope and counts, to verify what he has said.

10. The envelope flaps may be turned in rather than sealed, and the child would be asked to "mail *two* letters," *"three,"* etc.

11. Small pieces of paper with the child's name on each might be placed in each envelope before "mailing."

SUGGESTION 5

Aim

To give the child practice in the use of consonants which have already been introduced to him in the words and sentences natural to general and specific situations. Tactile, visual, and auditory approaches would be used.

Materials

Large chart of stiff cardboard with substantial support at its back.

Several envelopes, one for each consonant to be practiced. Envelopes pasted, flap-side out, on cardboard. Consonant printed on flap of envelope.

Several pictures of familiar objects for each envelope, all pictures for each envelope showing objects whose names begin with the particular consonant printed on the outside of the envelope.

Procedure

Pictures for practice of *b* would be taken from envelope marked *b*.

2. Adult points to the picture of the *b*ow, places the child's hand on her cheek as she says "Bow," and "bububu-bow," and encouarges child to repeat.

3. Sentences such as, "What color is the bow?" "It's a red bow," etc., would be incorporated into the discussion that should revolve about each picture, and child would imitate as much of the spoken language as is possible for him.

4. The picture of the bow is handed to the child and he, at the request of the adult, puts it in the *b* envelope.

5. All pictures that belong in the *b* envelope would be treated in a like manner.

6. Pictures in each of the other envelopes would be discussed, emphasis being upon the child's imitation of each word.

7. Attention may be directed to the printed form on the envelope in accordance with the child's age and readiness. The three-year-old or younger, instead of being exposed to the printed form of the consonant on the envelope, would find on each envelope a picture of an object whose name begins with a particular consonant, and in each envelope, there would be other words beginning with the same consonant.

8. Four- and five-year-olds, depending on the individual child, may have the printed word as well as the printed consonant on each envelope. Larger, hand-made envelopes may be necessary in this case, to accommodate words.

9. Vowels as they occur in words may be practiced in a similar manner.

SUGGESTION 6

Aim

To give the child practice in the use of color words in phrases and sentences.

Materials

Three-inch squares of cardboard each with a slit in center.
Pieces of colored ribbon, one drawn through the slit in each
card and tied in bows.
Hearing aid.

Procedure

1. Bows on cards placed before child, who wears earphones.
2. Adult indicates each bow, talks about it as child watches,
feels (hand on speaker's cheek), and listens. "That's a *blue bow*,"
"That's a *yellow bow*," "That's a *purple bow*."
3. With one hand on adult's cheek and other on his own
cheek, child imitates each phrase and says it into the microphone.
4. Adult says to child, "I'm going to tie a bow," and ties the
blue bow. Then she says, "I tied a bow. A blue bow." Adult
unties bow and says to the child, "You tie the blue bow." Child
ties bow as well as he is able, and adult guides him in saying,
"I tied a bow," and, "I tied a blue bow," as he watches, listens,
and feels.
5. Other bows would be used in a similar manner.
6. As the child progresses, he may lipread, "Tie a blue bow";
"Tie a purple bow"; "Tie an orange bow"; etc.
7. Throughout this exercise, emphasis is placed on the
child's lipreading and his use of the color words in phrases and
simple sentences. He should be permitted to "listen" to his own
speech patterns, as well as to the adult's, through the use of the
hearing aid.
8. The question form "What color" should be used whenever applicable.

SUGGESTION 7

Aim

To give the child practice in a play-way in the use of the
adjectives *big* and *small,* in phrases and sentences, combining
speech, lipreading, and auditory experience.

Materials

Several objects, bought or hand-made; for example, a big hat and a small hat, a big toy car and a small one, a big horn and a small one, a big wax apple and a small one, a big box and a small one.

Procedure

1. The objects would be shown to the child one at a time: first a big one, then a small one; and he would be encouraged to imitate the phrase or sentence used by the adult.

2. The objects would be placed in various positions about the room. Child goes with adult, and as each object is placed, the phrase would be repeated by adult and child.

3. Adult and child return to table with a mirror near by.

4. Adult says, "Find the *big* hat and bring it to me." Child gets hat and brings it to the adult. Adult says, "You have the *big* hat. Put it on." Then adult and child turn to the mirror and say in unison, or child after adult, "That's a *big* hat," or "A *big* hat." In this position, it is easy to speak near the child's ear as he watches in the mirror.

5. Other objects would be used in a like manner.

6. Adult must use the adjectives in irregular order, so that the child has to lipread, and cannot guess. That is, if a big object is asked for, then a small one, then big, small, etc., the child begins to reach for a big or small object automatically, without lipreading. The adult should ask for a small object, a big one, another big one, a small one, a small one, a small one, a big one, etc.

SUGGESTION 8

Aim

To make the child more familiar with the sequence of adjectives in phrases, using the visual, tactile, and auditory means. (Generally, this is for five-year-olds, although some four-year-olds have been ready for such specific work.)

Materials

A big, red hat; a small, red hat; a big, yellow hat; a small, yellow hat; a big, purple hat, a small, purple hat; etc.

Procedure

1. The child would be asked to indicate the big hats, the small hats; would describe each as "big" or small," with the adult's assistance if necessary; then he would place all the big hats together, and all the small ones together.

2. The adult would say, indicating each group. "These are *big* hats, and these are *small* hats."

3. The *big* hats would be discussed as to color, one by one. "That's a *blue* hat. It's *big* and it's *blue*. A *big, blue* hat." "That's a *red* hat. It's *big* and it's *red*. A *big, red* hat," etc. The child would watch the adult closely and he would repeat, "A *big, blue* hat," etc.

4. A similar procedure would be followed, using the small hats of various colors.

5. When the adult feels that the child has some idea of the differences in size or color or both, she would ask, "Show me the *big, blue* hat," etc.

6. The number of hats and number of colors are increased as the child grows in understanding of the situation and in lip-reading skills.

7. Throughout the exercise, the child is encouraged to use the phrases himself as frequently as possible, to establish the idea of sequence and to help prevent the use of incorrect sequence, which frequently happens among deaf children.

8. Question forms such as "How many," "What color," "Is it big," or "Is it small," should be employed as much as possible.

SUGGESTION 9

Aim

To improve the child's use and understanding of language revolving about animals. (Same idea for foods, transportation, etc.)

Materials

   Toy animals; pictures of each, some static, some involving activity such as walking, eating, etc.

Procedure

   1. Place a few toy animals before the child.
   2. Adult talks about each and the child repeats its names.
   3. The adult asks the child to indicate each animal as she asks, "Where is the dog?" "Where is the horse?" etc.
   4. Adult asks child to find the corresponding animals on the wall chart and to tell her the names of them.
   5. The animals on the chart are discussed as follows: "What is the horse doing?" "The horse is running." "What is the dog doing?" "The dog is jumping," etc.
   6. The adult presents three large envelopes containing pictures of each animal, varying in size, color, action, etc. The picture of each animal is pasted on the outside of the envelope, and also, for the older preschool child, the corresponding printed word and initial consonant of that word.
   7. An envelope is handed to the child, and the adult asks, a picture from it. The child pulls out another picture of a dog.
   8. The adult opens the envelope and asks the child to get a picture from it. The child pulls out another picture of a dog.
   9. The picture is discussed using as many of the following questions as possible: "What color is the dog?" "Is the dog big?" "What is the dog doing?" "Who is playing with the dog?" "What does the dog say?" "Show me the dog's tail?" "How many legs does the dog have?" The child is guided in an understanding of such questions and in answering them.
   10. Other animals would be discussed in a similar manner.
   11. The child should be able to use the hearing aid to listen to his own voice as well as to the adult's.

SUGGESTION 10

Aim

To give the child further practice in the use of vowels as they occur in words, in isolated form, and in the printed form. (For five-year-olds.)

Materials

A large chart for the vowels to be practiced, showing the printed form, a word containing the vowel, and a picture to illustrate the word; for example:

$\overline{oo}$ shoe   (picture of a shoe)
ī   pie   (picture of a pie)

Individual vowel cards, one vowel to a card, to correspond with those on the large chart.

Individual word cards, one word to a card, to correspond with printed words on large chart.

Hearing aid.

Procedure

1. Chart is placed near the child. Adult asks child to find the picture of the shoe. Then child and adult say the word "shoe" into the microphone.

2. Adult points to the vowel on the chart, places the child's hand on her cheek and says into the microphone, "$\overline{oo}$b$\overline{oo}$b$\overline{oo}$b$\overline{oo}$." Child repeats. Then, "sh$\overline{oo}$sh$\overline{oo}$sh$\overline{oo}$," and child repeats. Then "shoe," and child repeats.

3. Adult points to the chart, moving her hand from left to right, saying, "$\overline{oo}$" (for the vowel), "shoe" (for the printed word), and "shoe" for the picture. Child repeats.

4. Adult takes the separate vowel cards and word cards, and shows child how each is matched to the corresponding one on the chart.

5. Individual cards placed on the table before the child.

6. Adult points to the word *shoe* and asks the child what it says. The child says, "Shoe," into the micropohne, then matches the word on the card to the corresponding word on the chart.

7. The child matches the vowels in a similar manner.

8. Child and adult repeat, "$\overline{oo}$, *shoe*, shoe," indicating vowel, word, and picture on the chart.

9. A similar procedure using the other vowels and words on the chart would be followed.

10. Charts similar to those shown in Figure 2 for consonants may be made for vowel practice, so that a complete chart is supplied for each vowel.

11. This type of exercise gives the child a broader concept of sounds as they occur in words which he has become familiar with. Five-year-olds have learned to find a number of $\overline{oo}$ words from a series of pictures, a number of $\overline{\imath}$ words, etc. The printed forms should not be emphasized. In fact it is quite possible to carry out such an exercise without the use of printed forms. The adult is concerned mainly with lipreading and auditory discrimination.

Part III

The Preschool
for Deaf Children
and Parent Education

Chapter 15

Design for Preschool Center
with Parent Education

The following outline may be helpful to groups of individuals who are contemplating the establishment of a preschool center for children with serious hearing losses. Although these suggestions may not represent the ultimate to centers that are heavily endowed, the acquisition of everything in this outline may be far beyond the means of other groups. If, out of all that any group might select, they wonder what should be given first priority, the wisest decision, without doubt, would be to engage a highly qualified teacher of young deaf and hard of hearing children. A good teacher can give the parents and children an adequate start, something that even the most highly trained nursery school teacher of hearing children cannot be expected to do without the special qualifications. Costs, of course, will be greater, but the results should be considered worth the difference. In addition, as funds increase, the teacher of the deaf can guide the group or the Board in the selection of other requirements, whether another teacher or more equipment. It probably can be assumed that any group interested in establishing a preschool will proceed to organize a Board of Directors, which, in turn, will try to obtain strong and permanent financial backing.

A. STAFF

1. *Director, Supervisor, or Principal.*

In every center, designed for such purposes as educating young hearing handicapped children, there must be someone capable of and responsible for organizing and administering a suitable and effective educational program. Where there is more than one teacher, a nursery school and inclusion of parents in the program, there should be an efficient person to draw up and put into effect programs for each of these areas, and to supervise all aspects from day to day. Briefly, then, a Director or Supervisor must be appointed. There must be good supervision of teachers and teaching by a person capable of coordinating staff efforts, of knowing the field well enough that he or she evaluate needs and progress, and of being able to demonstrate for any teacher what and how to carry out recommended procedures. For best results, the qualifications of such a person should include at a minimum:

 a. Complete training, and experience as a teacher of the deaf and hard of hearing, including specialized training in the area of preschool education of the hearing handicapped.

 b. Training and experience in the guidance of the parents of hearing impaired children, particularly as this relates to the educational aspects.

 c. Training and experience with hearing children of preschool age, and in nursery school procedures.

 d. Some experience in organization of programs, and a familiarity with rulings and regulations pertaining to the running of preschool centers.

 e. A Director or Supervisor, trained in all of these areas, and therefore responsible for the nursery school program, would participate in the selection of the nursery school teachers(s).

2. *Nursery School Teacher.*

Unless the service to the children and parents is to be conducted on an individual or tutoring basis, there must be someone to supervise the children while the teacher of the deaf is attending to the specialized training in language, over and above what is given the children in the group. Whatever additional training such a teacher would have, she should be, at least, a Nursery School Teacher, with complete training in nursery school procedures as they are required in nursery education programs for hearing children.

Where there are just two teachers, the nursery school teacher might be a trained teacher of the deaf who is also a fully trained nursery school teacher. Although this is most desirable, such teachers are not available in very large numbers, and it is more likely that the preschool will have to start out with a nursery school teacher, under the direction of the Director or supervisor who has both qualifications.

If the population of children numbers above ten, possibly ten to twenty, there should be two full-time teachers besides the Director. It is preferable that the *third teacher* be a fully qualified *teacher of the deaf and hard of hearing.* However, since it is difficult to obtain such teachers, the preschool may have to engage another fully qualified nursery school teacher.

One of the dangers in staffing a new center, where funds are quite limited, is the possibility of accumulating a staff of untrained persons. Whoever is engaged should be trained to take responsibility for the task assigned, and no further responsibilities should be given that individual until she is adequately trained.

There are many highly qualified teachers of the deaf and hard of hearing who have not had training in nursery school procedures, and who have never worked with young hearing children in a nursery school atmosphere. There are many good teachers of the hard of hearing who have never worked with children with very serious hearing losses, such as the severely hard of hearing and deaf. There are many nursery school teachers, highly qualified with a good record of experience with hearing children, who have never worked with hearing handicapped children of any age. Each of these people has an area they can manage efficiently, and until they are trained in other areas, they should continue to perform efficiently in their own area. This cuts down on trial and error situations.

Frequent meetings among the teachers, with discussions of details to be attended to, give the nursery school teachers a deeper insight into the specific needs of the hearing-impaired child, and more confidence in their own efforts to provide adequately for these needs during each day's activities. The nursery school teacher has the advantage of knowing what little hearing children need and enjoy, and this is important from the standpoint of the deaf child. However, she will notice differences which may prevent her from doing what she might have done with a group of hearing children. Regular conferences during which these matters may be discussed usually result in the nursery school teacher learning how to approach the children in such a way that the seemingly "impossible" becomes possible.

The placement of volunteer helpers within the young hearing impaired child's nursery school environment, established for very specific purposes on behalf of the child, is not advisable unless each one is willing to take minimal training in certain tasks. In some new centers which are privately run with very limited financial resources, or are within agencies not oriented toward educational needs of the hearing impaired, there may be a serious shortage of professionally trained staff. Where young deaf children are mixed in group situations with children who have handicaps other than hearing loss or in addition to hearing loss, experience has taught us that proportionately more trained staff is required. Under these conditions, it may well be that trained volunteers can give strength to the program as their efficient functioning within the program permits trained teachers of the deaf and trained nursery school teachers to carry out effectively what they are specially trained to do.

Within preschool settings, there are numerous and necessary tasks to be carried out with and for the children, which can be done by conscientious, trained volunteers willing to take direction and to learn. Routines such as toileting, washing up, preparing and helping to supervise snacks, dressing and undressing, can be managed by volunteers who are interested, who have been given opportunity to observe, and who view such participation as important to the child as a whole and to the special training he requires. Volunteers, as well as professionally trained teachers, who view such tasks as menial and unrelated, should be avoided, if possible, or removed early from the child's environment. Placing them within the specific language guidance program may be reinforcing for them but could have a derogatory effect upon the children.

In time, supervisors and teachers may discover other ways in which selected volunteers can best provide for the child. In some instances, a volunteer has been able to participate in one-to-one situations with the individual child in the carrying out of a language activity with prepared materials. This works best where the basic concept has been established in some degree through professional tutoring and group experience. Follow-through by the volunteer after observation and direction provides added repetition and practice for the child, as does follow-through at home by the parents. Some volunteers can be most helpful in the playroom, working with small groups for language interaction through craft projects, as well as supervising free play.

Workable volunteer assistance requires regular attendance, whether the same day or days each week, or daily on a half-day or full-day basis. How many to be used in any one group of preschoolers will depend on readiness of the children to involve themselves with a growing number of adults, space available, the nature and goal of the program, the attendance schedule possible for the volunteer, and, of course, the ability of the individual teacher to work with and guide the volunteers.

Volunteers who involve themselves at highly emotional levels tend to overstimulate little deaf children and to diminish the attentional skills and persistence for learning which take so long to acquire, and without which the deaf child cannot progress. The good volunteer, however, accepts training and direction, comes to see the worth of what she does, and can make a valuable contribution to the little deaf child.

Parents of hearing impaired children have, on occasion, become involved in the program beyond their involvement with their respective children. A mother, expecting to contribute to the whole group within which her own child is placed, may be disappointed at the outcome, and may feel compelled to spend full time with her own child. The use of parents as potential volunteers must be considered from many viewpoints. Their primary role should be in relation to the training and guidance of their own child in the home, making full use of information and observation provided by the center. Many parents whose children are no longer preschoolers and have enjoyed reasonable success been able to contribute much to other hearing impaired children in the role of volunteer assistants.

B.   CONSULTANTS

Every center for the early education of hearing-impaired children should require a medical diagnosis of hearing loss by an ear specialist before the child is registered for continuing attendance. Hearing and developmental assessments should also be carried out by qualified professionals, preferably before entrance. Parents should have immediate help in the home through a social worker, welfare worker, or psychologist, and, depending upon the structure of the center, possibly a visiting teacher of the deaf. Since placement of the child may involve just tutoring at the center, with group attendance when ready in a nursery school or kindergarten with hearing children, or, a specific number of days or half-days in the preschool center, or other arrangements, it is wise to establish consultant contact with other early childhood guidance centers. All consultant services should be used effectively not only at pre-entrance or early attendance times, but for follow-up attention throughout each child's attendance in the center. The consulting staff would therefore consist of the following:

1. *An Otologist*
2. *A Clinical Audiologist*

3. *A Pediatrician*
4. *A Psychologist*
5. *A Social Worker*
6. *An Educational Consultant* from each of:
    a. An early childhood education center for hearing children
    b. The special education section of the elementary school system

If multihandicapped deaf children are to receive training from the same center, then professionally qualified personnel in areas of neurology, orthopedics, limited vision, and blindness, etc., should be, if possible, routinely available for pertinent consulting services.

C. AFFILIATIONS AND CONTACTS

1. The preschool should have on hand all pertinent and current *literature* from the various training centers in the world concerned with the education of the hearing handicapped.
2. *Affiliations* and contacts should be established with related, accredited educational organizations.
3. Subscriptions to journals such as *The Volta Review, The American Annals of the Deaf,* and at least one concerned with early childhood training, such as *The Association For Childhood Education, International.*
4. The parents of the preschool should join *The Parents' Section of the Alexander Graham Bell Association.*
5. Contacts and arrangements should be made with local nursery school and kindergarten centers for hearing children, whereby the teaching staff of the special center may visit periodically to maintain awareness of the functioning of young hearing children.

6. Provisions should be made whereby each staff member is able to attend selected conferences on the guidance of hearing, hearing-handicapped and multihandicapped children.

D. LICENSING

1. *Fire*
2. *Police*
3. *Nursery Education*
4. *Health and Welfare*
5. *City*

E. SECRETARIAL ASSISTANCE

Almost from the beginning, there is some secretarial and stenographic work to be attended to. Correspondence must be filed and answered. In addition, there are a number of items which must be collected and filed.

1. *Individual folders* for filing must be set up for each child.
2. *Interview forms* must be set up to record pertinent data regarding each child.
3. *Results* of *hearing tests* and *other* tests taken in the preschool and elsewhere (if the latter are available) must be recorded and filed.
4. *Report forms* on which each child's *progress* is recorded must be set up. One copy goes to the parents, the other filed in the preschool.
5. *Report forms* for use by the *parents* in reporting to the preschool the child's progress at home, must be set up and filed.
6. *Final report forms* for use when the child leaves.
7. *Reports* of *all children* who are brought to the preschool for interviews, whether or not they attend regularly, must be filed.

8. *Teacher's records* of each child's progress must be filed.

9. *Qualifications,* experience, letters of recommneda-tions, certificates of health and X-Ray, etc., of the teaching staff must be filed in the preschool.

10. *Periodic notices* to parents must be typed and mailed from time to time. Forms can be typed and duplicated in large numbers when they pertain to factors such as opening and closing of the pre-school, special meetings, and material for parents' classes.

F. A COOK

A cook is required, only if the program includes a full-day attendance and therefore lunch at noon hour, for the children.

G. A CLEANING WOMAN OR JANITOR

The nursery school premises should be cleaned thoroughly every day.

H. PHYSICAL FACILITIES

Outdoor Play Area

If the preschool program for each age-level is to be con-ducted on a full-day schedule, possibly 9 A.M. to 3:30 P.M., out-door play facilities will be required.

1. *Preschool quarters* must be on the ground floor.
2. *Play area* must be adjacent to toilet facilities.
3. *Playground* must be dry, well fenced and attractive.
4. *Play equipment* must be strong and securely placed. Swings, jungle gym, teeters, boxes, parallel bars, etc.

Playroom(s)

1. *Lighting*
   Rooms should be bright, with windows on the best side for sunlight, with eaves to cut off glare, and with good artificial lighting for dark days.
2. *Ceilings* should be about 12 ft. high.
3. *Wall* and *ceilings* should be acoustically treated, attractively decorated in light colors, and insulated.
4. Part of the wall space should be used for a generous *bulletin board* of soft material, at the eye-level of the children, and for a long strip of 8″ width *blackboard,* also at the eye-level of the children.
5. *Folding walls* at strategic places. These are convenient for such purposes as extra teaching area, apart from the group, and for isolation space in the event of a child being ill or tired.
6. The *building* should be *fire proof,* with no stairways, no heater or window guards, no exposed wiring, no concrete or highly polished floors, and no four-cornered posts, with which the children could come in contact.
7. *Flooring* should be of strong linoleum, or similar surfacing, over concrete or hardwood, clean, washable, level, safe, and quiet. Where possible, the playroom floor should be carpeted wall-to-wall, particularly if the room is equipped with a loop induction amplifying system. Large sheets of non-slip, durable, and washable plastic can cover areas used for painting and water play.
8. The *playroom(s)* should have a large *rug,* washable and reversible, for the chidren to sit on.
9. *Indoor play space* should be 40 to 60 square ft. per child. In some instances, 30 square ft. per child is permitted providing the group is very small, and the indoor period short.
10. *Storage space* should include built-in shelves, cupboards and closets, large enough and numerous

enough to take care of all equipment and supplies. Closets should be ventilated.

11. A *small room* or *alcove* off the playroom should be available for the child who may become ill or who needs extra rest. If this is not possible, the folding walls can be used.

12. *Heating* should be adequate for warmth. Temperature should be even. Rooms should be free of drafts. Ventilation should be good, and humidity should be at about 60 per cent. *Air conditioners* for very hot weather should be installed, and regulated to prevent extreme cold and drafts.

13. A *double sink* for each playroom situated in the work area.

14. An easily operated drinking *fountain,* about 20 in. high, should be installed, in a convenient place out of line of traffic.

15. *Electric outlets* should be above the reach of the children.

16. *Toilet facilities* should include one toilet and washbowl for every two children, with toilets about 10 ft. high and washbowls about 23 ft. high. There should be floor space of about 5 or 6 square feet per child. The bathroom should be off the main playroom, bright, with washable flooring, and good ventilation.

I. EQUIPMENT FOR PLAYROOM

Tables

1. Durable, attractive, steady, and washable.
2. About 20 in. in height, or according to size of child.
3. Possibly shaped as half circles, or other shapes, to be used separately or placed together.

Chairs

1. Durable, in attractive colors, steady, lightweight.
2. Suitable sizes, possibly seats 10 in. from the floor, and backs 20 in. to 22 in. high.

Science Corner

How much is included in this area will depend on the care that can be given pets and plants. Some nursery schools find it more efficient to bring in plants and animals frequently rather than to keep them in the nursery school.

Library Corner

1. A table different from other tables.
2. Placed near movable bookcases.
3. Tables and fitted chairs (perhaps cushioned) should be of suitable height.

Lockers
Books

1. In good condition.
2. Vary broadly in content.
3. Colorful and selected.
4. Replaced when necessary.

Easels

1. Movable and of suitable height.
2. Double for painting on both sides.
3. Equipped with paint trays.

Housekeeping Center

1. A partially enclosed area with false windows and doors painted on the sides.
2. Furniture includes: a sink, a refrigerator, a stove

with oven, a table, two chairs, a doll's high chair, doll's bed, and a rocking chair. (All of suitable height.)

3. Other playhouse equipment: telephone, dishpan, dishes, tablecloth, mirror, mop, broom, dustpan.

Work Corner

1. A workbench with vise.
2. Sturdy tools.

The Town or Workshop Village

1. About 25 ft. or more of continuous wall space, on which is painted an outdoor scene with trees, hills, buildings.
2. On the floor space along the wall, set up a series of small stores, houses, barns, garages, a post office, a firehall, a police station, etc.

The Play Store

1. Large enough to contain life-size articles.
2. Counter.
3. Shelves.
4. Cash register with toy money.

A Rocking Horse
A Small Slide
Two Trikes
One or Two Wagons
A Wheelbarrow
Storage Boxes

1. On Wheels.
2. Hinged lids.

One or Two Blackboards on Wheels
Audio-Visual Aids

1. A few good prints to be hung on the walls.
2. A large file of pictures of interesting activities.
3. A motion picture camera, slide machine, and projector.
4. Suitable slides and films.
5. Collection of good phonograph records.
6. Shades or other facilties for darkening room for the showing of slides.

Hollow Blocks

1. About 20 or 30, minimum, various sizes and shapes.

Piano
Record Player
Doll Buggy and Dolls
Flannel Boards

1. With sense training materials made of felt.
2. Nursery rhymes in felt.

Supplies

Supplies required for nursery school activities are too numerous to include here. Pamphlets on equipment and supplies for regular nursery schools are usually available through Child Welfare Offices. The following are a few of the essentials:

1. Powdered, washable, watercolor paint.
2. Long-handled paint brushes.
3. Plasticine, clay and asbestos.
4. Crayons.
5. Fingerpaint.
6. Paste and paste brushes.
7. Wooden tongue depressors (for creative activities, not speech).

8. Paper (construction, easel, newsprint, drawing, fingerpaint, folding, cutting, etc.)
9. Flannel board figures.
10. A multitude of toys such as balls, tops, cars, trucks, drums, boats, construction sets, puzzles, etc.
11. Doll clothes.
12. Scissors.
13. Costumes or dress-up apparel.

J. SPECIAL TEACHING ROOMS

1. About three or four small teaching rooms.
2. One of these rooms should be large enough to accommodate up to six children under active teaching conditions, tables, chairs, shelves, hearing equipment and other teaching materials.
3. Other rooms should be large enough to house a table, chairs, hearing equipment and a limited amount of teaching material, and be comfortably bright and ventilated for an adult's tutoring of a child.
4. All rooms should be bright and attractive.
5. All rooms should be sound treated, and if possible, soundproof. They should be in a part of the building farthest away from major sources of noise.
6. All rooms should be thickly carpeted.

K. OBSERVATION ROOMS

1. One-way mirror for observation of all play and teaching activities in every teaching room, including playroom(s).
2. Sound treated, carpeted and ventilated.

L. TESTING ROOMS

  1. For the testing of hearing.
  2. Soundproof.
  3. Observation window.

M. HEARING EQUIPMENT

  1. A good group hearing aid with all necessary controls.
  2. Earphones.
  3. Turntable.
  4. Three or four portable table model hearing aids with earphones.
  5. A tape recorder with accessories.
  6. A set of good auditory training records.
  7. Extra tapes to set up auditory training exercises adaptable to the particular group of children.

N. OTHER TEACHING EQUIPMENT AND SUPPLIES

  1. Mirror (adjustable) attached to teaching table.
  2. Several chart stands of suitable height.
  3. Flannel boards with cutouts, objects, actions, etc.
  4. Slot charts.
  5. Small blackboard.
  6. Picture file; objects, actions, activities.
  7. Special sense training materials.
  8. Northampton charts.
  9. Phonovisual charts.

O. LECTURE ROOM FOR PARENTS' CLASSES

P. CONSULTATION ROOM

Q. OFFICE

R. SOME SCHEDULES AND RULINGS

1. Daily schedules of planned children's activities should be posted daily.

2. Teachers should keep "day books" or "record books" of the activities planned for the children each day. At the end of the day, accomplishments may be checked off.

3. Each teacher is given a Staff Book which includes rules and regulations of the nursery school regarding parents, children, training philosophy and procedures, recommended readings, and several hundred examples of suggested lessons applicable to deaf and hard of hearing children of preschool age. Teaching is not restricted to these suggestions, although many of them are very basic and tend to be commonly used. In the keeping of a daily lesson record along with other activities, some teachers find it expedient to merely check off according to number, the planned lesson for the child each day. It may be sense training from Lesson #5, and Speech from Lesson #1. Since certain parts of the training are so individual, and certain recording, as in speech, so detailed, daily planning and recording of achievements can become quite time consuming. The one hundred lessons outlined in the Appendix are from the large number compiled for teachers' use in one center, and which other teachers and parents may find helpful.

4. The nursery school teachers should be on the premises about half an hour before official opening each morning, to be certain that all preparations have been made for the day, that temperature and ventilation are comfortable, and to greet the children when they arrive.

5. Early arrivals among the children are not encouraged any more than late. When a child arrives very early, he is apt to be unusually tired by closing time.

6. A child may attend mornings, afternoons, or both. Where the child attends for just a half-day, the two- and three-year-olds might attend in the mornings, and those closer to five in the afternoons.

7. The child's day in nursery school would include free play, toileting, creative activities, music activity, experiences in housekeeping, activities about the library and science corners. In addition to the language experiences he would experience in these situations, he would have at least one special training period devoted to the establishment of language skills through speech, lipreading, auditory training, sense training, and rhythm activities.

8. The parent's responsibility to her child includes:
   a. Her own regular attendance at classes and on assigned observation and teaching days.
   b. Bringing the child to school on time, and taking him home promptly at closing time.
   c. Bringing the child to school appropriately dressed, and clean.
   d. Providing the child with such items as a clean apron or smock, a blanket, etc., and taking these articles home regularly for laundering.
   e. Submitting reports on home training, etc.

9. Participation of the parents in the child's training includes observation of the child at play under special direction related to language development. During the course of attendance in the preschool, parents will see demonstrated, and will be involved in some way in the carrying out of, the experience-centered language concepts presented throughout this book.

S.   PARENTS' CLASSES

The following is a topical outline of some of the factors discussed in the classes for parents of young hearing impaired children. A detailed treatment of these topics is given in the text entitled "Early Guidance of Hearing Impaired Children," by the author.

1. Why you and your child attend the Preschool; philosophy, aims.
2. Problems of deafness; for you, for your child.
3. Child development; physical, emotional, intellectual, social.
4. Aspects and understanding of language, history, humanities.
5. Speech development; in the hearing child, in the deaf child, in the hard of hearing child. Deviations from normal; when they occur, detection, our task.
6. Lipreading or speech reading; what is it?—when is a child really lipreading?—approaches, procedures.
7. Sense training; what is it?—purpose, application to other developments.
8. Combined use of residual hearing, speech, and lipreading in real situations; in contrived situations.
9. Auditory training; what is it?—effect on general understanding, what is expected of the child?—does he hear and if so, what?—procedures.
10. Speech mechanism; production of speech, problems, awareness.
11. Hearing mechanism; the mind, reception, perception, interpretation, relation to speech, types of hearing losses, causes.
12. Intelligence; measurement, development, application, tempo, personality, and the hearing loss.
13. Measurement of hearing; hearing tests, tuning forks, ice-water tests, etc.
14. Interpretation of test findings; test findings and the use of hearing aids, meaning of speech range, hearing sound, hearing speech.
15. Training the deaf child; training the hard of hearing child; similarities, differences.
16. Vocabulary building; words, connected language, content, selection, colloquial.

17. Reading readiness; what is it?—getting ready for what?—word recognition, when is a child really reading?—where and to what extent does reading readiness and reading fit into the nursery school program?

18. Your child now; effects of training, summary of progress.

19. Review of the literature; discussion of books and pamphlets read.

20. Further review of the literature; changes in methods during the years, trends, the unchanged, history of education.

21. More about auditory training procedures; the individual child, evaluation, familiarity with sound. Practical listening from the standpoint of the hearing person; what is heard, what is missed, and why. Consideration of recommendations found in the literature in view of these difficulties as applied to the hearing impaired; aids.

22. Schools for the Deaf; residential, day, private, selection, basis.

23. The potentially deaf child; training, placement.

24. Controversy regarding the education of the hearing handicapped.

25. Vacation and the deaf child.

26. Discussion of parents' reports and running records.

27. The impact of parent participation.

28. Those who are leaving; what of their future?

Note—The order of consideration of the topics listed above will depend on the needs of the group and the individual, and on the period of time the parent will remain in training. There is a constant overlapping and correlation of subjects throughout the training program.

The responsibility of guiding the parents in an understanding of the problems of deafness and in the guidance of their children is a demanding one for the teacher. Some parents assimilate information and adjust to the "teaching situations" much more rapidly than others. The teacher must anticipate the needs and capabilities of the individual parent in relation to such situations. Through the cooperative efforts of the teacher and the psychologist, the parent should be guided and supported in achieving adequate independence of teacher and psychologist. The foregoing statement is not meant to imply that all parents should become independent of educators; there must always be some interdependence between the two.

The desired "independence" of the parent implies, first, acceptance of responsibility for the child "as a whole." Observation of the children in all situations, of the teacher and other parents at work with the children, and eventually, participation in the various guidance situations, promote the parent's self-assurance, and decrease the dependence upon the teacher. Failure to achieve adequate independence could result in the parent's placing the entire responsibility of guiding the child upon the teacher and the nursery school, and so would defeat the whole purpose of the program for parent and child.

The teacher is bound to offer information and intelligent guidance. The parent must be willing to learn and to grow, and to assume responsibility for guiding the child to oral communication and personal adjustment to the world in which he must live.

REFERENCES

(See Bibliography)
5, 8, 9, 10, 11, 16, 18, 21, 22, 25, 27, 32, 34, 48, 49, 55, 67, 78, 79, 81, 83, 84, 86, 90, 100, 102, 110, 114, 129, 136, 137, 138, 143, 146, 148, 151, 154, 155, 167, 169, 170, 173, 177.

CHAPTER 16

Records
and Record Forms

Pertinent and regular recording of planned, specific, language-learning situations for each child, of the child's responses to those situations, of how he carries out general and specific developmental tasks, and of the parents' participation in guidance of the child, is an important part of any ongoing preschool program for hearing impaired children. If used as they should be, records can be a reliable means of following and evaluating more objectively the progress of each child over a period of time.

The kind and the format of records may vary greatly, according to staff/child ratio, goals toward which training is directed, and the basis on which the child attends; for example, tutoring, group, or both. In order to have a recorded picture of each child as a whole developing being and of his progress in learning and therefore in language, report forms must be set up accordingly. Besides those for specific use by professional staff, there should be reports to parents. The amount of detail and use of terminology specific to the area of education would depend heavily upon the degree of involvement of parents, and staff time allowed for parent education. Written reports of the child's performance at home provides the parents, as well as teaching staff, with a more complete picture of the child, and parent-teacher interviews can work toward identifying discrepancies, as to home and preschool performance.

The record, which is essentially developmental, has been used rather extensively for some years, in reporting on hearing impaired children, as well as hearing children. It may be very general or specific, may identify beginnings of cognitive learning, and serves recording purposes well whether the child is in a group with other hearing impaired children, with just hearing children, or in a mixed group. The following areas might be described and reported on regularly, for specific periods of time:

—Description of the Child in experienced situations
—Description of the Child as to Specific Developmental Tasks (visual, auditory, tactile, kinesthetic, motor, social, emotional)
—Parents' Participation
—Individual Interviews With Parents
—Summary
—Home Situation (reported by Social Worker)

In addition to the foregoing information, teachers should have records of the child's progress in language development. The specific language report, done on a regular time basis, would have to include details of such areas of development as the following:

—Receptive Language Being Developed and Developed
—Evidence of Language Understanding Through Auditory and/or Visual Interpretation
—Expressive Language Being Developed and Developed
—Use and Quality of Voice
—General Awareness of Sound, Specific Auditory Responses to Sound Sources such as Gross Sounds, Music, Voice, and Spoken Words. Differentiation Sound to Sound, and Discrimination (Words, Sentences, etc.)
—Speech Usage (Detailed Description)

Reports to parents may be set up under headings such as:

—Language Understanding (Through Lipreading, Listening)
—Responses of the Child to Sense Training
—Imitation of Spoken Words

—Language Expressed Spontaneously Through Spoken Language

—Attitude and Interest of The Child in Language-Learning Situations

—Recommendations For Language Training At Home

The report to parents may, however, be better presented under the general heading of:

—Progress Report and Recommendations:

The report submitted by parents outlining home performance of the child, including responses to and with spoken language, seems to be easier for the parent to use when there are some areas specifically named or described on a report form. Report forms might be set up under headings and areas such as:

—*Sense Training* (Your child's use of his/her senses of sight, touch, smell, taste, hearing in recognizing similarities and differences in things, actions, people, colors, numbers (quantity), sizes, shapes, places)

—*Language Understanding* Through Lipreading and/or Auditory Awareness. (Comment on gestures and situational clues)

—*Words Imitated* (Wholly or Approximated)

—*Spoken Language* Uttered Spontaneously and Meaningfully

—*Comments*

If possible, the parent(s) of each child, on the scheduled observation day, once a week or more often, once every two weeks, or other, should have an opportunity to speak with the particular teacher on what was observed during that time. Where parent education is extensive and intensive, follow-up written reports on observations are done and submitted by the parents. Where parents are involved when ready for one-to-one participation in the preschool with their respective children, they are helped in advance to set up written planned procedures. When professional time and guidance are available to each involved parent, that parent profits in ways that promote understanding of the child and his general and specific needs; contrary to turning the parent's orientation toward training procedures where language is viewed apart from the child, a stronger and more secure grasp of the total situation evolves.[141]

Records and reports on each child should be reviewed routinely at set times, as well as at intervening times if necessary, by those teachers involved in any way with the child. In many instances, the entire disciplinary team should review the situation. All assessments (audiological, psychological, etc.) should be immediately discussed with involved teaching staff and the findings considered in relation to the present functioning of each child as recorded in reports on file.

CHAPTER 17

Excerpts from Records

The brief excerpts below are *not* presented merely to show what the young deaf child may accomplish in vocabulary, language skills, etc. They are meant to be of help to parents in understanding that the personality of the individual child largely determines the way he will respond to a particular situation. Parents are inclined to feel discouraged when their child does not "settle down" and perform in the way that some other child does, or in some way that would be more acceptable to them, the parents. Unfortunately, too many parents become so concerned with expediency, or with set standards of behavior and results, that they lose sight of the child and of what *their* feelings and behavior may be doing to him.

Many times, the parent and the teacher have to give time and thought and action to "clearing away the underbrush" in the child's personality before he is ready emotionally to accept direct guidance in specially designed activities. Some of the reactions of the child which disturb the parent are normal; others may be indications of deep problems which will demand months of guidance and readjustment for both parents and child.

LARRY

Larry was three years and two days old when he entered nursery school. His favorite activity was playing in the sandbox. He would cover himself with sand, run trucks through the sand, tear up sand hills, accompanying each of these activities with loud yells and squeals. Indoors, he would crawl over and under tables, turn chairs upside down, remove objects from shelves and shove them around the floor.

Any arbitrary attempts to "make" the child conform to more conventional standards of behavior would have resulted in equally unfavorable reactions: temper tantrums, passive resistance, etc. It became necessary to give special attention to the parents, while, in the meantime, trying to redirect Larry's energies.

One day, after Larry had done a very thorough job of making the room as untidy as possible, he ran to the children's lockers near the front door and climbed upon them. He began to poke and pull at the very colorful curtains behind the lockers. The teacher casually reached for some color cards. She pointed to the red cherries on the curtain, to the red in Larry's sweater, to the red in her blouse, and to the red card. "They're all red, Larry. That's red, and that's red, and that's red, and that's red. Red, red, red." Larry laughed and very vigorously poked each article with all his three-year-old strength.

Then the teacher pointed to the yellow in the curtains and to the yellow wall. Larry grabbed the cards, pulled the yellow one out, slammed it down on the locker and yelled, "Yayaya." He seemed to enjoy this activity, and went through the various cards matching the colors to corresponding colors within his reach. Each time, he pounded the object of a particular color, he would laugh at the teacher and use his voice in trying to say something, which might have been intended for the color name.

In the days that followed, Larry continued to use voice, but in a more controlled way, and to watch more quietly. Nevertheless, the learning process in the individual periods during the first few months was a most active one, and the teacher had to be prepared to follow Larry. As the months went by, and as the parents received help, Larry's behavior, although still very active, became healthier, and lipreading and speech began to make a favorable impression upon him.

The months of following Larry through his gymnastics were not wasted. His use of voice remained spontaneous and natural. At the end of that first year in nursery school, Larry was imitating the names of all the colors, and several nouns and verbs. His lipreading vocabulary and general language understanding had broadened. There was every indication that he liked to learn. The channeling of his energies by the guidance given to him and his parents required several months, but, in every respect, the time proved to have been well spent.

MOLLY

Molly was a three-year-old who had had some home training before entering nursery school. It soon became apparent that the previous training had been well managed by the parents. Molly was relaxed and cooperative in most situations, with the exception of auditory training. She refused to have anything to do with earphones for the first two months.

Before the family had discovered the real cause of the child's delay in speech development, she had been taken from specialist to specialist, and had been subjected to so many tests that any sustained contact with any part of her head caused an immediate and violent reaction by her.

Although no attempt was made to force earphones upon the child, steps were taken to help her overcome her fear of the equipment and training. The teacher tried the well-known method of wearing the earphones herself as a means of encouraging Molly to wear them. This met with failure.

One day, Molly came in to the training room with another child. The teacher proceeded to do some work on gross sounds with Jane, the other child. No earphones were used. Molly watched quietly, with her hands over her ears. By the time the third sound was introduced, Molly was over at the table trying to knock down blocks with Jane.

For some time, Molly's interest was primarily in the blocks. Before long, she accepted the idea of waiting until she "heard" a sound before knocking over a block. It seemed evident that Molly possessed some residual hearing, but for weeks after she was able to discriminate between two of the gross sounds, she continued to refuse to wear earphones.

Each day for three weeks Molly was allowed to come in with another child who would wear earphones, and finally she put on a pair for a few seconds. The next time she kept them on a little longer. The first listening experiences included music and some favorite stories.

Seven months after entering nursery school, Molly was very enthusiastic about auditory training. She had some usable hearing, and a systematic program was set up for her, whereby lip-reading and speech were combined as much as possible with daily auditory training.

Any other than a gradual, unforced, approach to auditory training for a child like Molly would have failed. As it was, Molly was trained to use what hearing she possessed, and was saying whole words intelligibly by her fourth birthday.

AUDREY

Audrey was a three-year-old who showed little interest in the activities of the other children. If she participated at all with other children, it was with older ones. In the training situation, she showed no interest in form boards, toys, etc. She wanted dolls, a doll carriage, the ironing board, etc. It was clear that parent and teacher would have to reach Audrey through her chosen interests.

The teacher set up a housekeeping corner which could be dismantled easily and which might also be used by some of the older children. A small table, a chair, a set of dishes, two dolls with identical clothes, and pairs of toys were a part of the equipment. Through the use of these materials, matching was introduced and carried out. If Audrey chose a red hat for one doll, she or the teacher would find a red hat for the other doll. Blue cups were matched to blue, blue doll shoes to blue ones, etc. If one doll were given a puzzle, the other would have a puzzle. Audrey would do a puzzle for one doll, then one for the other doll. If one doll were given three balls, the other would have three, and each doll would be given a number picture card for three to go with the objects.

By the end of that year, Audrey had developed a very impressive lipreading vocabulary connected with objects and activities of special interest to her, and about other objects and activities in which she had begun to develop interest. Being allowed to explore her special interest, to the extent she needed to explore, resulted in a broadening of her interests.

MIKE

Mike entered nursery school at two years and eleven months. His mother had begun his training at home, and Mike was able to do a large number of sense training exercises and had established an impressive lipreading vocabulary. The teachers noticed Mike's extraordinary capabilities in sense training and lipreading. But they also noticed that, in the speech preparation situations, his voice was strained and unnatural and his whole body became tense as soon as he tried to imitate speech.

Because of this obvious tension, the parents were strongly advised to refrain from "teaching speech" to Mike at home, and give more attention to his activities in the play situation.

During the painting period, he would take his completed page, look around furtively, then tear and mutilate the page until it was a crumpled, sodden mass. When he successfully completed a puzzle, he would throw it in the air, laugh hilariously, and then look around with a startled expression at the teacher.

In the speech and lipreading situation, however, he conformed to every direction, would be very particular about the order of the cards and objects on the table, and would sit very quietly and stiffly awaiting the next suggestion.

No attempt will be made here to interpret the parent-child relationship, nor the basic causes underlying the child's problems. Suffice it to say that the mother received individual attention and guidance; and Mike was given complete freedom in the nursery school, short of seriously endangering himself or others.

Before long, Mike went to the opposite extreme in the special training situation, and a little later the mother reported that Mike's behavior at home was as "bad" as it was at school. It took the parents some time to accept such behavior from their child, and to accept the teacher's acceptance of such behavior. For a while, things seemed to get worse instead of better. Now, when he used his voice, there was no question about its being spontaneous. He would yell and jump and often, during the rest hour, he would be heard babbling freely.

Approximately six months after the parents and child began to receive attention in the nursery school, Mike began to be more relaxed and spontaneous in the special training situation, and more controlled and relaxed in the play and expressive activities. His voice was less strained, and his lipreading, which had been outstanding, continued to improve.

The following statements taken from the running records written by a parent during observation of Mike may help to tell the story of the change in Mike.

October 26. . . . Mike sat in the sandbox, making hills of sand. When he finished each hill, he punched it. Billy came and sat beside Mike. Mike looked around carefully, then pushed Billy to the sand and ran to the swing. Miss —— went over to the swing. When Mike saw her, he "ducked" his head. Then when he saw the teacher smiling, he held up his hands to be lifted into the swing.

January 12. . . . Mike stood watching Danny and Laura playing on the teeter-totter. He picked up a toy truck, ran over to the teeter, and hammered the truck on the board until the wheels broke off. Then he took the pieces over to the teacher, showed them to her, threw them on the ground, and kicked them.

March 18. . . . Mike was going up and down the slide with one of the other children. He saw Miss —— coming out with some puzzles and cards. He poked Billy and pointed to Miss —— as he babbled and chattered. Both children ran to the box on which the puzzles were being spread. Mike pointed to the ball from one puzzle, and said, "Baw," for *ball*. He took Billy's hand, placed it on his (Mike's) cheek and repeated the word. Then he patted Billy on the shoulder when he (Billy) said the word. Then he took Billy's hand, and both children ran to the wagon.

Close observation of Mike and his parents during the following two years showed that the child's most serious problems had been dealt with successfully through the combined efforts of home and nursery school.

PAT

Pat was three years and four months old. He had been in the nursery school with other deaf and hard of hearing children for six months. He was deaf. It was almost a certainty that he would never hear a spoken sound as the normal ear hears it.

It was a sunny morning, late in April. Pat came into the nursery school playroom straining at his mother's arm, smiling but anxious to break loose. He ran to the center of the playroom, looked around with a look of possession in his eyes, then directed a smiling glance of satisfaction toward Miss Dane, his nursery school teacher. He said, "Bye bye," loudly and clearly to his mother, who waved her hand and went on her way.

He began to unbutton his jacket, but had difficulty with the top button. He turned to Miss Dane for assistance. She said, "Let's hear you say, 'Help me, please!'" The response after a few tries sounded like "Hemee, peas!" He completed the unbuttoning process, took off his jacket, carried it to his locker and hung it up.

He took a puzzle with stand-up figures of farm animals on it to a table, quickly took it apart and put it together again. Then he noticed a tricycle, and dashed across the room to enjoy a ride.

Before long, the other children began arriving, and each arrival was noted by Pat. When Gary started up the ladder to the slide, Pat ran after him. He followed closely behind Gary, yelling "Up, up." Knowing that Gary didn't hear him, he pulled one of Gary's legs to get his attention and repeated, "Up, up."

Gary evidently didn't mind being told to go up, but he objected to having his leg pulled. He shook the slide, and Pat jumped off the ladder, almost falling. As Gary reached the top of the slide, Pat yelled, "Babo," meaning "Bad boy." Miss Dane went over to Pat, and told him to say "Boy." Pat said the word clearly, then excitedly turned to point to Gary and yell, "Babo." After Gary had his slide, Pat went up the ladder, and Miss Dane said, "Where are you going now?" Pat laughed and said, "Down!"

The easels were set up for painting. Pat ran for his apron, put it on himself, and went quickly to a free easel. He spent several minutes covering the sheet with three brilliant colors—dots and strokes in large splashes. He pulled off the apron and walked to the bathroom to wash his hands. He came back into the playroom, pulled Miss Dane to his painting which was still drying on the easel, pointed to a lower corner of the sheet, and said, "Pa." He meant that "Pat" was to be printed on his painting. Miss Dane printed his name in the corner and said, "You may take it home with you at noon." Pat replied, "Ome." With a little help, he said "Home," more clearly.

Miss Dane pointed to the big black cardboard sheep pinned on the wall at the eye-level of the children, and to the three paper bags each containing wool taped to the wall, and told the children that they could have a sing-song. They gathered about the piano. Miss Dane began to play, with a decided beat, "Baa Baa Black Sheep." She swayed from side to side as she played. The children, each with one hand on the piano, swayed with her.

She began to sing "Baa Baa Black Sheep." "You sing with me, Pat." Pat sang, "Baa Baa Bashee." When the singing was over, the little group gathered on a mat near the black sheep on the wall for their story. Questions such as "Who can find the black sheep for me?" "Where is his black wool?" "How many bags of wool are there?" "Where did the wool come from?" "What color is it?" "Do you have any wool?", were asked and answered. To the last question, Pat giggled and said, "No!"

Now it was time to go with Miss James for a special speech lesson. He saw her coming and ran to meet her. This was always a special moment, so much attention and all for himself! When he went into the other room, his first action was to reach for the earphones. He took off his own hearing aid carefully, and put on the earphones with a little help. The lesson proceeded with moderate success, except of course for "g." In spite of failure to produce a "g" in words, he always enjoyed the process. Words containing the sound were connected with objects and activities he thoroughly appreciated. Dogs go "Bowow," guns go "bang," and garages were full of cars and trucks that "go, go, go."

Pat understood the words easily enough. He spent considerable time each day "gassing" not only cars and trucks for the other children, but also their trikes and wagons. He insisted that nothing would go without "gas." When he would finish "gassing" a vehicle, he would point away to the child riding it, and say, "O-e," meaning "Go." Some day he would say "g" in all the right places.

After this lesson, he ran back to the playroom and directly to the workshop village. Mary was playing hospital with dolls and bed. Pat grabbed a doll and tried to look into its mouth, which wouldn't open. Mary grabbed the doll back, and glared at Pat. Before a fight could start, Miss Dane directed Pat to the housekeeping center. He went in, opened the refrigerator, and put a doll in it. Sally slapped his hand and said, "No." Miss Dane said to Pat, "We won't put the doll there. It's too cold. Poor dolly will freeze. Poor Dolly." Pat looked seriously at her and said, "Poo doll." Pat went on to help Sally play house by washing clothes, and dishes.

After a midmorning snack of juice and cookies, the children sat around a table with Miss Dane. Each one had a little box, a little toy table and a little ball. Miss Dane showed them how to play the "In and Out" game. It was fun putting the ball "on the table" and "in the box," especially when you did it correctly, and everyone clapped for you and laughed.

Library time was fun too, even though it was quiet. Pat picked a book about The Three Bears. He sat down beside Miss Dane. He watched the book and Miss Dane alternately as she told him the story. He pointed to the three figures and said, "Father, Mother, Baby."

When his mother came for him at noon, Pat ran to her to

show her his painting. He smiled happily when she admired it. He put on his jacket, took his mother's hand, and said "Bye bye" smilingly to Miss Dane.

Pat was responding to the challenges of his nursery school environment, and language was growing with him. Tomorrow he would come in and once again look about this cherished environment possessively. Having been assured that all was still in place, he would proceed to enjoy another day. The feeling of well-being which he brings with him from his home each morning and with which he leaves the nursery school is the result of having exceptionally understanding parents who make it possible for a good nursery school program to work for him. He is learning to think for himself and to express his thoughts through spoken language. Perhaps Pat will be one of those fortunate deaf children for whom a good and early start in life will lead to the achievement of a successful status in a hearing world.

Teachers and parents of deaf children have contributed a great deal to the progress of society through their cooperative efforts. The guidance of the young deaf child presents many problematical situations. Many a parent has felt puzzled in spite of the guidance available to her, has wondered if she is walking up a blind alley. A problem seems to be solved, and then suddenly it may seem farther away than ever from solutions. The parent of the deaf child does not stand alone in this; the educator often feels the same way. Indeed, the parents and educators who have the moral courage to admit that they do not have all the answers are clearing a swath in the forest of problems created by deafness. In the meantime, parents and teachers have the privilege of working together in leading the young deaf child to oral communication.

Appendix

LESSON #1

Sense Training   Matching Objects: ball, shoe, airplane.

Lipreading   Objects: ball, shoe, airplane.

Speech   Babbling sounds using colors: blowing, p.
    bububu
    mmmmmm—.

Auditory Training   "Listening" to music. "On" and "Off."
    Gross sounds: drum, cowbell.

LESSON #2

Sense Training   Matching Objects: ball, shoe, airplane.

Lipreading   Objects: ball, shoe, airplane.

Speech   Babbling sounds using colors: blowing, wh, p.
    bububu
    mmmmmm—.

Auditory Training   "Listening" to music. "On" and "Off."
    Gross sounds: drum, cowbell.

LESSON #3

Sense Training	Matching Objects: ball, shoe, airplane.
Lipreading	Objects: ball, shoe, airplane.
Speech	Babbling sounds using colors: blowing, wh, p, th.
Auditory Training	"Listening" to music. "On" and "Off." Gross sounds: drum, cowbell, whistle.

LESSON #4

Sense Training	Matching Objects: ball, shoe, airplane.
Lipreading	Objects: ball, shoe, airplane.
Speech	Babbling sounds using colors: blowing, wh, p, th, f.
Auditory Training	"Listening" to music. "On" and "Off." Gross sounds: drum, cowbell, whistle, flute.

LESSON #5

Sense Training	Matching Objects: ball, shoe airplane, boat, bus.
Lipreading	Objects: ball, shoe, airplane. Verbs: run, jump.
Speech	Babbling sounds using colors: blowing, wh, p, th, f, sh. Imitation of whole words, using objects and the tactile, visual and auditory approaches: ball, shoe.
Auditory Training	"Listening" to music. "On" and "Off." Gross sounds: drum, cowbell, whistle, flute, banjo. Animal sounds: dog barking.

LESSON #6

Sense Training	Matching Objects: ball, shoe, airplane, boat, bus.
Lipreading	Objects: ball, shoe, airplane. Verbs: run, jump.

Speech	Babbling sounds using colors: blowing, wh, p, th, f, sh.
	bububu, bawbawbaw.
	bababa, booboooo.
	mumumum—.
	Imitation of whole words, using objects and the tactile, visual and auditory approaches: ball, shoe.
Auditory Training	"Listening" to music. "On" and "Off."
	Gross sounds: drug, cowbell, whistle, flute, banjo.
	Animal sounds: dog barking, cow mooing.
	Dropping peg in a box in response to "hearing" boo.

LESSON #7

Sense Training	Matching Objects: ball, shoe, airplane, boat, bus.
	table, chair, bed, house, piano.
Lipreading	Objects: ball, shoe, airplane, boat.
	Verbs: run, jump.
Auditory Training	Babbling sounds using colors: blowing, wh, p, th, f, sh, bubu, bawbaw, baba, booboo, mumum—.

LESSON #8

Sense Training	Matching Objects: dog, boy, man, ball, doll, horse.
	cat, girl, woman, wagon.
	store, school, house, barn, table.
	train, duck, airplane, car.
Lipreading	Objects: airplane, car, train, doll, boat.
	Verbs: run, jump.
Speech	Babbling sounds using colors:
	blowing, p, th, f, wh, sh.
	bububu, dududu, gugugu.
	bababa, dadada, gagaga.
	booboo, doodoo, googoogoo.
	boeboe, doedoe, goegoegoe.
	mumumum—, mmmmmm.

Auditory Training	"Listening" to music. "On and "Off."
	Gross sounds: drum, cowbell, whistle, flute, banjo.
	Animal sounds: dog barking, cow mooing.
	Dropping peg in a box in response to "hearing" *boo*.
	Dropping peg in a box in response to "hearing" *baw*.
	Dropping peg in a box in response to "hearing" *ball*.

LESSON #9

Sense Training	Matching Objects: dog, horse, cat, pig, cow, duck.
	boy, girl, man, woman, baby.
	store, school house, barn.
	train, airplane, car, bus, wagon.
	ball, doll, shoe, cup, table.
Lipreading	Objects: ball, shoe, airplane, car, train, doll, boat.
	Verbs: run, jump.
Speech	Babbling sounds using colors, leading into whole word:
	bububu, booboo, bawbaw—ball.
	babababa, babababababa—bath.
	dawdawdaw—doll.
	gugugugu—gun.
	mamamama—mama.
Auditory Training	"Listening" to music. "On" and "Off."
	Gross sounds: drum, cowbell, whistle, flute, banjo.
	Animal sounds: dog barking, cow mooing, lamb baaing.
	Dropping peg in a box in response to "hearing" *ball*.
	Dropping peg in box in response to "hearing" *airplane*.
	"Listen" to *oo* spoken in very *high* tone.
	"Listen" to *oo* spoken in very *low* tone.

LESSON #10

Sense Training   Matching Objects to Pictures: ball, shoe, airplane.

Lipreading   Objects: house, barn, woman, man, baby, boy, girl, cow, pig, cat, horse, dog, duck.

Question and follow-up activity with attempt at answer:

    Show me all the things that go in the barn.

    Now, put them in the barn.

    Who lives in the house?

    Put them in the house.

Verbs: run, jump. Make the dog run.

    Make the dog jump.

Speech   Babbling sounds using colors, leading into whole word:

    bububu, bawbawbaw—ball.

    bawbawbaw—barn.

    baebaebae—baby.

    boeboeboe—boy.

    bubububu—bus.

Auditory Training   "Listening" to music. "On" and "Off."

"Listening" to recorded sounds of animals:

    Dog *barking*.

    Cow *mooing*.

    Lamb *baaing*.

Gross sounds: drum, whistle, cowbell, flute, banjo.

    Listen for the beat of the drum.

    Drop peg in a box.

    Listen for the sound of a whistle.

    Drop peg in a box.

    Same for cowbell, flute and banjo.

Dropping peg in a box in response to "hearing" the word "airplane" spoken.

Dropping peg in a box in response to "hearing" the word "shoe" spoken.

"Listen" to *oo* spoken in very *high* tone.

"Listen" to *oo* spoken in very *low* tone.

LESSON #11

Sense Training	Matching Objects to Pictures: ball, shoe, airplane. dog, horse, cat, pig, cow, duck. boy, girl, man, woman, baby, barn, house.
Lipreading	Get the basket of toys. Find all the things that go in a barn. (cow, duck, dog, cat, pig, horse) Put them in the barn. Find the people that live in a house. (man, woman, boy, girl, baby) Put them in the house. Verbs: run, jump. Make the dog run. Make the dog jump. Make the cow run. Make the cow jump. Make the horse run. Make the horse jump.
Speech	Babbling sounds using colors leading into whole words: h–, h–, horse, house. p–, p–, pig, airplane. t–, t–, train, table. c–, k–, cat, duck, school, car. s–, s–, store, school, horse, house. bubububu, ball, boy, baby, barn, bus. dudududu, doll, dog, duck. wuwuwuwu, woman, wagon. mumumumu, man, woman. n—, man, woman, train, airplane, wagon.

Auditory Training Repeat #10.

LESSON #12

Sense Training	Matching Objects to Pictures: dog, horse, cat, pig, cow, duck. boy, girl, baby, woman, man. store, school, house, barn.

train, airplane, car, bus, wagon.
ball, doll, shoe, cup, table.

Lipreading   Get these things from the barn:
    a cow, a duck, a dog, a cat, a pig, a horse.
Put the cow in the barn.
Put the duck in the barn.
Make the dog run to the barn.
Make the cat run to the barn.
Make the pig run to the barn.
Make the horse run to the barn.
Show us how the horse runs and jumps.

Get these things from the house:
    a man, a woman, a boy, a girl, a baby.
Make the man walk to the house.
Make the woman walk to the house.
Make the boy and the girl run to the house.
Carry the baby to the house.

Speech   Repeat #11.

Auditory Training   Repeat #10.

LESSON #13

Sense Training   Matching Colors: red, yellow, blue.
    1. Puzzle: with red, yellow and blue forms.
    2. Red yarn in a red box, yellow yarn in a yellow cup, blue yarn in a blue cup.

Lipreading   Where is the house?—the barn?—the store?—the school?
Get all the things that go in a barn, and put them on the table.
Get all the things that go in a house, and put them on the table.
Get all the things that go in the store, and put them on the table.
Get some things that go in a school, and put them on the table.
Make all the animals jump.
Make all the animals run to the barn.

Make all the people run to the house.
Make the boy and the girl go to school.
Put some food in the store.

Speech

Combination of vowels and consonants leading to whole words.

Group all the things and figures used under *lip-reading* (above), according to identical initial (or beginning) consonant. Emphasize whole word in simple statement. For example: h–, house, horse.

I live in a *house. House. House.*

The *horse* lives in a barn. *Horse. Horse.*

Also: p—pig, pie.
       b—boy, baby, barn, bread.
       m—man, meat, milk.
       d—dog, doll.
       t—table, towel.
       n—nail.
       c, k—cat, cow, cup.
       g—gum.
       f—fish, food.
       sh—shoe.
       ch—chair.
       s—school, store.
       w—woman, water.

Auditory Training

Listen to each of the above words as they are said.

Watch as they are said.

After each has been said, drop peg in a box.

Listen to each of the above words without watching.

Drop a peg in a box in response to each word heard.

Select two toys, airplane and shoe.

Listen as *airplane* is said. Indicate the right toy.

Listen as *shoe* is said. Indicate right toy.

Listen, without watching, to *airplane* spoken.

Indicate correct toy—airplane.

Same procedure with *shoe*. (Learning to differentiate).

LESSON #14

Sense Training   Matching Colors: red, yellow, blue.
Repeat 1. and 2. of Lesson #13.
3. Match two red bows, two yellow bows, two blue bows.
4. Match red blocks, yellow blocks, blue blocks.
5. Match according to colors, red, yellow and blue, toys such as chairs, tables, cups, spoons.

Lipreading   Let us go to the store.
Here is some bread, some milk, some meat, a pie.
What do you want to buy?
(Some bread. Some milk. Some meat. A pie.)
Give me some money, and I shall give you a pie.
Give me some money, and I shall give you some meat.
Etc.
You be the grocer. I shall buy some food.
I want a pie, please. Here is the money.
I would like some meat. Here is the money.
Etc.

Let us walk to the house.
Oh, look at the people in the house.
Who are they?
    A man like Daddy.
    A woman like Mummy.
    A boy like John.
    A girl like Mary.
    A baby like your baby at home.
What else do you see in the house?
    A dog.
    A cat.

Help the man and woman go to the store. Let the baby go, too.
Make the boy and girl walk to school.
Tell the dog and cat to run to the barn. Make them run.

Speech   Repeat #13.

Auditory Training	"Listening" to music.
	Say "Off," when the music stops.
	Say "On," when the music plays.
	"Listening" to recorded sounds of animals:

Bow-wow. What did you "hear?" A dog saying *bow-wow*.

Moo-moo. What did you "hear?" A cow saying *moo-moo*.

Baa-baa. What did you hear?" A lamb saying *baa-baa*.

Mew-mew. What did you "hear?" A cat saying *mew-mew*.

Neigh–. What did you "hear?" A horse saying *neigh*.

What says bow-wow?

What says moo-moo? Etc.

LESSON #15

Sense Training	Matching Shapes: round, square, triangle, rectangle.
	1. With puzzle.
	2. With cardboard cutouts.
	Matching Colors: Repeat #14.
Lipreading	A visit to the store, as in #14.
	A visit to the house. Who lives in the house?
	Let us look at some things in the house.
	A table, a chair, a bed, a fridge, a stove, a sink.
	Put the fridge in the kitchen.
	Put the stove in the kitchen.
	Put the sink in the kitchen.
	Put the table in the kitchen.
	Put the chair in the kitchen.
	Where does the bed go? In the bedroom.
	Put the bed in the bedroom.
Speech	Repeat #13, adding words, stove, sink, under *s*,
	bed and bedroom, under *b*,
	fridge, under *f*,
	chair, under *ch*,
	kitchen, under *k*.

Auditory Training   Repeat #14.

Introduce airplane, car, telephone.

Play recorded sounds of each.

"Listen" to the airplane.

"Listen" to the car.

"Listen" to the telephone.

Make a sound like an airplane. (Lip trill).

Try to make a sound like a car. (Engine growl).

Try to make a sound like a telephone. (Ling-a-ling).

Play sound produced by one of the above.

What did you "hear?"

Play the others, one at a time, repeatedly.

What did you hear?

"Listen" to *oo low*.   Say it.

"Listen" to *oo high*.   Say it.

Use picture of "Baa Baa Black Sheep."

Use large, black cutout of a sheep, three paper bags of cotton wool, and three cutout figures, to go with the rhyme.

Play the recorded music and words of the rhyme.

Keep time with clapping.

Tell story using "props" and matching them to corresponding objects and figures in the picture.

What is this? A black sheep.

What are these? Three bags of wool. Etc.

Listen to recorded music and words again, clapping.

Using fitted aid, dramatize story.

LESSON #16

Sense Training   Matching Colors as in #14.

Matching Shapes as in #15.

Matching Sizes:

    two big blocks, two small blocks;

    two big balls, two small balls;

    two big shoes, two small shoes;

    two big hats, two small hats;

    two big cups, two small cups.

Lipreading	Repeat #14 and #15.
Speech	Repeat #13 and #15.
Auditory Training	Repeat #14 and #15.

LESSON #17

Sense Training	Repeat #16. Combine matching of colors with speech and lip-reading. For example: Match a number of red objects. This is a *red* ball. What is it? A *red* ball. This is a *red* shoe. What is it? A *red* shoe. This is a *red* bow. What is it? A *red* bow. Similarly for *blue* and *yellow*.
Lipreading	This is the doll's house. We found a table, a chair, a bed, a fridge, a stove, and a sink in the doll's house. Now, let us go to your big play house and see what we can find.

Here is a table.   Here is a chair.
Here is a fridge.   Here is a stove.
Here is a sink.   Here is a bed.

Let me hear you say what you have in your play house.
Now, let us find some more things.
Here are some dishes. A cup, a plate, a spoon, a bowl.
Let us set the table.
What did you put on the table?
What do you do with the dishes?
What do you put in the cup? Milk.
Who do you put on the plate? Meat and potatoes.
Who do you put in the bowl? Soup, Cornflakes.
What do you eat them with? A spoon. A fork.

Speech	Repeat #13 and #15, adding new words selected from *Lipreading* (above). For example: p-plate; b-bowl, etc. Use simple sentences regarding use, etc.

Auditory Training   Repeat #14 and #15. Emphasis on oral response.
                       Some casual reference to "What color," and "How
                       many?"

LESSON #18

Sense Training   Repeat #16 and #17.

Lipreading   Repeat #17.
                       Add flour, water, sugar. Let us bake a cake.
                       Put the flour in the bowl.
                       Put the sugar in the bowl.
                       Put some water in the bowl.
                       Mix them with a spoon.
                       Pour the cake into the pan.
                       Put it in the oven.
                       Now, the cake is baked. (Use toy food to replace
                           batter.)
                       When the cake is baked in the big oven, we shall
                           have some.

Speech   Repeat #13, #15, #17.
                       Add new words to speech play period. For ex-
                           ample: f-flour; w-water; s-sugar; c-cake; p-pan.
                       Use expressions such as "Bake a cake."

Auditory Training   Listen to recording of "Pat-a-Cake." Clap in time.
                       Talk about the cake, baking a cake, the baker,
                           oven.
                       Use picture of the rhyme. Use real objects.
                       Play record again, encouraging speech in time and
                           clapping.

                       Talk about home. Use pictures of family.
                       Who is this? Father, Daddy, man.
                       Who is this? Mother, Mama, woman.
                       Use words used at home to designate parents.
                       Where is Daddy? Where is Mama?
                       Show us the picture of Daddy. The picture of
                           Mama.
                       "Listen" to yourself say "Daddy," "Mama."
                       Let us learn to shake hands and say "Hello."
                       Let us learn to wave our hands and say "Bye Bye."

Do you have a baby at home?
What is the baby's name?
Here is a picture of your baby brother (sister).

You are at school now. You will go home later.
Do you walk home? Do you go hme in the car?
Do you go home on a bus?
Here are some pictures of little girls and boys
    going home. (Walking, on a bus, in a car.)
Let us hear you try to say, "I'm going home soon."

Let us "listen" to some music. We shall play some
    music quickly like this, and you must clap
    quickly.
We shall play some music slowly and you must
    clap slowly.

LESSON #19

Sense Training

Repeat #16 and #17.
Sense of smell:
    Smell the flower.
    Smell the onion.
    Smell the coffee.
    Smell the bread.

Shut your eyes and smell. Select one of the above.
What did you smell?
Etc.

Sense of touch. Various shapes to be placed in
    corresponding openings in top of box. Toy.
Put this where it should go. Etc.
Remove shapes.
Shut your eyes like this, and put this piece in the
    box.
Now put this one in the box. Etc.
Get a doll and a shoe from the basket of toys.
Shut your eyes. Place doll in hands. Remove doll.
Eyes open. What did you have? Similarly for shoe.

Lipreading

Let us go to your play house.
Find your doll. Get some clothes for your doll.
What is this? A dress, panties, hat, socks, shoes.

Put the panties on the doll. Put the socks and shoes on.

Put the dress on your doll. Now put on the hat. What is your doll wearing?

Is your doll going to go to bed after a while?

Where are the pajamas? Oh, they need ironing. Where is the iron? Where is the ironing board? Iron the pajamas. Put them on the bed.

Where does your doll sleep? What does she wear to bed?

Let us go to your workshop.

Here is some wood. What are you going to make?

What will you need? Some wood. Some nails. A hammer.

Do you want to saw the wood first? Make two pieces.

Put the wood together with a nail. Hammer the nail.

What did you do?

Speech
Add new words with initial consonants to former group.

For example: d-dress; p-panties; h-hat; s-socks; etc.

Review complete group of words from #13 to #19.

Use simple sentences.

Auditory Training
Repeat #14, #15 and #18.

Place emphasis on acute observation as well as on listening.

Emphasize accent and syllable.

Emphasize "key" words in simple sentences.

Emphasize correct timing and fluency with clapping.

LESSON #20

Sense Training
Repeat #16, #17 and #19.

Lipreading
Repeat #19.

Speech
Review at least one word beginning with each of the initial consonants introduced to the present.

For example: h-hat; p-pie; t-table; k-kitchen; c-cake; f-fish; th-thumb s-stove; sh-shoe; ch-chair; w-water; b-baby; d-doll; g-grocer; th-the ball, the shoe, etc.; j-jam; l-lamp; r-round; y-yes; m-Mother; n-name; wh-what.

Group words according to initial consonants with voice, without voice and those that are nasal.

Use colors to classify each group.

Deep breathing. Say sounds or words as breath is exhaled.

Breathe deeply, exhale and blow out candle.

Breathe deeply, exhale and blow feather.

Breathe deeply, exhale and blow balloon.

Blow up balloon.

Auditory Training   Listen to music with decided "beat."

In unison, say Pum-pum-pum-pum.

Attempt some emphasis, along with music, on accented beat of music. Possibly, PUM-pum-PUM-pum, or PUM-pum-pum-PUM-pum-pum. Yankee Doodle Dandy, for example, has a different "beat" than "Little Boy Blue."

Follow this with simple statements, emphasizing accent, fluency and breathing, in unison:

I came to SCHOOL. MOther is at HOME.

Each is given a ball.

HERE is a BALL.

Emphasize *pitch.*

Say in Unison: pumpumpumpumpum.

Say in unison, voice pitched high:
    pumpumpumpumpum.

Say in unison, voice pitched low:
    pumpumpumpumpum.

Say in unison, normal pitch: pumpumpumpum-pum.

Combine high and low, Pum (high), Pum (low). Pum (low), Pum (high).

Each is given a drum and stick.

Listen. Beat drum three times and count:
one, two, three, one, two, three.
Beat your drum three times (in unison):
one, two, three.

Stand up. Listen to marching music.
In unison, keep time with feet.
All say: lalalalala.
Listen to music. Keep time, say in unison:
lalalalala.

LESSON #21

Sense Training   Puzzles:
one-piece puzzle; a car, an animal, etc.
two-piece puzzle; a dog, a car, etc.
puzzles increasing in number of pieces per
puzzle up to about twenty-five.

Colors:
Matching colors; red, yellow, blue.
Use squares of flannel on flannel board.
Match colored objects:
Red chairs.
Blue chairs.
Yellow chairs.
Put all the red chairs together, the blue chairs
together, and the yellow.
Use other colored objects in the same way.

Lipreading   Use one red chair, one blue chair, one yellow
chair.
Lipread these phrases and identify correct one.
Put the red chair at the table.
Put the blue chair at the table.
Put the yellow chair at the table.

Speech   Review #20.
Group together a few objects with names contain-
ing the same vowel, such as hat, bath, wagon.
Say each word as a whole several times.
Get the hat, say what it is; now, but it in the box.

Take all the "a" words as a group, asking that "hat," "bath" and "wagon" (objects) be taken from the box and put out on the table. Say the words.

Auditory Training

Review #20.
Also: Listen and Say.
  Here is a *hat*.
  Here is a *bath* (or bathtub).
  Here is a *wagon*.

Everybody say: aaaaaaaaaaa aaaaaaaaaaaa
  hat, hat, hat
  bath, bath, bath
  wagon, wagon, wagon

With piano: Everybody say, at high, medium and low pitches)

hat	hat	hat
(low)	(medium)	(high)
bath	bath	bath
(low)	(medium)	(high)
wagon	wagon	wagon
(low)	(medium)	(high)
-a-	-a-	-a-
(low)	(medium)	(high)

LESSON #22

Sense Training

Puzzles as in #21. Increasingly difficult. Up to thirty-five pieces per puzzle.

Colors: Matching colored objects (red, yellow, blue) as introduction to understanding of spoken phrases and use of phrases in speaking. Use familiar objects.

Match other colors as for red, yellow and blue introduced in #13.

Lipreading

Follow up sense training exercises above with use of phrases containing names of familiar objects and their respective colors, red, yellow and blue.

Use of dolls' clothing from doll house and/or from larger play house, on the basis of colors, especially red, yellow and blue. Discussion of: a red dress, a blue dress, a yellow dress, a red hat, a blue hat, a yellow hat, etc.

Speech

Enlarge upon speech vocabulary as outlined in #20.

For example: h-hat, house, hello; p-pie, pipe, play; t-table, tie, top; k-kitchen, kite, key; c-cake, cooky, come; f-fish, father, feather; th-thumb, throne, thimble; th-the ball, the bee, the thimble; s-stove, see, sink; sh-shoe, ship, sheep; ch-chair, cheese, children; w-water, want, wall; wh-wheel, whip, what; b-baby, ball, bus; d-doll, door, down; g-grocer, go, girl; j-jam, jar, Jack and Jill; v-violin, vase; l-lamp, lamb, love; r-rabbit, run, red; m-mother, man, mat; n-name, no, now, not now; y-yes, you, yellow.

A few of the above in phrases with red, yellow and blue.

Auditory Training

Review #21.

Similar treatment of "aw," using familiar words such as, *ball, water, father.* Use of piano for pitch.

LESSON #23

Sense Training	Review #22.
Lipreading	Review #22.
Speech	Review #22.
Auditory Training	Review #22.

LESSON #24

Sense Training

A puzzle: A tower of interlocking forms, circular, and graduated.

Matching colored cutouts: chairs, tables, umbrellas, horns, bows, butterflies, balls, bells, shoes, houses, airplanes.

Lipreading	Phrases with colors, red, yellow and blue, using the above cutouts. For example: a red shoe, a blue shoe, a yellow shoe.
	A visit to the play village consisting of houses, a store, a barn, a garage, etc., to find objects that are red, yellow and blue.
Speech	Review #22.

Use of short, simple sentences.

Help the girl (miniature wooden cutout) walk to the *house*. The woman is standing in front of the house.

Say *"Hello"* for the girl. Say *"Hello,"* for the woman. The woman said, "What a pretty *hat*." This provides practice in the use of *h—*.

Use of other simple sentences to provide practice of other initial consonants in words and sentences. For example: Let us look at this picture: The woman is baking a pie. The man is smoking a pipe. The children are playing. Encourage conversation.

Occasional use of red, yellow and blue in statements and questions.

Auditory Training   Listen and say:

Hat, bath, wagon. a-a-a-a-a
Ball, water, father. aw-aw-aw-aw
Shoe, tooth, boot. oo-oo-oo-oo
Top, hot, pot. O-O-O-O-O-O
Book, cook, look. oo-oo-oo-oo
Boat, coat, stove. oa-oa-oa-oa

Listen and say: (Use of pictures.)
The girl has a hat.
The boy is having a bath.
The boy has a wagon.
The ball is in the water.
Father is tall.
The boy lost his shoe.
The man lost his boot.
The girl lost a tooth.
The baby has a top.

The pot is hot.
The boy looks at a book.
The cook has a pie.
The stove is hot.
The coat is red.
The boat is in the water.

LESSON #25

Sense Training   A puzzle. A tower. A stacking figure (soldier).

Matching all colors, using various shapes and objects.

Matching various objects of red, yellow and blue.

Lipreading   Red, yellow and blue in phrases with familiar nouns.

Finding red, yellow and blue objects in houses, the barn, the garage, the store, the toy storage boxes, etc.

Speech   Continued practice with initial consonants.
In words, in phrases, in simple sentences.
Use of mirror in speech teaching and training.
Use of color for breath sounds. Kleenex, candles.
For example: say *t* and blow the Kleenex.
   Say *t* and try to blow out the candle.
   Watch in the mirror. Say *t*.
   Say, *Table, top, tie.*
   Similarly for other initial breath consonants.

Auditory Training   Using pictures and objects, review -a- sound.

Using pictures and objects, review *oo* sound.

Listen, watch and say: *a a a oo oo oo*

listen, with eyes shut: *a a a*

What did you hear?

Listen, with eyes shut: *oo oo oo*

What did you hear?

Listen, watch and say: *apple apple apple*

Listen, watch and say: *shoe shoe shoe*

Listen with eyes shut: *apple*

What did you hear?

Listen with eyes shut: *shoe*

What did you hear?

The lamb says, *"Baa."* The cow says, *"Moo."*

Listen, with eyes shut, and say what you hear.

LESSON #26

Sense Training	A puzzle. A tower. A stacking figure (cat).

A form board for matching colors and shapes.

A peg board. A See-Quees puzzle (Going to school).

Lipreading   Repeat #25.

Find red, yellow, blue, green, orange, purple, brown, black, gray, pink, and white objects in play area, using colors in form board above.
Is the ball red? No.
Is it yellow? No.
Is it blue? No.
Is it orange? Yes, this is an orange ball.
Etc.

Follow up with: What color is the . . . . ?
What color is the . . . . ?
Etc.

Place three large blocks, all the same color, in a row. Place right hand on block farthest to the right. Count, one, two, three.
Now, you count with me.
Put your hand on the blocks and count.
Here are some more blocks. These are red.
Let us count these.
One, two, three.

Here are three balls. You have three blocks.
I shall put one ball on the table.
You put one block on the table.
You take your block back, and I shall take the ball.
Now, I shall put two balls on the table.
You put two blocks on the table.
You take back your two blocks and I shall take the two balls.
Now, I shall put three balls on the table.
You put three blocks on the table.
Now, let us play a "Giving Game," with one block, two blocks and three blocks; and with one ball, two balls, and three balls.

Speech   Repeat #25.

Auditory Training   Repeat #25.

LESSON #27

Sense Training   A puzzle. A tower. A stacking figure (clown).

Mail Box: Place shaped blocks into corresponding openings.

Form Board for matching shapes (8 different shapes).

Peg Board, inserting three pegs at a time.

See-Quees puzzle, (Going to School, Flower Growing, etc.)

Lipreading   Repeat #26.

Set up six small baskets or boxes in groups of one, two and three.
Here is one basket. Here are two baskets.
Here are three baskets.
Here is one airplane. Put it in the right basket.
Here are two airplanes. Put them in the right baskets.
Here are three airplanes. Put them in the right baskets.

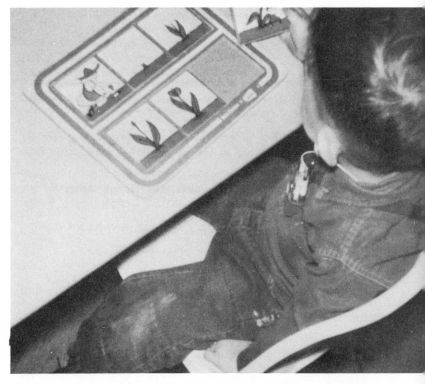

Plate XXXIII. Deaf two-year-old doing a See-Quees (Sequence) puzzle, as in lesson No. 27. The pictures must be in order to tell the story correctly.

Let us count the baskets.
How many are here? One.
How many are here? Two. (One, two.)
How many are here? Three. (One, two, three.)

Find one airplane. How many did you find? One.
Find two airplanes. How many did you find? Two.
Find three airplanes. How many did you find? Three.

Here are three puzzles (Peg boards).
In this one we can put one peg.
In this one we can put two pegs.
In this one we can put three pegs.

Here are two pegs. Put them in the right board.
Here are three pegs. Put them in the right place.
Now, put the one peg in the right place.

How many eyes do you have?
How many noses do you have?
How many mouths do you have?
How many ears do you have?
How many hands do you have?
How many feet do you have?
How many arms do you have?
How many legs do you have?

Speech   Repeat #25.

Auditory Training Introduce o-e, following procedure as in #25.
Learn to differentiate between "coat" and "boat."
Listen, watch and say: *a oo o-e.*
Listen, and say what you hear: *oo* or *a* or *o-e.*

LESSON #28

Sense Training   Another puzzle. A tower. A stacking figure (Penguin).

Repeat: Mail box, form board, peg board and See-Quees.

Lipreading   Visits to play house, store, barn and garage for practice in the use of "What color" and "How many?"

Let us set the table. Get enough dishes for the three of us.

Let us count the plates. Let us count the cups.

Count the spoons. Count the forks.

What color is your plate? Etc.

What color is my plate? Etc.

Speech   Let us say some words beginning with *b*—.

Let us find some things around the room that begin with *b*—. When you find one, say the word.

Let us say some words beginning with *d*—.

Let us find some things around the rooms that begin with *d*—. When you find one, say the word.

Now, let us talk about what we found.

What did you find?

What color was it?

What else did you find?

What color was it?

Etc.

How many things did you find?

Let us find some pictures of the things you found.

Put all the *b*— words together. Say them.

Put all the *d*— words together. Say them.

Auditory Training   Repeat #24.

LESSON #29

Sense Training   Another puzzle. Lacing wooden boot.

Putting letters in and out of envelopes.

Placing a block on each circle or picture on a series of number picture cards. One block placed on the one boat illustrated on large card. Two blocks placed on two dogs illustrated on large card. Three blocks placed on three monkeys illustrated on large card. Same for four and five.

Lipreading   Words: boat, dog, monkey, elephant, airplane, with
                    corresponding toy objects—five boats, five dogs,
                    five monkeys, five elephants, five airplanes.

                    Begin with counting each group of identical
                    objects.
                    One, two, three, four, five. Five boats.
                    One, two, three, four, five. Five dogs.
                    Same for the other objects.

                    Let us find one dog. One airplane. Etc.

                    Let us find two elephants. Two monkeys. Etc.

                    Follow through for three, four and five of the re-
                    maining objects.
                    Here is a big card. There is room for just one
                    thing. Find one boat and put it on the card.

                    Here is another big card. There is room for two
                    things. Find two airplanes and put them on the
                    card.

                    Here is another card. Etc. (Three, four, and five).

                    How many boats are here? One.

                    How many elephants are here? Five. Etc.

                    Continue with various arrangements using all the
                    objects on the number picture cards.

Speech   Using the same procedure as for #28, practice
                    p- and *t-* words, including simple sentences, and
                    the question forms *What color?* and *How many?*

Auditory Training Repeat #25.

                    Using the same procedure as in #25, practice
                    listening to *o-e* and *ow;* following up with the
                    use of words *boat* and *house.*

                    Finish lesson with recorded songs for children
                    about boats and houses, or at the piano. Clap
                    time.

LESSON #30

Sense Training Puzzle: with stand up figures—15 to a puzzle, figures fit into slots in puzzle—a doll, a dog, a clock, a duck, a tree, a boot, a house, a bird, a teapot, a chair, a teddy bear, a hen, a jug, a cat, a boat.

Match each figure to a corresponding flannel cutout and place on flannel board.

Lipreading Using matching along with lipreading and speech, place corresponding pictures of above objects and flannel cutouts on ledge or table.

Hide a few pitcures at a time, lipread what is asked for, find the correct picture, put on ledge, say the word, and find two other dolls, or houses, etc. For example: Find the doll. What did you find? Show me another doll. Where is the other doll?
Etc.

Repeat #29.

Speech Using the same procedure as for #28, practice *m*- and *n*- words; including simple sentences and the question forms *What color?* and *How many?*

Auditory Training Repeat #25 and #29.

Using the same procedure as in #25, practice listening to *oo* as in *cookies* and *-o-* as in *top*.

With piano, say at high and low pitches, the following sounds: *a, oo, o-e, ow, oo,* and *-o-*.

Listen to recorded spoken words, using pictures: apple, shoe, boat, house, cookies, top. (Or taped)

Listen again. (record or tape)
Sometimes you will hear a word like apple. You will hear someone speaking. Point to the right picture. Sometimes you will hear a drum, like this. You will not hear anyone speaking.

Play the tape or record. This gives practice in learning to identify spoken language from gross sounds.

Follow up with record such as "Bing Town" which includes singing, marching music, speaking, and the playing of a bass drum.

LESSON #31

Sense Training

Tactile (*tadoma,* or sense of touch in relation to speech).
Hand on cheek and cupped around under chin.
Shut your eyes. (Say *oo.*)
Open eyes.
What did I say? Watch now, and say *oo.*
Eyes shut. (Say "shoe.")
Open eyes.
What did I say? Watch now and say *shoe.*
Find a *shoe* in the bag.
Tell me what you did? "I found a shoe!"

Similar procedure for five or six familiar words.

Lipreading

Repeat #29 and #30.

Review the fifteen words in #30 under *Sense Training.* Include question forms such as What color? Where? How many? in relation to each object or picture.

Speech

Using the same procedure as for #28; practice *wh-* and *k-* words, including simple sentences and the question forms What color? How many? Where?

Combine sense training and lipreading, as above, with speech, with specific emphasis on oral production of both questions and answers.

Review the sounds: *a, oo, o-e, ow, oo,* and *-o-.*

Review the words: apple, shoe, boat, house, cookies, top, whip, and kite.

Play Hide and Find Game. Hide the apple. Etc.
Find the apple. What did you find? "An apple."
Now, say what you did. "I found an apple."

Auditory Training Using the same procedure as in #25, practice
listening to *aw* as in *father,* and *ee* as in *tree.*

Here is a little tree, and here is a cowbell.

Listen closely (Record or tape)

If you hear someone saying "tree," point to the
little tree, and say, "tree."

If you hear the cowbell, point to the cowbell and
say "cowbell."

Continue using a word (object) and a gross sound
in pairs until all have been used: apple, shoe,
boat, house, cookies, top, drum, whistle, xylo-
phone, clicker, banjo, tambourine.

LESSON #32

Sense Training Sense of touch in relation to speech as in #31.

Concentrate on vowel sounds:
  oo as in *shoe.*
  a as in *apple.*
  o-e as in *boat.*
  ow as in *house.*
  oo as in *cookies.*
  -o- as in *top.*
  aw as in *father.*
  ee as in *tree.*

Lipreading A counting exercise ,one to five.

Use number pictures and objects.

Use of question form, How many?

Find two babies. Put them in the carriage (or
buggy).

Find three blocks. Put them in the basket. Etc.

Find four elephants. Count them.

A color exercise, concentrating on two or three such as red, yellow, and blue.

Use of objectes and pictures in these colors.

Use of question form, What color?

Find a yellow bird. Put it near the yellow house. Find a red wagon. Put it near the red house. Etc.

Find all the blue things. Say what each one is: e.g. This is a blue hat.
This is a blue bird.
Etc.

Speech   Using the same procedure as for #28, practice *h-* and *w-* words, such as *house* and *water*.
Include simple sentences and the question forms, What color? and How many?
Group words and objects or pictures or both according to initial sounds: b-, d-, p-, t-, m-, n-, wh-, k-, h-, w-.

Auditory Training   Using the same procedure as in #25, practice listening to *a-e* as in *table,* and *-i-* as in *pig.* Through listening alone, identify *table* and *pig.*

Listen to tape, alternating a word spoken and a gross sound, as in #31, adding *table* and *pig.*

LESSON #33

Sense Training   Repeat #32
A puzzle with various vehicles: airplane, car, boat, wagon, truck, train, bus, sled.

A See-Quee puzzle, putting pictures in correct order to tell a picture story, e.g., a flower from the time of planting until it dies, or a house being built.

A word-lotto game.

Lipreading   A number exercise as in #32.

A color exercise as in #32.

More formal introduction of *on* and *under,* with the question form, *Where?* following possibly weeks (or months) of casual use of same in play situations.

Several familiar objects on and under chairs, tables, stoves, fridges, sinks, beds, etc.

Where is the ball? Under the table.
Where did you put the doll? On the bed. Etc.

Say what you did with the top.
"I put the top (or, it) on the table." Etc.

Speech   Using the same procedure as for #28, practice *g-* and *l-* words, such *as girl* and *lamp.*
Include simple sentences and the question forms, What color? How many? and Where?
Review all initial consonants to date, in groups.
A box with a sample picture on each one to represent the initial consonant. For example, the *b-* box might have a picture of a boy on it.
What is this? A lamp.
Put it in the right box.
After all words have been placed in correct boxes, select any one box at a time.
Say all the words you have found. Now, let us find a doll in the playhouse, a dog in the barn, etc.

Auditory Training   Using the same procedure as in #25, practice listening to *-e-* as in *bed,* and *a(r)* as in *barn.*
Listen. What did you hear? Bed? Barn?
Listen to tape of words spoken one at a time and to various gross sounds. Did you hear a word spoken? Did you hear one of these sounds. (Drum, etc.)

LESSON #34

Sense Training   Repeat #32 and #33.

Lipreading   A color exercise with at least three colors and several familiar nouns (objects, pictures).

A number exercise with at least three to five of various familiar nouns (objects, pictures).

The question form *Where?* with the prepositions, *on* and *under*.

Emphasize oral use of question and answer.

Speech   Using the same procedure as for #28, practice *r-* and *f-* words, such as *rabbit* and *fish*.

Use of question forms, *What color? How many? Where?*

Review of initial consonants to date—in words, phrases and simple sentences.

Boxes for pictures or objects placed here and there.
Finding a requested object or picture, or a group according to beginning sound, saying the words as clearly as possible when found.

Auditory Training   Using the same procedure as in #25, practice listening to *-u-* as in *umbrella, ur(ir)* as in *bird*.

Listen. What did you hear? Umbrella? Bird?

Listen to tape of words and gross sounds. When you hear a word like shoe, apple, boat, house, cookies, top, father, tree, bed, barn, table, pig, umbrella bird, put your hand up. Here is a shoe, and it sounds like this: *shoe.*
Here is an apple, and it sounds like this: *apple.*
Etc.
This is a drum, and it sounds like this: (A beat of the drum)

Use just the one gross sound at this point. Whether tape is used, or other means, instead of saying a word, then producing a gross sound, then another word followed by a gross sound, two words or three or one or four might be said between each drum beat. For example; shoe, (drum), rather, pig, (drum), barn, cookies, umbrella, (drum), bird, (drum), etc.

LESSON #35

Sense Training

Repeat #32.

Lacing the wooden shoe. Try tying a bow.

Button and unbutton using Button Board (frame with cloth and buttons and button holes).

Lipreading

A color exercise as in #34.

A number exercise as in #34.

The question form *Where?* with the prepositions *on* and *under* in answers.

A Hiding and Finding Game with such questions and answers as:

Where did you hide the shoes?
Where did I hide the feather?
I found the umbrella, *on the shelf.*
You found the ball *under the bed.*

Use of colors and numbers in hiding and finding.
Hide three bears somewhere.
Hide the yellow cup somewhere.
Oh, I found the three bears under the chair.
You found the yellow cup on the table.
Where did I find the three bears?
Where did you find the yellow cup?
Etc.

Speech

Using the same procedure as for #28, practice *v* and *th* words, such as *violin* or *valentine,* and *thimble* or *thumb.*

Use of question forms, *What color? How many? Where?* in relation to various words beginning with all previously introduced consonants.

Game involving grouping of words (using objects or pictures) using the boxes or another idea.

Emphasize good speech, awareness of similarity and differences among speech sounds in words, phrases and meaningful, simple sentences.

Auditory Training   Using the same procedure as in #25, practice listening to *i-e* as in *pie* and *oi* as in *boy*.

Use of tape, recording or other means as in #34.

LESSON #36

Sense Training   Repeat #32, including with other sounds and words:
a-e as in *table*.
-i- as in *pig*.
-e- as in *bed*.
a(r) as in *barn*.
-u- as in *umbrella*.
ur as in *bird*.
i-e as in *pie*.
oi as in *boy*.

Repeat #35.

Lipreading   A color exercise as in #34, adding another color, such as *green*. What color?

A number exercise as in #34. How many?

Repeat as in #35, the game with questions and answers, numbers and colors.

Introduce *big* and *little*. (These have been put to considerable use in casual play situations for weeks and months before this time.)

Use of several objects, with decided differences in size:
a big ball, a little ball
a big cup, a little cup
a big house, a little house

Big and *Little* objects in games.
Also: I have a *big* hat. You have a *little* hat.
You have a *big* brush. I have a *little* brush.

What color is the little book?
What color is the big elephant?
How many big balls do you see?
Where is the big plate?

Speech	Using the same procedure as for #28, practice *s*- and *z*- words, such as *stove* and *zoo*.
	Repeat #35, adding *s*- and *z*- words.
Auditory Training	Using the same procedure as in #25, practice listening to *u-e* as in *music* and *mule*.
	Use of tape, recording or other means as in #34.
	Let us play some music. Listen and clap time.
	Try to say lalala in a high voice in time to music.
	Try to say lalala in a low voice in time to music.

LESSON #37

Sense Training	Repeat #32 and #36, including:
	oi as in *boy*.
	i-e as in *pie*.
	u-e as in *music*.
	Repeat lacing and unbuttoning as in #35.
	Brief review of matching of shapes, sizes, colors, numbers (pictures), pictures.
Lipreading	Repeat #36.
Speech	Using the same procedure as in #25, practice *sh*- and *ch*- words, such as *shoe* and *chair*.
	Repeat #35, and #36, adding *sh*- and *ch*- words.
Auditory Training	Use of tape, recording or other means, as method of training the ear to distinguish between spoken language and other sounds. For example:
	Let us play a listening game.
	Here is a bird. Here is a drum.
	Listen, and you will hear the word, *bird*.
	Now, listen, and you will hear a *drum*.
	Listen again.
	You heard the word, *bird*. Point to the *bird*.
	Say "bird."
	Listen.
	You heard the *drum*. Point to the *drum*.
	Beat the *drum*.

Play the tape which may go in the following order: "Bird." "Bird." (Drum). "Bird." (Drum). Etc.

Now, let us play a listening game with *cookies* and a *cowbell*.

When you hear "cookies," point to the cookies and say "cookies."

When you hear the *cowbell,* point to the *cowbell* and ring it, like this.

Now, let us put all of these together: the bird, the cookies, the drum and the cowbell.

Listen. You heard "cookies." point to the cookies and say, "cookies."

Listen. You heard "bird." Point to the bird and say "bird."

Now, you heard a drum. Beat it. That was the cowbell. Ring it.

Listen and we shall play all of them. Point to what you hear. If you hear a word, say it.

LESSON #38

Sense Training	Repeat, using tactile or sense of touch in relation to speech production, lessons under *Sense Training,* from #32 to #37.
Lipreading	Repeat all exercises as in #36, adding another color, perhaps *orange,* to the color exercise.
Speech	Using the same procedure as in #28, practice *j*- and *y*- words, such as *jar* and *yarn.*
	Repeat #3, #36, #37, adding *j*- and *y*- words.

Auditory Training Watch, listen, point to, and say:

shoe	shoe	shoe	Say oo oo oo
apple	apple	apple	Say a a a
boat	boat	boat	Say oa oa oa (o-e)
house	house	house	Say ou ou ou (ow)
cookies	cookies	cookies	Say oo oo oo
top	top	top	Say o-o-o-
father	father	father	Say aw aw aw
tree	tree	tree	Say ee ee ee
table	table	table	Say a-e a-e a-e
pig	pig	pig	Say i-i-i-
bed	bed	bed	Say e-e-e-
barn	barn	barn	Say a(r) a(r) a (r)
umbrella	umbrella	umbrella	Say u-u-u-
bird	bird	bird	Say ir ir ir (ur)
pie	pie	pie	Say i-e i-e i-e
boy	boy	boy	Say oi oi oi (oy)
music	music	music	Say u-e u-e u-e

Here is a shoe. Here is an apple.

Turn around and listen. Shoe. What did you hear? (Point to the shoe, and say "shoe.")

Turn around and listen. Apple. What did you hear? (Point to the apple and say "apple.")

Use pairs of words from above group, including a one syllable and a two-syllable word in each pair. For example:

  boat and cookies
  father and tree
  table and barn
  umbrella and boy
  music and pie
  cookies and bird
  table and bed
  top and apple
  father and house

Here are all your toys (or pictures).

Hold up a toy like this; speak into the "mike" like this and say what you have. For example: Here's a barn. Etc. Now you "hear" your own voice.

LESSON #39

Sense Training	Repeat #38.
Lipreading	Repeat #38, adding another color, perhaps purple.
	Introduce preposition *"in"* in action games, such as: hiding in the cupboard, putting things in boxes, cups, baskets, etc., sitting in the rocking chair, etc.
	Use of the question *Where?* with answer in phrases, using *on, under* and *in*.
Speech	Using the same procedure as in #28, practice *qu*-words such as *queen*.
	Repeat procedures as in #35, #36, #37, #38, adding *qu-* words.
Auditory Training	Repeat #38.
	Now, I shall shut my eyes, and you say any of these words. I shall try to guess what word you say. Speak up clearly. (Use words (and objects or pictures) as in #38).

LESSON #40

Sense Training	Repeat #32 to #38.
Lipreading	Repeat #38. Introduce any other colors.
Speech	Using the same procedure as in #28, practice all words (singly, in phrases and sentences, beginning with the various consonants.
Auditory Training	Repeat #38.
	Emphasize listening to own voice.
	Develop awareness of two syllable word as compared with one syllable word.
	Select a few one syllable and a few two syllable words. Use piano to demonstrate "beat" and accent.

LESSON #41

Sense Training   Picture Lotto: picture of animals.

Lipreading   Names of animals as in picture lotto.

What is this? *A monkey.*
Find the other *monkey* (or, another monkey).
Put the *monkeys* together.
The *monkey* is funny.
He does *funny* things. (Use pictures to illustrate.)

He has *big, big* feet.
He has a *big, big* mouth.
He has *little* eyes.
He has a *long, long* tail.

What is this? *An elephant.*
Find the other *elephant* (or, another).
Put the *elephants* together.
The elephant is very *big.*
He has a *long, long* trunk.
He has *little* eyes.
He has *big, big* ears.
He has a *little* tail.
He has very *funny* feet.

Other animals in the group may consist of: a bear, a tiger, a lion, a camel, a dog, a cat, a mouse, a horse, etc.

Make use of *adjectives* such as *big, little, funny, long, cross, slow, fast.*

Speech and
Auditory Training   Review consonants in beginning or initial position in words. At least one word for each consonant.
Use of words in phrases and sentences. Consonants include: b, d, p, t, m, n, wh, k, h, w, g, l, r, f, v, th, s, z, sh, ch, j, y, qu.

Select one consonant. For example: *b*.
   Use *b* with each vowel, followed by a word.
   For example: ba ba ba   bath
                             boobooboo   boot
                             boobooboo   book
                             bo bo bo   bomb
                             bawbawbaw   ball
                             beebeebee   bee
                             boeboeboe   boat
                             bowbowbow   bow
                             baebaebae   bear
                             bi bi bi   bib
                             be be be   bed
                             ba(r)ba(r)   barn
                             bu bu bu   bun
                             burburbur   bird
                             biebiebie   bike
                             boiboiboi   boy
                             buebuebue   bugle

Use pictures depicting activities revolving about
   these words. Select pictures which have as many
   of the above objects, actions, etc., contained
   within one picture, if possible.
   For example: a picture of a *boy* having a *bath*,
      and playing in the water with a *ball* and a
      boat.
   Initiate a discussion of the picture, using the
      words orally and listening to the words
      spoken, including own voice. For example:
   What is the boy doing? He is having a *bath*.
   Where is he? *In the bathtub.*
   What do you see in the water? *A ball.*
   What else do you see? *A boat.*
   What is this *in the boat? A bee.*
   Do you see something else on the water? *A bird.*
   Now, tell a story about the picture.
      A *boy* is having a *bath*.
      He is playing with a *boat*.
      There is a little *bee* in the *boat*.

I see a *bird* sitting on the water.
A *ball* is going up and down in the water.
The *boy* is having fun.

Pretend you are having a *bath*.
Yes, this is the way we have a *bath*. Rub. Rub.
Rub.

Rhythm

Use of recording or piano.
Listen. Play,
    "This is the way we have a *bath*,
    Have a *bath*, have a *bath*;
    This is the way we have a *bath*,
    Before we go to *bed*."
Fold your arms like this. (Right hand is placed on
    left upper arm; left hand placed on right upper
    arm.) Rub your hands up and down on your
    arms.
Keep time to music with up and down movements
    of hands on upper arms.
Now, put your hands on your legs and rub up
    and down. Keep time to music.

Listen to the music. Now, say, "I had a *bath*."
    (If piano is used, middle C, then F, G, A.)
Try for some variation in pitch as words are said.

Work out various rhythmic movements for speech
    and action with music, following each picture
    story.

LESSON #42

Sense Training

Picture Lotto:
    pictures of animals
    pictures of a family
    pictures of flowers

Lipreading

Names of aniamls as in picture lotto, using same
    procedure as outlined in #42.
Names of members of a family, using same proce-
    dure as outlined for names of animals.
Names of some flowers, such as lily, rose, daisy.

Speech and
Auditory Training   Review consonants in beginning or initial position
                        in words. At least one word for each consonant.
                        Use of words in phrases and sentences. Conso-
                        nants include: b, d, p, t, m, n, wh, k, h, w, g,
                        l, r, f, v, th, s, z, sh, ch, j, y, qu.

                        Select one consonant, other than *b*. For example:
                        d. Use *d* with each vowel, followed by a word.
                        For example:

dadada	daddy
doodoodoo	do
doedoedoe	door
do do do	dog
dawdawdaw	doll
deedeedee	deer
dowdowdow	down
daedaedae	daisy
di di di	dinner
de de de	desk
da(r) da(r)	dark
du du du	duck
durdurdur	dirty
diediedie	diningroom
doidoidoi	doily
dueduedue	duel

                        Use pictures depicting activities revolving about
                        these words. Select pictures which have as many
                        of the above objects, actions, etc., as possible
                        contained within one picture.
                        For example: a picture of *Daddy* standing at a
                        door waiting for a *dog* that is running *down*
                        the steps, with a *doll* in its mouth.
                        Initiate a discussion of the picture, using a pro-
                        cedure similar to that in #41.

Rhythm   Use of recording or piano.
                        Select or "make up" a song about any or several of
                        the items or activities indicated above.
                        Emphasize keeping time, pitch, volume, and rhyth-
                        mic movements for speech and action with
                        music.

LESSON #43

Sense Training

An exercise relating to size: *big* and *little*.
Five big objects and five little objects:

a big ball	a little ball
a big shoe	a little shoe
a big boat	a little boat
a big house	a little house
a big flower	a little flower

Place the big objects in one row, the little ones opposite in another row, as above.

Here is a big ball.	Here is a little ball.
Here is a big shoe.	Put the little shoe here.
Here is a big boat.	Find the little boat.
	Where does it go?
	Etc.
These are *big*.	These are *little*.

Gather all the objects into one group.
  Now, we will put all the big things together, and all the little things together, like this.
  These are *big*.   These are *little*.
Gather all the objects into one group.
  Now, you put all the big things here, and all the little things there.

Lipreading

Big. Little. In phrases, using above objects.

Begin with *a big ball* and *a little ball.*

Find *a big ball*. Find *a little ball.*

When these have been understood and fairly well established, introduce a *big* shoe, a *little* shoe. etc.

Review, names of animals, members of a family and names of a few flowers as in #42.

Speech,
Auditory Training,
and Rhythm

Repeat #41 and #42 in detail.
Listen to music, varying in volume and pitch.
  Play high chord on piano.

Say "meow" like the cat.
Say it softly. Say it loudly.
Play low chord on piano.
Say "Bowow" like the dog.
Say it softly. Say it loudly.
Play marching music. Quickly. Slowly.
March in time, quickly, then slowly.

LESSON #44

Sense Training

Review *Big* and *Little,* as in #43.
Introduce pictures or cutouts of same objects, in large and small sizes.
Use in similar way as the objects were.
Place little object (ball) on little cutout (ball).
Place little object (ball) on little cutout (ball).
Similarly for other objects and cutouts.

Lipreading

Big. Little. In phrases with nouns, naming the objects and cutouts.
Use several cutouts of *big* balls, several of *little* balls.
Here is a *big* ball. Here is another *big* ball. Find another *big* ball.
Here is a *little* ball. Here is another *little* ball. Find another *little* ball.
Here is a *big* basket.

Find a *big* ball.	Put it in the *big* basket.
Find a *little* ball.	Put it in the *big* basket.
	Etc.

Use several cutouts of *big* and *little* shoes, boats, houses and flowers.

Find a *big* boat.	Put it in the *big* basket.
Find a *little* shoe.	Put it in the *big* basket.
Find a *big* house.	Put it in the *big* basket.
	Etc.

Speech and Auditory Training

Review consonants in beginning or initial position in words. At least one word for each consonant. Use of words in phrases and sentences. Consonants include: b, d, p, t, m, n, wh, k, h, w, g, l, r, f, v, th, s, z, sh, ch, j, y, qu.

Select one consonant other than *b* or *d*.

For example: *p*.

Use *p* with each vowel followed by a word.

For example:

papapa	pat
poopoopoo	pool
poopoopoo	put
po po po	pot
pawpawpaw	paw
peepeepee	peek
poepoepoe	pole
powpowpow	powder
paepaepae	paper
pi pi pi	pin
pe pe pe	pet
pa(r)pa(r)	pardon
pu pu pu	puppy
purpurpur	purple
piepiepie	pie
poipoipoi	point
puepuepue	pure

Use pictures depicting activities revolving about these words. Select pictures which have as many of the above objects, actions, etc., as possible contained within one picture.

For example: a little girl *pointing* to a *pie* with one hand, and *patting* a *pet puppy* with the other. Perhaps, a *pool* of water is nearby as well as a *pot* of *purple* flowers. Etc.

Initiate a discussion of the picture, using the words orally, and listening to the words spoken. Listen to own voice.

For example:

What is the little girl doing?

She is *pointing* to the *pie*.

She is *patting* the *puppy*.

The *puppy* is a *pet*.

You have a *pet*. It is a *pussy cat*.

Here is a top *puppy*.

Can you *point* to the *puppy*?

Pat the *puppy* on the head.

What is this?

A *pool.*

The boy is going to swim in the *pool.*

What is this?

A *pot* with some flowers in it.

We have a pot of flowers over there.

Point to our flowers.

What color are the flowers by the pool?

Purple.

What color are our flowers?

Pink.

Now, tell a story about the picture.

Rhythm   Use of recording or piano.

Select or "make up" a rhyme to music. Act out and say, while record is playing or piano is being played, something similar to:

"*Pat* your *pretty puppy,*
And *point* to the school.
Point to your *pal,*
And *pull* her to the *pool.*"

"*Pull* a *pink poppy,*
Put it in a *pot.*
Take a *piece* of *pie,*
And eat it while it's hot."

Try for variation in pitch as expressions are said along with piano: I have a *puppy.* I have a *pie.* Etc.

LESSON #45

Sense Training   Repeat #43 and #44, using more pictures of objects, *big* and *little.*

Go on excursion about the nursery school looking for *big* and *little* objects.

Use pictures of animals and flowers in lotto game and try to find larger pictures illustrating larger animals and flowers to match them.

Use *big* and *little,* with furniture in use in the playroom, as the colors, red, yellow and blue, were used with these objects in #21. Adult chairs should also be used to clearly define differences.

Speech and
Auditory Training   Review consonants with words as in #44.
Select one consonant other than *b, d,* or *p.*

For example: *t*

ta ta ta	tap
tootootoo	tooth
tootootoo	took
to to to	top
tawtawtaw	talk
teeteetee	teeth
toetoetoe	toe
towtowtow	towel
taetaetae	tail
ti ti ti	till
te te te	tell
ta(r)ta(r)	tar
tu tu tu	tub
turturtur	turn
tietietie	tie
toitoitoi	toy
tuetuetue	tune

Picture description using as many of above words as possible. Discuss. Ask questions. Answer questions.

Rhythm   Use of recording or piano. Act out, and say:
Tap your *toe,*
And *turn* around.
Take a *top,*
And spin it now.

Try for variation in pitch as expressions are said along with piano: The dog as a *tail.* I *try* to *talk.* Etc.

Match accented words in sentences with emphasized chords or notes on piano: I *spun* the *top.* Etc.

LESSON #46

Sense Training   Heavy paper cutouts of: a big red ball
                                                 a big red house
                                                 a big red umbrella
     a big red flower
     a big red butterfly
     a little red ball
     a little red house
     a little red umbrella
     a little red flower
     a little red butterfly.

These may be matched across according to size; down according to object.

Thus: a big red ball   a big red house
        a little red ball   a little red house.
                                Etc.

Lipreading   *Big* and *little* in phrases with the color word "red," as above, using just two phrases to begin with, and adding other phrases one or two at a time.

Speech and
Auditory Training   Review consonant with words as in #44.

Select one consonant other than *b, d, p,* or *t.*

For example: *m*

ma ma ma	man
moomoomoo	moon
mo mo mo	mop
mawmawmaw	Momma
meemeemee	meat
moemoemoe	more
mowmowmow	mouth
maemaemae	make
mi mi mi	milk
me me me	melon
ma(r)ma(r)	marble
mu mu mu	money
miemiemie	mine
muemuemue	music

Picture description using as many of the above words as possible. Discuss. Ask questions.
Answer questions
Use of *big* and *little* where possible.

Rhythm	Use of recording or piano, and illustrations.

> "The *man* in the *moon*
> Has a *mouth* like *me,*
> But he doesn't drink *milk,*
> And he doesn't eat *meat.*"

Using piano chords, practice above sentences for accent on correct word.

LESSON #47

Sense Training
Heavy paper cutouts of objects as in #46, in red, yellow and blue.

These may be matched according to size, object or color.

Lipreading
Big and *little,* in phrases with red, yellow or blue. First, use the color red all the way through; then yellow, then blue, then in any order.

Speech and Auditory Training
Review consonants with words as in #44.

Select one consonant other than those already used.

For example: *n*

na na na	nap
noonoonoo	noon
noonoonoo	nook
no no no	(k)nob
nawnawnaw	(g)naw
neeneenee	(k)nee
noenoenoe	nose
nownownow	now
naenaenae	name
ni ni ni	nickel
ne ne ne	neck
nu nu nu	nut
nienienie	night
nuenuenue	new

Picture description using as many of the above words as possible. Discuss. Ask questions. Answer questions.

Use of *big* and *little, red, yellow* and *blue,* also.

Rhythm   Use of recording or piano, illustrations, and
                  dramatizations.
                      "I have a *knee,*
                      A *nose* and a *name.*
                      I have a *nickel,*
                      To go to the game."

                  Use simple, short sentences to practice accent.

                      I have a *nickel.* Etc.
                      (Heavy piano chord; heavy accent.)

                  Free running to music. Free walking to music.
                  Listen. What do you do? Walk? Run?
                  When you "hear" running music, *run.*
                  When you "hear" walking music, *Walk.*

LESSON #48

Sense Training   Repeat #47.

Lipreading   Visit the store in the Workshop Village or Town
                   and "buy" various objects, *big* and *little* in red,
                   yellow and blue colors. Requests may take the
                   form of:
                       I want to buy a big red umbrella,
                       or
                       A big red umbrella, please.
                       Etc.

Speech and
Auditory Training Review consonants as in #44.

                   Select another consonant, for example: *wh*
                       whawhawha   wham
                       whoowhoowhoo
                       whowhowho
                       whawwhawwhaw   what
                       wheewheewhee   wheel
                       whoewhoewhoe
                       whowwhowwhow
                       whaewhaewhae   whale

whiwhiwhi	whip
whewhewhe	when
wha(r)wha(r)	
whuwhuwhu	
whurwhurwhur	whirl
whiewhiewhie	white
whoiwhoiwhoi	
whuewhuewhue	whew!

Picture description with questions and answers, and where suitable, with *big* and *little* and colors red, yellow and blue.

Rhythm Use of recording or piano with illustrations.
"The big white boat,
 And the big white whale,
 Whip through the water,
 And sail and sail."

Practice *high* and *low* pitches, using a word such as *Whee!*

Play suitable music. Movements to music.
Run. Walk. Whirl. Wham (Bang).

Now, listen to the music. What does it tell you to do? Do what the music says.

Say (as heavy and light chords are played on piano), with accent in correct places:

The big white boat, Etc.

LESSON #49

Sense Training Repeat #47.

Include additional cutouts of same objects of other colors, such as orange, green and purple. These may be matched according to color, size (big or little, and object.

Lipreading Continued experience with objects, both big and little), and in various colors.

Speech and
Auditory Training   Review consonants as in #44.

Select another consonant, for example: *k,* and *c.*

ca ca ca	cat
coocoocoo	coo (like the dove)
coocoocoo	cook
co co co	cot
cawcawcaw	caw (like the crow)
keekeekee	key
cowcowcow	cow
caecaecae	cage
ki ki ki	kiss
ke ke ke	kennel
ca(r)ca(r)	car
cu cu cu	cup
curcurcur	curl
kiekiekie	kite
coicoicoi	coil (stove)
cuecuecue	cucumber

Picture description with questions and anwers, with adjectives *big* and *little,* and with colors.

Rhythm   Use of piano or recording, with illustrations.
"The cat saw the crow,
    The cook saw the kite.
    The cow ate the hay,
    And slept all night.

"The monkey in the cage,
    Sat up all night,
    Got a kiss from the lady,
    With curls all white."

Use the four lines of the first verse, with piano, to practice the saying of sentences with accent on the correct words, and with fluency.

For example: The cat saw the crow. Etc.

Practice humming to music and swaying in rhythm.

Fun with rhythmic movements and music. (Run, walk, etc.)

LESSON #50

Sense Training   Repeat #47. Include other colors.

Lipreading   Picture description, using phrases containing adjectives *big* and *little* with various colors.

Speech,
Auditory Training,
and Rhythm   Experience with initial consonant *h* as from #41, on.

LESSON #51

Sense Training   Quantity. Matching numbers of objects, for example:

one block to one block;
two blocks to two blocks;
three blocks to three blocks.

Gather together, nine small open top boxes,
one block, one airplane, one cup;
two blocks, two airplanes, two cups;
three blocks, three airplanes, three cups.

Arrange boxes, three across and three down.

Each of the boxes across the top are for the *ones*.
Each of the boxes in the second row across is for the *twos*.
Each of the boxes in the third row across is for the *threes*.

Put one block in one box, one airplane in one box, one cup in one box.
Put two blocks in one box, two airplanes in one box, two cups in one box.
Put three blocks in one box, three airplanes in one box, and three cups in one box.
Make number picture cards—a large black spot for each unit: X   X   X
                              X
                                   X   X

Place one block on the *one* card, two on the *two*, etc.

Lipreading	Counting toys, arranged in row from left to right: one, two, three.
Speech, Auditory Training, and Rhythm	Experience with initial consonant *w,* as from #41, on.

LESSON #52

Sense Training	Repeat #50 and #51.
Lipreading	Repeat #50 and #51. Repeat #35 and #39.
	Additional experiences with *in, on* and *under,* using *big* and *little* objects of various colors, as in *hide* and *find* games.
Speech, Auditory Training, and Rhythm	Experience with initial conosnant *g,* as from #41, on.

LESSON #53

Sense Training	Repeat #50 and #51.
Lipreading	Repeat #52.
Speech, Auditory Training, and Rhythm	Experience with initial consonant *l,* as from #41, on.

LESSON #54

Sense Training	Make several sets of number picture cards, illustrating familiar objects in groups of one, two, three, four, five.
	Match all the *ones.* Match all the *twos.* Etc.

Lipreading   Repeat #52.

Use of number picture cards.
  How many are here? Two.
  How many are here? One.
  How many are here? Three.
  How many are here? Five.
  How many are here? Four.
Put two blocks on any picture of *two*.
Put four blocks on any picture of *four*, Etc.
Count to five, any group of five objects, arranged
  in row. Count from left to right.

Speech,
Auditory Training,
and Rhythm   Experience with initial consonant *r*, as from #41,
                     on.

LESSON #55

Sense Training   Repeat #50 and #54. Repeat #31 and #32.

Lipreading   Repeat #52 and #54.

Speech,
Auditory Training,
and Rhythm   Experience with initial consonant *f*, as from #41,
                     on.

LESSON #56

Sense Training   Repeat #50 and #54. Repeat #31, #32 and #33.

Lipreading   Repeat #52 and #54.

Speech,
Auditory Training,
and Rhythm   Experience with initial consonant *v*, as from #41,
                     on.

LESSON #57

Sense Training   Repeat #54. Repeat #31, #32, #33.

Lipreading   Gather together a number of objects (or cutouts) of various colors, from *one* to *five* of each object, both *big* and *little*.

Take one object or cutout.
   Here is a bow. It is big. It is red.
   This is a big red bow.
What is this? A big red bow.

Take two objects or cutouts, little and red.
   Here is a car. Here is another car.
   How many cars are there? Two.
   Here are two cars.
   What color are the cars? Red.
   Here are two red cars.
   Are the cars big? No.
   Are the cars little? Yes.
   Here are two little red cars.
What do we have here? Two little red cars.
   Etc.

Speech,
Auditory Training,
and Rhythm   Experience with initial consonant *th*, as from #41, on.

Review of selected consonants and words from #41 to #56.

LESSON #58

Sense Training   Pairs of familiar objects, old and new.
Put all the new things together.
Put all the old things together.
Match in pairs.

Lipreading   Repeat #57.

Discussion of old things and new things, with emphasis on the adjectives *new* and *old*.

For example: a new ball, an old ball,
a new hat, an old hat,
a new book, an old book.
Etc.

Speech, *Auditory Training,* *and Rhythm*	Experience with initial consonant *s,* as from #41, on.

LESSON #59

Sense Training	Repeat #58.
Lipreading	Repeat #57 and #58.
Speech, *Auditory Training,* *and Rhythm*	Experience with initial consonant *z,* as from #41, on.

LESSON #60

Sense Training	Repeat #58. Introduce matching and recognition of dirty things and clean things.
Lipreading	Repeat #57 and #58.
	Discussion of things that are, *old, new, dirty* or *clean,* with an emphasis on the adjectives.
Speech, *Auditory Training,* *and Rhythm*	Experience with initial consonant *sh,* as from #41, on.

LESSON #61

Sense Training	Repeat #60.
Lipreading	Repeat #60.
Speech, Auditory Training, *and Rhythm*	Experience with initial consonant *ch,* as from #41, on.

LESSON #62

Sense Training
and *Lipreading*   Review of adjectives, *big, little, old, new, dirty, clean,* in phrases and sentences, followed by questions and answers.
Introduce *quiet* and *noisy*. Dramatize.

Speech, Auditory Training,
and Rhythm   Experience with initial consonant *j,* as from #41, on.

LESSON #63

Sense Training
and *Lipreading*   Repeat #62.

Speech, Auditory Training,
and Rhythm   Experience with initial consonant *y,* as from #41, on.

LESSON #64

Sense Training
and *Lipreading*   Repeat #62.

Speech, Auditory Training,
and Rhythm   Experience with initial consonant *qu,* as from #41, on.

LESSON #65

Sense Training
and *Lipreading*   Repeat #62. Introduce: *That's mine.*
                                                That's yours.
Locate a series of personal possessions for this lesson.

Speech, Auditory Training,
and Rhythm   Select initial consonants from #41 to #64, with words. Use in phrases and simple sentences. Review speech with listening.

LESSON #66

Sense Training
and Lipreading   Repeat #65.

Speech, Auditory Training,
and Rhythm   Introduce plurals for practice in use of final *s*.
Two ball*s*, three shoe*s*, four elephant*s*, etc.

LESSON #67

Sense Training
and Lipreading   Repeat #65.

Speech, Auditory Training,
and Rhythm   Use of plurals to provide practice in developing
the final *s*. Besides phrases with one, two, three,
four and five, expressions such as, a few blocks,
many blocks, some blocks, (and other nouns)
may be introduced.

LESSON #68

Sense Training
and Lipreading   Repeat #65. Introduce: I am (Miss _____)
You are (Mary).
Then: I am Mary
You are Miss _____.
Etc.
Then: He is (John).
She is Ann.

Speech, Auditory Training,
and Rhythm   Repeat #67. Continue with I am _____,
You are _____,
He is _____,
She is _____.

Questions and answers.
What is *your* name?
What is *my* name?
What is *his* name?
What is *her* name?

LESSON #69

Sense Training
and *Lipreading*   Review adjectives (color, number, descriptive), in
                        phrases, simple sentences and with question and
                        answer games.
                        Using illustrations, review health rules, and drama-
                        tize.

Speech, Auditory Training,
and *Rhythm*   Select one nursery rhyme. Dramatize story. Once
                        idea has been fairly well established, select each
                        word from rhyme which can be either illustrated
                        or acted out, and practice for speech and listen-
                        ing. Review rhyme in full to music. Use props.
                        Baa Baa Black Sheep is usually easily under-
                        stood.

LESSON #70

Sense Training
and *Lipreading*   Repeat #68 and #69.

Speech, Auditory Training,
and *Rhythm*   Repeat #68 and #69.

LESSON #71

Sense Training
and *Lipreading*   Play Store. Practice counting pennies to five.
                        Practice counting purchased articles.
                        Practice asking for things to buy.
                        Practice asking "How much is it?"
                        Practice use of colors of requested
                            items.
                        Practice asking an answering one an-
                            other.

Speech, Auditory Training,
and *Rhythm*   Play a game, "Pass the Plate." On each paper plate
                        print a consonant. Make a number of speech
                        cards, each containing a picture of an object or
                        verb beginning with a specific consonant. Make

several for each initial consonant. Each person gets a card from the "h" plate. When a particular word beginning with "h" is asked for, the one holding the word card must raise hand and say, "I have it." Plate is passed, and card is dropped into it. All "h" words illustrated with picture must go on the "h" plate, "p" words on the "p" plate.

LESSON #72

Sense Training
and *Lipreading*

A visit to a real Bakeshop.

Upon return, glance through many pictures of bakeshops, and of bakers with baked goods.

Bake a real cake.

Pictures of ingredients. Practice vocabulary: flour, sugar, milk, mix, spoon, pan, stove, oven, hot, turn on, oven door, shut, wait, finished, cool, ice, butter, spread, cut, a piece of cake, eat.

Playhouse: use of stove, toy utensils.

Playtown: Go to the baker's. Use of standups for baker and foods. Use of flannel board figures.

Speech, Auditory Training,
and *Rhythm*

Repeat #71.

LESSON #73

Sense Training
and *Lipreading*

Bakershop vocabulary. Many different pictures for discussions, flannel, cardboard and wooden figures. Setting up and decorating a shelf for a bakeshop. Buying baked goods. Review of counting, and vocabulary of buying.

Speech, Auditory Training
and *Rhythm*

"Pass the Plate-Speech Game."
Rhyme "Hot Cross Buns."

Plate XXXIV. Having used a prepared "mix," the children, with teacher, are waiting for the brownies to bake in the portable electric oven. (See Lesson #72.)

LESSON #74

Sense Training
and *Lipreading*   A See-Quee puzzle, with pictures of baking proce-
                      dures in sequence, with vocabulary and conver-
                      sation.

Speech, Auditory Training,
and *Rhythm*   "What Do I Hear?" game. Alternate gross sounds
                      and words. First, with lipreading and speech.
                      Then listen without watching.

LESSON #75

Sense Training
and *Lipreading*

A visit to real Post Office.

A talk with a real mailman.

Mailing real letters in a mailbox.

Collecting real mail from mailbox at school.

Playing mailman with uniform, mailbag and letters.

Vocabulary: letter, stamp, mailbox, mailman, post office, mail a letter, open your own letter, etc.

Take a group of small envelopes to fit small mailbox. In each envelope place a small picture of an object.

Mail your letter. Whom did you send the letter to? Tell him to get his letter. Tell him to open his letter. Ask him what is in the letter. "I got '*a wagon*' in my letter." Etc.

Speech, Auditory Training,
and *Rhythm*

Rhyme, "I Sent A Letter To My Love."

"Pass the Plate" Speech Game. Select consonants relative to words in Post Office vocabulary.

Repeat #74. Use vocabulary of Post Office.

LESSON #76

Experience For General Language Development
(Understanding and Speech)

A visit to a real fire station.
On return to nursery school:
Collecting toys, fire engine, fire stations, fireman, etc.
Learning the names of things and persons.
Safety rules.
Dramatizing. Discussion.
Specific practice in lipreading vocabulary.
Opportunity for conversation.

Speech, Auditory Training, and Rhythm

Experience with consonants in initial position in words as outlined in Lessons #41 to #64.

Attention to production of *final consonants* in familiar words. For example: *b*. Use as many vowels as possible in combinations.

_____b	ab ab ab	cab
*oob*ooboob		
*oeb*oeboeb		robe
ob ob ob		knob
*awb*awbawb		sob
*eeb*eebeeb		
*owb*owbowb		
*aeb*aebaeb		babe
ib ib ib		bib
eb eb eb		web
*a(r)b*a(r)b		
ub ub ub		tub
*urb*urburb		curb
*ieb*iebieb		
*oib*oiboib		
*ueb*uebueb		tube

Rhymes in which some of these words appear: (Illustrations)

Old King Cole	robe
Rockabye Baby	babe bib
Little Miss Muffet	web
Little Bo Peep	sob
RubaDubDub	tub

Speech play with rhyming syllables:
bab, cab, dab, fab, gab, hab, jab, lab, mab, etc.
boob, coob, doob, foob, goob, hoob, joob, etc.
bobe, cobe, dobe, fobe, gobe, hobe, jobe, etc.
bob, cob, dob, fob, gob, hob, job, lob, mob, etc.
Etc.

LESSON #77

Experience For General Language Development
(Understanding and Speech)

A visit to a real Police Station.
On return to the Nursery School:
Collecting toys, police wagon, traffic signs and lights, policeman, etc.

Learning the names of things and persons.
Safety rules. Stop. Wait. Go.
Dramatizing. Discussion.
Specific practice in lipreading vocabulary.
Opportunity for conversation.

Speech, Auditory Training, and Rhythm

Experience with consonants in initial position in words as outlined in Lessons #41 to #64.

Attention to production of *final consonants* in familiar words. For example: *d.*

_____d.	*ad* ad ad	lad
	*ood*oodood	food
	*ood*oodood	good
	*oed*oedoed	road
	od od od	nod
	*aw*dawdawd	rod
	*ee*deedeed	bead
	*ow*dowdowd	cloud
	*aed*aedaed	maid
	id id id	hid
	ed ed ed	head
	*a(r)d*a(r)d	hard
	ud ud ud	mud
	*ur*durdurd	heard
	*ie*diedied	ride
	*oid*oidoid	
	*ued*uedued	

Rhymes in which some of these words appear.

"Make up" rhymes to include words. Stories. Pictures.

Through listening identify words and gross sounds.

Speech play through rhyming syllables:
  bad, cad, dad, fad, gad, had, jad, lad, mad, nad, etc.
  bood, cood, dood, food, good, hood, jood,
  bode, code, dode, fode, gode, hode, jode, mode, etc.
  bod, cod, dod, fod, god, hod, jod, lod, mod, nod, etc.
  Etc.

LESSON #78

Experience For General Language Development
(Understanding and Speech)

A visit to a real Farm
On return to the Nursery School:
Collecting toy animals (stands up) placed about the barn.
Learning the names of the animals, (review of earlier play experiences).
The farmer, hens, eggs, ducks, geese, etc.
Dramatizing feeding of the animal, poultry, etc.
Specific practice in lipreading vocabulary.
Opportunity for conversation.

Speech, Auditory Training, and Rhythm

Experience with consonants in initial position in words as outlined in Lessons #41 to #64.

Attention to production of *final consonants* in familiar words. For example: *t.*

_____t	*at* at at	hat
	*oot*ootoot	boot
	*oot*ootoot	foot
	*oet*oetoet	coat
	ot ot ot	cot
	*awt*awtawt	caught
	*eet*eeteet	beet
	*owt*owtowt	out
	*aet*aetaet	ate
	it it it	hit
	et et et	pet
	*a(r)t*a(r)ta(r)t	cart
	ut ut ut	cut
	*urt*urturt	dirt
	*iet*ietiet	bite
	*oit*oitoit	
	*uet*uetuet	

Rhymes in which some of these words appear.
"Make up" rhymes to include words. Stories. Pictures.

Plate XXXV. After a visit to a real farm, a mural was drawn and painted while the children watched. Follow-up conversation takes place. (See Lesson #78.)

Through listening identify words and gross sounds. (Differentiate)
Speech play through rhyming syllables:
bat, cat, dat, fat, gat, hat, jat, lat, mat, nat, etc.
boot, coot, doot, foot, goot, hoot, joot, moot, etc.
bote, cote, dote, fote, gote, hote, jote, mote, etc.
bot, cot, dot, fot, got, hot, jot, lot, mot, not, etc.
Etc.

LESSON #79

Experience For General Language Development
(Understanding and Speech)
A visit to a real Grocery and Meat Market.
On return to the Nursery School:
Collecting foods to place in play store.
Learning the names of the foods.
Buying and selling. Storekeeper. Customer.
Specific practice in lipreading vocabulary.
Opportunity for conversation.

Speech, Auditory Training, and Rhythm
Experience with consonants in initial position in words as outlined in Lessons #41 to #64.
Attention to production of *final consonants* in familiar words. For example: *p*.

———p	*ap* ap ap	tap
	*oop*oopoop	hoop
	*oop*oopoop	Oops!
	*oep*oepoep	rope
	op op op	top
	*awp*awpawp	stop
	*eep*eepeep	peep
	*owp*owpowp	
	*aep*aepaep	tape
	ip ip ip	lip
	ep ep ep	step
	*a(r)p*a(r)p	harp
	up up up	up
	*urp*urpurp	
	*iep*iepiep	pipe
	*oip*oipoip	
	*uep*uepuep	

Rhymes in which some of these words appear.
"Make up" rhymes to include words. Stories. Pictures.
Through listening differentiate between words and gross sounds.
Speech play through rhyming syllables:
bap, cap, dap, fap, gap, hap, jap, kap, map, nap, etc.
boop, coop, doop, foop, goop, hoop, joop, moop, etc.
bope, cope, dope, fope, gope, hope, jope, mope, etc.
bop, cop, dop, fop, gop, hop, jop, lop, mop, nop, etc.
Etc.

LESSON #80

Experience For General Language Development
(Understanding and Speech)

A visit to an Animal Hospital and Kennel.
Follow-up language experiences in Nursery School.

Speech, Auditory Training, and Rhythm

Experience with consonants in initial position in words.

Final consonant _____m. (As in Lesson #76)

Follow-up activities with rhymes, listening and speech play.

LESSON #81

Experience For General Language Development
(Understanding and Speech)

A visit to a Pet Shop.
Follow-up language experiences in Nursery School.

Speech, Auditory Training, and Rhythm

Experience with consonants in initial position in words.

Final consonant _____n. (As in Lesson #76)

Follow-up activities with rhymes, listening and speech play.

LESSON #82

Experience For General Language Development
(Understanding and Speech)

A visit to a Hardware Shop.
Follow-up language experiences in Nursery School.

Speech, Auditory Training, and Rhythm

Experience with consonants in initial position in words.

Final consonant _____k. (Use #76 as example)

Follow-up activities with rhymes, listening and speech play.

LESSON #83

Experience For General Language Development
(Understanding and Speech)

A visit to a Garage.
Follow-up language experiences in Nursery School.

Speech, Auditory Training, and Rhythm

Experience with consonants in initial position in words.

Final consonant _____g. (Use #76 as example)

Follow-up activities with rhymes, listening and speech play.

LESSON #84

A visit to a Drug Store.   Final consonant _____l.

LESSON #85

A visit to a Magazine Shop.   Final consonant _____r.

LESSON #86

A visit to a Lumber Mill.   Final consonant _____f.

LESSON #87

A visit to a City Hall.   Final consonant _____v.

LESSON #88

A visit to a Camp with boats.   Final consonant _____th.

LESSON #89

A visit to an Airport.   Final consonant _____s.

LESSON #90

A visit to a Book Store.   Final consonant _____z.

LESSON #91

A visit to a Dress Shop.	Final consonant _____sh.
A visit to a Men's Shop.	Final consonant _____ch.

LESSON #92

A visit to a Flower Shop. Final consonant _____j.

LESSON #93

A visit to a Furniture Store. Final consonant _____y.

LESSON #94

A visit to a Big School. Final consonant _____ng.

LESSON #95

A visit to a Train Station. Review of consonants in words, in final or initial positions.

LESSON #96

A visit to a Park. Review of consonants as in #95.

LESSON #97

A visit to a Bus Depot. Review of consonants as in #95.

LESSON #98

A visit to a Music Shop. Review of consonants as in #95.

LESSON #99

A visit to an Art Shop. Review of consonants as in #96.

LESSON #100

A visit to the Docks & Ships.   Review of consonants
                                       as in #96.

LESSON #101

A visit to a Doctor's Office.   Review of consonants
                                       as in #96.

LESSON #102

A visit to see a Hospital   Review of consonants
Building and grounds.   as in #96.

LESSON #103

A visit to a Dentist's Office.   Review of consonants
                                       as in #96.

LESSON #104

A visit to a Toy Shop.   Review of consonants
                                       as in #96.

LESSON #105

A visit to the Armories.   Review of consonants
                                       as in #96.

LESSON #106

A visit to a Photographer's Studio.   Review of consonants
                                       as in #96.

LESSON #107

A visit to a Candy Shop.   Review of consonants
                                       as in #96.

LESSON #108

A visit to a Bank.   Review of consonants
                                   as in #96.

LESSON #109

A visit to a Restaurant.   Review of consonants
                                   as in #96.

LESSON #110

Experience For General Language Development
(Understanding and Speech)

A Health Rule: Keeping clean.   Vocabulary.
                                   Dramatization.
                                   Conversation with questions
                                       and answers.

Speech, Auditory Training, and Rhythm

Experience with consonants in medial position in words.

For example:

___d_____	daddy
___b_____	baby
___p_____	paper
___m_____	momma
___n_____	dinner
___l_____	elephant
___r_____	tree
___f_____	elephant
___v_____	cover
___th____	mother
___s_____	saucer
___z_____	puzzle
___sh____	brushing
___ch____	catching
___g_____	bugle

Etc.

LESSON #111

Experience For General Language Development
(Understanding and Speech)

A Health Rule: Fresh air, breathing deeply.
                 Breathe deeply, shoulders down, breath out.
                 Say "aw" when breathing out.
                 Other sounds while breathing out.
                 Attention to vocabulary and conversation.

Speech, Auditory Training, and Rhythm

Select any consonant. Establish a group of words with the consonant in initial, medial and final position. For example: *p*.
Initial—*p*ie.
Medial—pa*p*er.
Final—to*p*.
Practice sentences containing these words. Select those which are used commonly in everyday life.
Use good illustrations and interesting real experiences.

LESSON #112

Experience For General Language Development
(Understanding and Speech)

A Health Rule: Eating good food.   Vocabulary.
                                        Conversation.

Speech, Auditory Training, and Rhythm

Select any consonant. Practice in a group of words where consonant is situated in initial, medial and final positions.

Practice rhyming words: bat, cat, fat, hat, mat, pat, rat, sat.

Choral speaking in the group: The fat cat sat on a mat.

Individual attention to initial and final consonants.

LESSON #113

Experience For General Language Development
(Understanding and Speech)

A Health Rule: Sleeping.　Go to bed early.
　　　　　　　　　　　　　　Stay in bed.
　　　　　　　　　　　　　　Do not play.
　　　　　　　　　　　　　　Sleep.

　　Vocabulary.
　　Conversation.

Speech, Auditory Training, and Rhythm

Select any consonant to be used in a group of words in initial, medial and final positions.

Practice rhyming words: ball, call, doll, fall, hall, tall, wall.

Choral speaking in the group:　The tall doll,
　　　　　　　　　　　　　　　Leaned on the wall.
　　　　　　　　　　　　　　　The pretty ball,
　　　　　　　　　　　　　　　Rolled in the hall.
　　　　　　　　　　　　　　　Don't fall, doll.
　　　　　　　　　　　　　　　I'll get the ball.

LESSON #114

Experience For General Language Development
(Understanding and Speech)

A Courtesy Rule:　Please and Thank you.
　　　　　　　　　Taking Turns.
　　　　　　　　　Don't push.
　　　　　　　　　Etc.

Speech, Auditory Training, and Rhythm

Consonants in initial, medial and final position in words.
Practice rhyming words.

Choral speaking, with attention to rhythm in speech, accent, and speaking in unison.

Individual attention to initial and final consonants in words.

LESSON #115

Experience For General Language Development
(Understanding and Speech)

What does Mother do at home?   Use of Play House Center.
    Mother gets up.
    She wakes me up.
    She gets breakfast.
    We eat it.
    She helps me get ready for school.
    Then, she brings me to school (in the car, on the bus).

Helping Mother.   I try to dress myself.
                         I eat my breakfast.
                         I put on my coat and hat.
                         I sit still in the car (on the bus).
                         I walk into school myself.
                         I take off my coat.
                         I say "good bye" to Mother.
                         Sometimes, she stays at school.
                         I am good, then, too.

Speech, Auditory Training, and Rhythm

Attention to words beginning with a blend of two sounds.
    For example: br, cr, dr, fr, gr, pr, tr. (*br*own, *cr*y, etc.)
                  bl, cl, fl, gl, pl, sl. (blow, cloud, fly, etc.)
                  sm, sl, sc, sp, st, tw. (smell, sled, etc.)

Emphasis on listening to these words.

Suggested Content for Additional Lessons, with Emphasis on Conversation and Active Participation, with Follow-up Attention to Specific Speech Difficulties.

A. The *different* object in a small group of identical objects. "Find the thing that is *different*."

B. Practice with *ACTION VERBS* such as run, jump, sit, stand, hop, fall, ride, play, read, sleep, eat, go, come, look, see, cut, fold, draw, paint.

C. Practice in simple sentence form with *HAVE* and *HAS*.

D. Practice with *THESE* and *THOSE, THIS* and *THAT,* in every day situations.

A WORD TO THE TEACHER

As you glance back over these suggested "lessons," either as a teacher in the formal sense of the word, or as a teacher in the sense that a parent teaches, too, you realize how many experiences a young child can enjoy during the process of growing, and of developing language skills.

Probably, you realize, too, how much easier it is for the hearing child to accumulate all the vocabulary that goes with these experiences, and how much easier it is for him to recall the right words and expressions when the need arises. In your application of these ideas, you will find it necessary to select part of this lesson, and part of that one, to assist the child in learning to use situations already experienced in order to explain the new to himself. You cannot do his learning for him. His mind must be trained to respond sharply to each new experience. The "teaching" of one lesson after the other, will not solve the language problems incurred by the handicap of deafness. Everything you teach him must have some linkage with his everyday life and his developing mind, so that his training will not become mere superficial activities to keep him occupied. As soon as possible, have him *use spoken language*. It will only be through real experiences with language, and continuous practice of it, on his part, that he will understand and will learn to use it meaningfully and with ease.

It is not expecting too much of a preschool age deaf child with at least average learning ability to learn the language of his world as do little children everywhere. Neither is it asking too much of parents and teachers to make it their job to study each individual child in their care, to discover what to do and how to do it. It is their responsibility. Deaf children can learn to manage language at a normal level, providing they are not mentally incompetent. BUT, they must be trained and taught. It is up to the parents and teachers.

Bibliography

1. Adams, S., "Analysis of Verb Forms in the Speech of Young Children and Their Relation to the Language Learning Process," *Journal of Experimental Education,* 7:141, 1938.
2. Anderson, J., "The Development of Motor, Linguistic and Intellectual Skills in Young Children," *Child Development,* 144–174, 1929.
3. Anderson, W., and Stageberg, N., *Introductory Readings On Language.* New York: Holt, Rinehart and Winston, 1966.
4. Avery, C., "The Social Competence of Preschool Acoustically Handicapped Children," *Volta Review,* June 1948.
5. Bangs, T., *Language and Learning Disorders of the Pre-Academic Child.* Washington, D.C.: The Volta Bureau, 1968.
6. Baruch, D., "An Experiment with Language Expression in Nursery School," *Childhood Education,* 139, 1931.
7. ———, *New Ways in Discipline.* New York: McGraw-Hill, 1949.
8. Bell, A., *Memoir Upon the Formation of a Deaf Variety of the Human Race.* Washington, D.C.: The Volta Bureau, 1969.
9. Bender, R., "A Child's Hearing," *Audecibel,* Vol. 19, 1970.
10. ———, and E. Wiig, "Binaural Hearing Aids for Young Children," *Volta Review,* June 1962.
11. ———, *The Conquest of Deafness.* Cleveland, Ohio: Case Western Reserve University Press, 1965.
12. Biber, B., "Children's Drawings: From Lines to Pictures," New York: *Bureau of Educational Experiments,* 1934.

13. Bigge, M., and Hunt, M., *Psychological Foundations of Education*. New York: Harper & Row, 1962.
14. Birch, H., "The Role of Motivational Factors in Insightful Problem Solving," *Journal of Psychology*, 1945.
15. Blatz, W., *Understanding the Young Child*. New York: Morrow, 1944.
16. Brunschwig, L., "A Study of Some Personality Aspects of Deaf Children," *Teachers College, Columbia University*, No. 687, 1936.
17. Carmichael, L., Ed., *Manual of Child Psychology*. New York: John Wiley, 1946.
18. Cherry, C., *On Human Communication*. Cambridge, Mass.: M.I.T. Press, 1965.
19. Christopherson, J., "Teaching Numbers to Young Children in Spanish Schools," *Young Children*, 20:119–122, 1964.
20. Cockrell, D., "Design in the Paintings of Young Children," *School Arts Magazine*, 30:33–39; 112–119, 1930.
21. Conn, J., "The Child Reveals Himself Through Play: The Method of Play Interview," *Mental Hygiene*, 23:49–70, 1939.
22. Carmmatte, A., *Deaf Persons in Professional Employment*. Springfield, Ill.: Charles C Thomas, 1967.
23. Cranston, M., *Philosophy and Language*. Toronto: T. H. Best & Co., 1969.
24. Crocker, E., "Depth Consultation With Parents," *Young Children*, 20:91–99, 1964.
25. Cruickshank, W., Ed., *Psychology of Exceptional Children and Youth*. Englewood Cliffs, N.J.: Prentice-Hall, 1963.
26. Dale, D., *Deaf Children at Home and at Play*. England: London University Press, 1967. In America, The Volta Bureau, Washington.
27. Dawson, M., and Zollinger, M., *Guiding Language Learning*. New York: Harcourt Brace Jovanovich, 1957.
28. Denner, P., *Language Through Play—For Hearing Impaired Children*. New York: Arno Press, 1969.
29. Dewey, J., *Experience and Education*. New York: Macmillan, 1938.
30. Drevdahl, J., "Factors of Importance for Creativity," *Journal of Clinical Psychology*, 12:21–26, 1956.
31. Erickson, E., "Studies in the Interpretation of Play." *Genetic Psychology Monographs*, 22:557–671, 1940.
32. Ewing, A., "Linguistic Development and Mental Growth in Hearing Impaired Children, *Volta Review*, 65:4, 1963.

33. ———, and Ewing, I., *New Opportunities for Deaf Children*. Washington, D.C.: The Volta Bureau, 1958.

34. Fellendorf, G., *Bibliography on Deafness*. Washington, D.C.: The Volta Bureau, 1966.

35. Fender, M., *A Structural View of English*. Boston, Mass.: Harcourt Brace Jovanovich, 1949.

36. Fiedler, M., *Deaf Children In A Hearing World*. New York: Ronald Press, 1952.

37. ———, *Developmental Studies of Deaf Children*. Washington, D.C.: American Speech and Hearing Association, 1969.

38. Fisch, L., "The Assessment of Hearing in Infants and Small Children," *Talk*, London, England, 1969.

39. Fowler, W., "Cognitive Learning in Infancy and Early Childhood," *Psychological Bulletin*, 59:116–152, 1962.

40. Frank, L., "The Fundamental Needs of the Child," *Mental Hygiene*, 20:353–379, 1938.

41. French, S., "To Parents of Young Deaf Children: Some Suggestions for Child Management," *Volta Review*, April, 1968.

42. Freud, S., *The Problem of Anxiety*. New York: Norton, 1936.

43. Froechels, E., *Psychological Elements in Speech*. Boston: Expression Co., 1932.

44. Gates, A., *The Improvement of Reading*. New York: Macmillan, 1937.

45. Gesell, A., "Normal and Deaf Children in the Preschool Years," *Volta Review*, November, 1946.

46. ———, *The First Five Years of Life*. New York: Macmillan, 1940.

47. Gibson, J., and Gibson, E., "Perceptual Learning: Differentiation or Enrichment?" *Psychological Review*, 62:32–41, 1955.

48. Giolas, T., Webster, E., and Ward, L., "A Diagnostic-Therapy Setting For Hearing Handicapped Children," *Journal of Speech & Hearing Disorders*, 33:345–350, 1968.

49. Goldstein, M., *Problems of the Deaf*. St. Louis: The Laryngoscope Press, 1933.

50. Goodenough, F., "Use of Pronouns by Young Children," *Journal of Genetic Psychology*, 52:333, 1938.

51. Goodman, M., "Language Development in a Nursery School Child," *Child Research Clinical Seminar 2*, #4, 1936.

52. Gordon, A., "Speech for the Deaf Child," *Special Education Review*, June 1948.

53. Gray, G. and Wise, C., *The Bases of Speech*. New York: Harper & Row, 1934.

54. Gregory, I., "A Comparison of Certain Personality Traits and Interests in Deaf and in Hearing Children," *Child Development,* 9:277–280, 1938.

55. Griffing, B., "Supervision of Instruction," *Volta Review,* 70: 678–683, 1968.

56. Groht, M., *Natural Language for Deaf Children.* Washington, D.C.: The Volta Bureau, 1958.

57. Gruenberg, S., *We, the Parents.* New York: Harper & Row, 1939.

58. ———, *Your Child, Today and Tomorrow.* Philadelphia: Lippincott, 1934.

60. Guthrie, V., "Creative and Expressive Activities for Young Deaf Children," *Volta Review,* December 1945, January 1946.

61. Hall, R., *Linguistics and Your Language.* New York: Doubleday, 1960.

62. Hanford, H., *Parents Can Learn.* New York: Holt, 1940.

63. Harley, C., "Art in the Nursery School," *Progressive Education,* 8:570–575, 1931.

64. Harris, G., "A Consideration of Priorities in Preschool Education of the Hearing Impaired," *Journal of Ontario Speech & Hearing Association,* 1971.

65. ———, *Early Guidance of Hearing Impaired Children.* Washington, D.C.: The Library of The Volta Bureau, 1964.

66. ———, "For Parents of Very Young Deaf Children," *Volta Review,* Reprint No. 807, 1964.

67. ———, "Recent Trends in Preschool Education of the Deaf," Canadian Speech & Hearing Association, Edmonton, 1971.

68. ———, "The Hearing Impaired Preschooler in Regular Nursery Schools," *Ontario Nursery Education,* 1965.

69. ———, "The Very Young Hearing Impaired Child," *Rehabilitation in Canada,* 1966.

70. ———, and Weber, L., "Babies with Hearing Loosses," *Volta Review,* October 1967.

71. Havighurst, R., *Human Development and Education.* New York: Longmans, 1953.

72. Hayakawa, S., Ed., *The Use and Misuse of Language.* Greenwich, Conn.: Fawcett, 1962.

73. Haycock, S., *The Teaching of Speech.* Washington, D.C.: The Volta Bureau, 1941.

74. Hudgins, C., "Speech Breathing and Speech Intelligibility," *Volta Bureau,* November, 1946.

75. Isaacs, S., *Intellectual Growth in Young Children.* New York: Harcourt Brace Jovanovich, 1930.

76. ———, *Social Development in Young Children*. New York: Harcourt Brace Jovanovich, 1933.

77. Johnson, H., *The Art of Block Building*. New York: John Day, 1933.

78. Johnson, R., and Medinnus, G., *Child Psychology*. New York: John Wiley, 1967.

79. Kaiser, E., *The School for the Deaf*. Switzerland: Riehen School for the Deaf, 1969.

80. Kendler, H., *Basic Psychology*. New York: Appleton, 1963.

81. Kopp, H., *Curriculum: Cognition and Content*. Washington, D.C.: The Volta Bureau, 1968.

82. Korner, F., *Hostility in Young Children*. New York: Grune & Stratton, 1949.

83. Lane, H., "Influence of Nursery School Education on School Achievement," *Volta Review*, 44:677–681, 1942.

84. Leopold, W., *Speech Development of a Bilingual Child*. Evanston, Ill.: Northwestern University Press, 1949.

85. Levin, C., "The Teacher Is the Nursery School," *Young Children*, 20:110–115, 1964.

86. Levine, E., "Mental Assessment of the Deaf Child," *Volta Review*, February 1971.

87. ———, *The Psychology of Deafness*. New York: Columbia University Press, 1960.

88. Ling, A., "Advice For Parents of Young Deaf Children: How to Begin," *Volta Review*, May 1968.

89. Lippitt, R., "An Experimental Study of Authoritarian and Democratic Group Atmospheres," *Studies in Topological and Vector Psychology*, 16, No. 3, 1940.

90. Lowell, E., and Stoner, M., *Play it by Ear*. Washington, D.C.: The Volta Bureau, 1961.

91. Lukens, H., "A Study of Children's Drawings in Early Years," *Pediatrics Seminar*, 4:79–110, 1896.

92. Luterman, D., "A Parent-Oriented Nursery Program For Preschool Deaf Children," *Volta Review*, 72:106–112, 1971.

93. Mannen, G., *Conversational Language*. Washington, D.C.: The Volta Bureau, 1959.

94. MacKinnon, D., "The Nature and Nurture of Talent," *American Psychologist*, 17:484–495, 1962.

95. MacMillan, D. and Forness, S., "Behaviour Modification: Limitations and Liabilities," *Exceptional Children*, 37:291–297, 1970.

96. McCarthy, D., "Research in Language Development: Retrospect and Prospect," Monograph, *Child Development*, 24:3–24, 1959.

97. McDermott, E., "Storytelling—Lipreading, Language and Reading," *Volta Review,* 73:54–57, 1971.

98. McElwain, E., "The Importance of Communication," *Volta Review,* December 1970.

99. Meltzer, H., "Children's Attitudes to Parents," *American Journal of Orthopsychiatry,* 5:244–265, 1938.

100. Menninger, K., *The Human Mind.* New York: Knopf, 1946.

101. Meyers, C., "The Effect of Conflicting Authority on the Child," *Studies in Topological and Vector Psychology III,* 1944.

102. Millar, S., *The Psychology of Play.* Baltimore, Penguin Books, 1968.

103. Miller, J., "Oralism—A Way of Life," *Volta Review,* April 1970.

104. Millichamp, D., *Priorities in Preschool Education.* Toronto: The Brora Center, 1970.

105. Monaghan, A., "Educational Placement for the Multiply Handicapped Hearing Impaired Child," *Volta Review,* Reprint, 1964.

106. Montague, H., "Home Training for Preschool Deaf Children Through Correspondence," *Journal of Speech and Hearing Disorders,* 14:131–134, 1949.

107. Moulton, W., *A Linguistic Guide to Language Learning.* New York: Modern Language Association, 1966.

108. Murchison, C., Ed., *Handbook of Child Psychology.* Worcester: Davis Press, 1931.

109. Mussen, P., Conger, J., and Kagan, J., *Child Development and Personality.* New York: Harper & Row, 1963.

110. Myklebust, H., *Your Deaf Child.* Springfield, Ill.: Charles C Thomas, 1950.

111. New, M., "Color in Speech Teaching," *Volta Review,* Reprint #511, 1940.

112. Nielson, D., "Gay, Profitable Rhythm Class," *Volta Review,* January 1948.

113. Noll, V., and Noll, R., *Readings in Educational Psychology.* New York: The Macmillan Co., 1967.

114. Northcott, W., "An Experimental Summer School: Impetus For Successful Integration," *Volta Review,* November 1970.

115. Numbers, M., "Using the Hearing of Children so Deaf that They Entered School Speechless," *Volta Review,* March, 1937.

116. Numbers, M., and Hudgins, C., "Speech Perception in Present Day Education for Deaf Children," *Volta Review,* 50:449–456, 1948.

117. O'Neil, J., Ed., *Foundations of Speech.* Englewood Cliffs, N.J.: Prentice-Hall, 1941.

118. Osborne, K., Bellefleur, P., and Bevan, R., "An Experimental Diagnostic Teaching Clinic for Multiply Handicapped Deaf Children," *Exceptional Children,* 37:387–389, 1971.

119. O'Shea, M., "Some Aspects of Drawing," *Educational Review,* 14:263–284, 1897.

120. Pelles, G., *Art, Artists, and Society.* Englewood Cliffs, N.J.: Prentice-Hall, 1963.

121. Pennington, J., *The Importance of Being Rhythmic.* New York: Putnam, 1925.

122. Perrine, V., *Let The Child Draw.* New York: Stokes, 1936.

123. Piaget, J., *Play, Dreams and Imitation in Childhood.* New York: Norton, 1951.

124. ———, *The Child's Conception of Physical Causality.* London: Kegan, Trench, Trubner, 1930.

125. ———, *The Child's Conception of the World.* New York: Harcourt Brace Jovanovich, 1932.

126. ———, *The Language and Thought of the Child.* New York: Harcourt Brace Jovanovich, 1926.

127. ———, *The Moral Judgment of the Child.* New York: Harcourt Brace Jovanovich, 1932.

128. ———, *The Origins of Intelligence in Children.* New York: Columbia University Press, 1952.

129. Pollock, M. and Pollock, K., "Letter to the Teacher of a Hard of Hearing Child," *Childhood Education,* 47:206–209, 1971.

130. Pringle, M., and Bossion, V., "A Study of Deprived Children— Language Development and Reading," *Vita Humana,* 1:142–170, 1958.

131. Quigley, S., Ed., *Preparation of Teachers of the Deaf.* Washington, D.C.: U.S. Department of Health, Education and Welfare, Bulletin No. 8, 1966.

132. Rabinovitch, S. and Golick, M., "Loops To Learn By," (Films), *National Film Board,* New York: McGraw-Hill, 1968.

133. Ray, H., "The Multi-Sensory Experience Center," *Journal of Association for Childhood Education,* 47:255–258, 1971.

134. Read, K., "Teachers' Verbal Contacts With Children," *Peabody Journal of Education,* 18 No. 5, 1941.

135. Reese, E., *The Analysis of Human Operant Behaviour.* Dubuque, Iowa: Wm. C. Brown, 1969.

136. Reichstein, J., "Integration of Deaf Children at Preschool Level," *Proceedings of I.C.O.E.D.,* Washington, 1967.

137. Roberts, D., "An Evaluation of the Term 'Central Deafness'," *Journal of Australian College of Speech Therapists,* June, 1968.

138. Rogers, C., *Counselling and Psychotherapy,* Boston: Houghton Mifflin, 1942.
139. Rooney, A., "Parent Education—Emphasis on the Preschool," *Volta Review,* December 1946.
140. Ross, A., *The Exceptional Child in the Family.* New York: Grune & Stratton, 1964.
141. Rotter, P., *A Parents' Program in a School for the Deaf.* Washington, D.C.: The Volta Bureau, 1969.
142. Russell, B., "Two Very Different Types of Teachers," in *Ideas that Matter,* New York: Ronald Press, 1961.
143. Sapir, E., *Language,* New York: Harcourt Brace Jovanovich, 1949.
144. Seth, G., and Guthrie, D., *Speech in Childhood.* New York: Harcourt Brace Jovanovich, 1935.
145. Shaw, R., *Finger Painting.* Boston: Little, Brown, 1934.
146. Silverman, R., "Behavioural Research Problems in Deafness," *Research on Behavioural Aspects of Deafness,* Washington, D.C.: U.S. Dept. of Health, Education and Welfare, 1965.
147. ———, and Davis, H., *Hearing and Deafness.* New York: Holt, Rinehart and Winston, Inc., 1970.
148. ———, "Education of Deaf Children—Past and Prologue," *Proceedings I.C.O.E.D.,* Washington, 1964.
149. Simmons, A., "Motivating Language in the Young Child," *Proceedings I.C.O.E.D.,* Washington, 1967.
150. ———, "Teaching Aural Language," *Volta Review,* January 1968.
151. Slavson, S., Ed., *The Practice of Group Therapy.* New York: International University Press, 1947.
152. Smith, A., "Parent Education and Group Therapy," *Journal of Clinical Psychology,* 4:214–217, 1948.
153. ———, "Psychology Testing of the Preschool Deaf Child," *Proceedings I.C.O.E.D.,* Volta Bureau, Washington, 1967.
154. Sorokin, P., "Living in an Age of Testocracy," in *Contemporary Sociology.* New York: Philosophical Library, Inc., 1958.
155. Spock, B., *The Pocket Book of Baby and Child Care,* New York: Pocket Books, 1950.
156. Staats, A., *Complex Human Behaviour.* New York: Holt, Rinehart and Winston, 1963.
157. ———, *Learning, Language and Cognition.* New York: Holt, Rinehart and Winston, 1968.
158. Staats, A., and Staats, C., *Verbal Behaviour and Learning.* New York: McGraw Hill, 1963.

159. Stalmaker, E., "Language of the Preschool Child," *Child Development,* 4:229, 1933.

160. Stepp, R., "A Medium for Programming Learning for Deaf Children," *Midwest Regional Media Center for the Deaf,* Nebraska, 1967.

161. Symonds, P., *The Psychology of Parent-Child Relationships.* New York: Appleton, 1939.

162. Thielman, V., Ed., *Correpondence Course.* Los Angeles: The John Tracy Clinic, 1965.

163. Tolstoy, L., "Art Like Speech Is a Condition of Human Life," in *What Is Art?* New York: Crowell, 1899.

164. Travis, L., *Handbook of Speech Pathology.* New York: Appleton, 1957.

165. ——— and Baruch, D., *Personal Problems of Everyday Life.* New York: Appleton, 1941.

166. Underwood, B., and Schulz, R., *Meaningfulness in Verbal Learning.* New York: Lippincott, 1960.

167. Utley, J., "A Test For Lipreading Ability," *Journal of Speech Disorders,* 11:109–116, 1946.

168. ———, *Auditory Training Album—What's Its Name.* Washington, D.C.: The Volta Bureau, 1950.

169. van Uden, A., "New Realizations in the Light of the Pure Oral Method," *The Volta Review,* December 1970.

170. ———, *A World of Language for Deaf Children.* The Netherlands: Institute for the Deaf, 1968. In U.S.A., The Volta Bureau.

171. Washburn, R., *Children Have Their Reasons.* New York: Appleton, 1942.

172. Waterman, E., *The Rhythm Book.* New York: A. S. Barnes, 1936.

173. Wedenberg, E., "Auditory Training of Deaf and Hard of Hearing Children," *Acta Oto-laryng.,* Supplement 94, 1951.

174. ———, "Experience From Thirty Years Of Auditory Training," *Proceedings I.C.O.E.D.,* The Volta Bureau, 1967.

175. Weir, M. and Stevenson, H., "The Effect of Verbalization in Children's Learning as a Function of Chronological Age," *Child Development,* 30:143–149, 1959.

176. West, R., Ed., *Russian Translations on Speech and Hearing.* Washington, D.C.: American Speech & Hearing Association, 1968.

177. Whitehurst, M., "Testing the Hearing of Preschool Children," *The Volta Review,* Pamphlet, 1961.

178. Wilson, D., "The Hearing Team," *The Volta Review,* May 1962.

179. Wolff, W., *The Personality of the Preschool Child.* New York: Grune & Stratton, 1947.

180. Woodbridge, F., "Art Tells Us What Life Really Is," in *Ideas That Matter*. New York: Ronald Press, 1961.

181. Zimmern, A., "The Pre-Instruction Stage in Education," from *Learning and Leadership*. London: Oxford University Press, 1961.

Index